THE MANY LIVES OF
JAMES BOND

THE MANY LIVES OF
JAMES BOND

HOW THE CREATORS OF *007* HAVE DECODED THE SUPERSPY

MARK EDLITZ

LYONS PRESS

GUILFORD, CONNECTICUT

To Mom, my late Dad, Tracy, Joan, Irving, Gail, and Elliot,
for their love and support.

To my wife Suzie and my children Ben and Sophie,
for their love and lunacy.

CONTENTS

Pick a Bond, any Bond. When you hear the name James Bond, what comes to mind? For many, it is likely to be a favorite Bond movie or one of the actors who has portrayed the secret agent. After all, it is natural to think first of the cinematic Bond. The multibillion-dollar franchise has retained its remarkable box office power for nearly sixty years—the first Bond movie, *Dr. No*, appeared in 1962—and its popularity shows no signs of waning. Still, another Bond aficionado might think first of the twelve novels and nine short stories written by Bond's creator, Ian Fleming.

But the movies and books are just the most prominent facets of the diverse and ever-expanding James Bond universe. Bond fandom extends to continuation novels, video games, comic books, comic strips, radio dramas, and even to an animated television series.

The James Bond movies and books have been a lifelong passion of mine. My first exposure to the cinematic Bond was seeing *Moonraker* when I was eight years old. After watching 007 duel the giant, steel-toothed villain Jaws in space, I was hooked. From there, I devoured every Bond movie. In elementary school, I scribbled "Roger Moore #1" on a piece of loose-leaf paper and pinned it to my T-shirt. I watched *Thunderball* on my grandparent's small television set in Boca Raton, Florida. I'd run home from school to watch and rewatch my VHS copies of the series, which I recorded while watching the ABC Sunday Night Movie. I wept when I ran out of tape partway through *The Spy Who Loved Me* and I couldn't record it in its entirety. My dad's generous offer to tape over one of his treasured New York Giants games didn't immediately assuage my outsized grief.

I read faded Pan editions of the Fleming novels as I walked between classes in middle school. The walls of my bedroom during high school were covered with stills of Sean Connery and George Lazenby and posters for the Timothy Dalton and Roger Moore Bond movies. My shelves bulged with Bond books and memorabilia, including the Corgi Lotus Esprit and my aunt and uncle's gift of the Gilbert figures from *Dr. No* and *Goldfinger*. I had vivid anticipatory dreams of the not-yet-released *Never Say Never Again*, and I saw *A View to a Kill* in a theater on two consecutive nights. In my mid-twenties, I went to a James Bond convention where I asked Pierce Brosnan to introduce himself as Bond would. He graciously played along.

As an adult, I had the pleasure of meeting Roger Moore, and true to Bond form, we were wearing tuxedos. I stuttered and stammered at first, but he helped calm my obvious nerves with his natural charm. Like many Bond fans, I was gutted when Moore passed away in 2017. I spent all of my childhood and most of my adult life trying to be Moore's Bond. It's safe to say that Bond in particular, and my love of movies in general, have consumed much of my life.

Although my love of Moore has never diminished, I have stopped worrying about whose 007 is best and learned to love all the Bonds. For me, Sean Connery, George Lazenby, Roger Moore, Timothy Dalton, Pierce Brosnan, and Daniel Craig have all become "my Bond"—each of them is a rightful heir to the Bond throne.

Despite my long and unwavering fascination with Bond, his psyche always has been an irresistible mystery to me. Beyond his dedication to queen and country and his unquenchable desire to devour life's finer things in all their pleasurable forms, I have often wondered who James Bond is, what drives him, and what—if anything— he really wants.

In an effort to find out, I have interviewed the writers, directors, actors, and other creators of Bond films, graphic novels, video games, radio dramas, songs, and audiobooks to learn how they attempted to understand this enigmatic and malleable character.

This book is composed of five parts. In "Bond on Film," I ask the directors, writers, and lyricists to talk about their artistic and practical decisions in bringing the cinematic 007 to life. In "Bond in Print," authors and comic book creators explain how they got inside the mind of Bond. In "Being Bond," actors discuss their interpretations of the character and reveal what it's like to "become" the agent. The artists in "Designing 007" have visually represented Bond in print, on film, and in video games. "Bond Women" takes a look at how the women Bond becomes involved with help to illuminate his character.

These interviews explore the ways the artists got involved with their projects, examine how they approached their work, scrutinize their thoughts and feelings about the character, and consider the extent to which they felt a sense of responsibility to earlier interpretations of James Bond and to the franchise. Many of the artists also reflect on our collective need for a character like Bond.

Through these wide-ranging conversations, I attempt to provide a behind-the-scenes look at the artists' goals, the challenges they faced, and how they met them. As I talked with these creative people, a through line emerged. It involves a series of fundamental questions about Bond that artists must reckon with when interpreting the character. Who is James Bond and, beyond successfully completing a mission, what does he want? Why did he become an agent? What is the nature of his inner life? Would he be capable of a satisfying life away from the high-octane adventure and danger of his work as a spy?

I've scoured his cinematic and literary adventures for clues. But finding answers to these questions has not been easy. When I asked the three-time Bond screenwriter Tom Mankiewicz about Bond's personal life, the late great wordsmith and raconteur confessed, "Bond's personal life is a cipher to me."

So who is James Bond? What motivates him? And what creative decisions do artists make when interpreting the character?

This book is my attempt to explore and answer those questions.

AUTHOR'S NOTE

In different novels, Ian Fleming, who was not fussy about continuity, rendered Bond's elite section as "Double-O" (with a dash), "Double O" (without a dash), and "double-o" (in lower case). Similarly, in different media M, Bond's superior, is styled with and without a period. For consistency, I have chosen to use "Double-O," except when quoting Fleming or someone else who depicts it differently, and to exclude the period from M. For aesthetic reasons, I have opted for "Eon Productions" rather than "EON Productions" and to identify the animated series *James Bond Jr* as *James Bond Jr.* (with a period) and the Bond film *SPECTRE* as *Spectre*.

The Many Lives of James Bond is meant to serve as a companion to the original works of art—the movies, books, songs, video games, and radio dramas—that I write about. I was not able to publish reproductions of all the Bond posters, actors, and assorted other images that are referenced in this volume. So during the discussion about the *Moonraker* poster, for example, I encourage you to stop reading, search the internet for the relevant image, and then return to the book. Although I refer to scores of Bond adventures, I have written in depth only about projects for which I've been able to obtain a primary interview. If your favorite Bond tale or artist is absent from this volume, I offer my apologies—and add that I probably wanted to include them but was unable.

All of these interviews have been edited for length and clarity.

I have referred to many Bond books, fanzines, experts, super fans, websites, podcasts, and message boards that have informed my thinking about 007. I have benefited greatly from their scholarship, their insights, and their passion, and I am deeply indebted to them all.

Finally, it is my hope that these interviews will help bring deeper insight into the artists' crafts, expand our appreciation of Ian Fleming's multifaceted creation, and generate even greater enjoyment of the works themselves.

PART I

BOND ON
FILM

DIRECTING BOND MOVIES

MARTIN CAMPBELL

As the director of *GoldenEye* (1995) with Pierce Brosnan and *Casino Royale* (2006) with Daniel Craig, Martin Campbell set the template for two radically different periods of Bond films. Campbell's *GoldenEye* confidently continued the Bond traditions when skeptical pundits questioned the viability of the series. His *Casino Royale* subverted the audience's expectations by eschewing the franchise's tropes while at the same time deepening Bond's character and delivering the requisite thrills. Campbell established Brosnan's Bond as a sophisticated and charming veteran who dutifully serves his country and launched Craig's as an unformed, reckless, unestablished agent who joined MI6, as love interest Vesper Lynd (Eva Green) describes, as a "maladjusted young man" with "a chip on [his] shoulder."[1] Whereas Brosnan's Bond eschews long-lasting relationships as a survival mechanism, Craig's Bond draws women close, falling in love and eager to leave the spy game for both Lynd and Madeleine Swann (Léa Seydoux in *Spectre* [2015]). These eras of Bond films, established by Campbell, are as different as their singular characterizations.

Making a Bond film is always a challenge. But when you made *GoldenEye* and *Casino Royale* you had the additional responsibility of establishing a relationship between the audience and a new James Bond that, if successful, could last more than a decade. Is that daunting?
You know, it's not. Although, quite honestly, *Casino* was a slightly more daunting task than directing *GoldenEye*, simply because it was a change of gear for Bond. The producers [Barbara Broccoli and Michael G. Wilson] felt that the previous one [*Die Another Day* (2002)], with its invisible car and its Ice Palace, was perhaps a bit too fantastical. We all wanted to bring the whole thing back down to earth. The idea was to go back to the books where the character was darker. Clearly, *Casino* was a different direction than the previous Bond films. So it was slightly nerve-racking because we were concerned as to how the audience would respond to our new direction.

When you were hired, was Craig already cast as Bond?
No, absolutely not. We tested a lot of Bonds. We tested eight people.

Wow, that many?

Yeah, that's standard practice for casting a new Bond, and Daniel was one of the eight [a group that also included future Superman Henry Cavill]. It was Barbara Broccoli who was the engine behind picking Daniel. She loved the idea and she felt that he would be absolutely terrific as Bond. Barbara was the one who really pushed for him.

Could any of those eight actors have done it or was it down to just a couple?

They could've done it but not nearly as well as Daniel. Daniel was clearly the best actor. He also fits Fleming's description of Bond in that he's certainly more rugged than what we've had previously.

All eight actors had a full screen test?

Everyone had a full day.

What do you remember about the screen test?

It's the scene we always test: the scene in *From Russia with Love* (1963). In it, Bond enters his hotel room, takes off his jacket, his gun, his shoulder holster, and he turns on the bath. He senses that someone's in the bedroom. So he crosses the terrace, opens the door, and there's a blonde girl in bed. He knows he has to seduce her because he wants the information about the Lektor, the decoding machine. The scene covers all the aspects of Bond's character. I think every Bond actor has been tested on that scene.

Can you recall the moment when you thought Craig was the guy?

It did take me a little adjustment to say, "He would be absolutely great for this new incarnation of Bond." When Daniel came over to England, he was shooting a movie in America. He came off with red eyes and he literally had no sleep. I felt sorry for him. He came off the plane, did the test, did very well, and then was straight back on a plane and away again. We looked at them all and Barbara had no doubts at all. I had no doubts about his acting abilities, but I sort of questioned whether—with Pierce having worked out as the old incarnation of Bond—audiences would accept this new approach. Then I saw the crime drama [*Layer Cake* (2004)] starring Craig again and thought, "There's no question. The guy's terrific." He also has a wicked sense of humor. That kind of did it for me. [*Note*: Craig, who shares Campbell's estimation of the condition he was in during the screen test, said, "If (Barbara) hasn't destroyed that piece of film yet, I hope she will. It's awful. I don't want anybody to ever see it. My eyes were just swimming.[2]]

Daniel Craig as James Bond.

ILLUSTRATION BY PAT CARBAJAL

After Craig was cast as Bond, I watched *Layer Cake*. I thought, "This guy's a good actor but he's not James Bond."

I think a few of us thought that. We were a little unsure not about his acting because he's obviously a superb actor, but if he was right for Bond. The template of Bond had always been the traditional good-looking actor. Daniel is handsome but rugged, tougher, darker, and grittier.

Can you expand on how casting Daniel helped change the direction of the series?

Pierce was an obvious Bond, right? Great-looking guy and, frankly, there was no one else at the time who was as good. Although we tested maybe two or three people [including Sam Neill], beyond that, Pierce was it. Roger Moore was it for [producer] Cubby Broccoli at that time. He is very good looking, fit the image perfectly. Though Tim Dalton is good, he was not as successful as either Roger or Pierce. After Pierce, we initially were looking at the kind of actors that we were brought up with for Bond. With that comes the humor, the great action, the women, and the misogyny. That was the formula. With Daniel, the template changed.

We went back to the tone of the books and made an effort to make the films tougher, grittier, and more realistic. We wanted to make Bond a darker character and tougher, but also more human. In the books, he smoked too many cigarettes; he smoked seventy a day [as Fleming established in the first chapter of *Casino Royale* (1953)]. He drank too much and his liver was dodgy. All that was in the book. We didn't [explicitly] go that far with it. We had to adjust our own thinking about where we were headed with the tone of the movie, which was very different than the other ones.

Because we were doing an entirely different Bond, that required casting somebody unique and somebody different. We all had to adjust to the idea that we were doing an entirely different Bond. And that took some thinking.

Once he was cast, was there time for rehearsals?

Yes, we were able to do rehearsals as much as we could. We rehearsed on set and Daniel was so committed to making it a success. Not only had he obviously worked out tremendously, but he also just got the character. He did a hell of a lot of work on it.

What concerns did Craig have in terms of finding and honing the character?

He may have had personal concerns but he never expressed them. He came in absolutely ready to go. There was a lot of criticism about him before we even had shot a foot of film. They said, "He's a blonde Bond. He doesn't look like the traditional

Bond. He's not pretty-boy handsome." There was a lot of rubbish that went on in the press, and Daniel decided just to work his ass off and prove everybody wrong, which he did in spades.

Do you recall what kind of character work he did?

Casino is an emotional story for Bond. Also, he's not yet the Bond we know, and he hasn't yet achieved his Double-O status. Emotionally, he's pretty raw and he thinks with his heart instead of his head. It's only at the end of the movie, after his experience with Vesper Lynd, that he ultimately becomes the Bond that we know and love. It was quite an arc for him to arrive at that point.

It's one of the most romantic Bond films. It's also interesting because most Bond movies traditionally end with a woman in Bond's arms. But in *Casino Royale*, the story continues after that moment. We see their relationship develop.

Indeed, Bond actually falls in love with her. What he believes is her betrayal is the thing that tears him apart. The fallout from the betrayal and their relationship causes him to become the Bond we know.

And we don't get that Bond until the final shot of the film.

No, you don't. You absolutely don't. Then he's setting out on the long road to all those Bond movies. Because he feels betrayed and emotionally torn apart by what happened with Vesper, he has a different attitude toward women. [But the irony is that] he feels betrayed by Vesper when in fact she saved his life.

Do you recall filming that last shot where he says, "My name is Bond, James Bond?"

Oh, yeah, I do recall it. Just to get it perfect, we did many different deliveries. I did seventeen or eighteen takes on it. We picked the one that we felt was the winner but there were a lot of good ones.

When audiences watch Bond movies there's a list of scenes that they demand. One of the joys of watching them is seeing the different ways those moments play out. But in *Casino Royale*, you withhold many of those scenes. But rather than frustrating the audience, the film ultimately becomes more rewarding.

You're right. It was different. The humor was also different from what we've seen in the past, and the famous scenes and iconic moments haven't been introduced yet. But in the subsequent films like *Skyfall* (2012) and *Spectre*, those elements are reintroduced. The relationship between Bond and Q (Ben Whishaw) has been expanded.

Spectre is fantastic. There's more humor and Daniel is absolutely terrific in it. I have nothing but the highest of praise for that movie. [Director] Sam Mendes did a marvelous job.

There's a moment in *Casino Royale* when Bond kills a man by shooting him in the eye with a nail gun—and here, because we're conditioned to it, we expect him to say something like, "He got the point." But this Bond is not ready for that.
You can't get away with those types of lines in something like *Casino*; it's a totally different film. The nearest he went to a line like that was when he comes back to the card table after he was poisoned, he says, "That last hand nearly killed me." I felt even that was pushing it a bit. Tonally that line was on the edge for me—the film doesn't suit those wisecracks and groaner lines that we're all so used to with Bond. But it worked and we got away with it.

Vesper teaches him how to dress properly; she gives him what might be his first tux. In the final shot of *Casino*, he's wearing fitted clothes, whereas earlier in the film he was dressed much more casually. It seems like everything he does in the films that follow—meaning from *Dr. No* to *GoldenEye*—is a reaction to his relationship with Vesper. So every time he drinks a martini, which we all previously assumed was a sign of sophistication, is actually a way of reminding himself of Vesper and the pain he's in.
Right, that's the point. And that's because the relationship between Daniel and Eva Green really worked in the film. It's similar to *On Her Majesty's Secret Service* (1969), with Lazenby, who was probably the worst of all the Bonds. But the story was rather marvelous. Lazenby's Bond saves a woman's life, ends up marrying her, and then Blofeld murders her. That film had a similar kind of emotional impact as *Casino*.

There is a danger in knowing too much about Bond. However, his past is cleverly revealed in *Casino Royale*. On the train, Vesper speculates about his personal life. She says that *maybe* he had a bad childhood, *maybe* he was an orphan, and *maybe* someone paid his way through school. Although we get insight into Bond's character, it's not definitive and there's room for latitude.[3]
There is latitude, but what's interesting about *Spectre* is that there's a lot of connective tissue with the previous Daniel Craig movies. It's very interesting; it connects [*Casino Royale*'s villain] Le Chiffre and *Skyfall*'s [villain as indirect and direct agents of SPECTRE]. It's all cleverly interwoven together. SPECTRE is the organization that Blofeld runs and that's cleverly integrated into the movie. The emotional spine

James Bond (Daniel Craig) enjoys a "Vesper Martini" in *Casino Royale*.

ILLUSTRATION BY PAT CARBAJAL

of the book and movie of *Casino* is what was so fascinating to me. They continued that in *Spectre*.

It's risky to reveal too much about his personal character. It's important to maintain some of the mystery.
Look at the box office numbers for *Skyfall* and *Spectre*, two movies that go into his personal life, and you'll see that it obviously works. Huge box office. [With worldwide grosses of $1.1 billion and nearly $900 million, *Skyfall* and *Spectre* are respectively the highest grossing films in the series.]

Before *GoldenEye*, Brosnan was already sort of the people's Bond. We, the public, cast him because we saw his Bondian qualities in his series *Remington Steele* (1982–1987). Was he officially cast when you joined?
No, he wasn't but he obviously was going to be cast. He was really the only one in contention. We saw other actors just to be sure, but he was always the front-runner. Of course, he was going to play Bond earlier, but he lost it because the *Remington Steele* producers wouldn't let him out of his contract.

I wanted him to play Bond at the time, but he was probably too young.
You're absolutely right. He was. Ultimately, he came in at the right time.

Brosnan wanted to do the type of Bond film that Craig is doing, but he had his foot or perhaps his leg firmly in the Roger Moore camp.
I think we all have our leg in the Moore and Connery camp. Our thinking at the time of *GoldenEye* was to make it perhaps a little more grounded than the Roger Moore ones. I thought Pierce was a terrific Bond. I thought he was absolutely great. Of all the various Bonds—with the exception of Connery, who is always remembered with great affection because of how bloody good he was—Pierce was the best. Before Daniel, when Pierce came on after Connery, he was the best of all the Bonds.

How did Pierce find the character? What was his process for finding Bond?
There are certain Bond characteristics that we all discuss and talk about—his misogynist attitude, the way he walks, the way he takes off his coat, the way he takes off his gun, and the way he fights. The man is totally and utterly grounded. He is comfortable in his own skin. Even during the action, he is always calm and focused. All that was developed during the Connery days and it has subsequently bled into all the other Bonds.

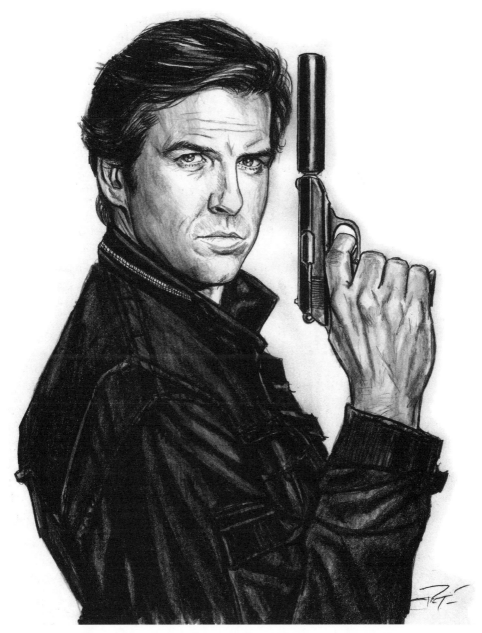

The trailer for *GoldenEye* reassured, "When the world is the target and the threat is real, you can still depend on one man."

ILLUSTRATION BY PAT CARBAJAL

Was there something that you thought was the most important part of Pierce's persona that you wanted to convey or establish in the new Bond?

No, all these guys bring their own baggage to Bond. Both Pierce and Daniel were prepared when they came in. They both had worked hard. They both had obviously thought deeply about Bond, and clearly about the humor in Pierce's case. He's obviously not as dark as Daniel Craig's Bond but he was much in the tone of all the previous Bonds. Especially in terms of the humor and his attitude toward women. The look of the film had the established Bond signature stamped all over it. Whereas with Daniel, it was a big change of gear, and it became something different.

Do you think that the Bond in *GoldenEye* is the same Bond in *Casino Royale*?

I don't. I see them as different characters. Largely because of Bond's flaws, I see Craig as a much more interesting and complex character. One of the things that I liked in the books is that when Bond is killing somebody, he has great difficulty with it if it's messy. At the beginning of *Casino*, he strangles the guy and tries to drown him in the basin. It's an ugly fight. It's awful and he doesn't like it. Once he killed the guy, there's a close-up of Bond and you see that he's not at all at ease with it. Putting a bullet in a guy's head is simple and fine and he's perfectly okay with it. But not this.

But it's also Bond's impetuousness—thinking with his heart instead of his head. He never should have gone after that guy [the bomb maker] and shot him in the opening sequence. A cooler head would never have gone into that embassy. A cooler head would wait. But Bond is fired up and reckless. His sense of injustice took over and he was just determined to get the guy no matter what the circumstances. In doing so he creates an international incident and he kills the guy when M needed Bond to take him alive.

What do you think motivates Craig's Bond? Is it a sense of injustice?

I think so. It's his sense of right and wrong. There is a sense of king and country and a sense of England but in *Casino Royale*, he's a rough diamond. He fucks up and makes mistakes. He's just a much more complex character. In terms of his personality, he's a much darker character.

Can you pick a moment from the film that helps reveal that character?

Do you remember the big fight down the stairway? [With Bond against the guerrilla leader Steven Obanno. Obanno's] got the machete and they're fighting like crazy. At the end of the scene, Bond is strangling the guy, but the guy just won't lie down.

I remember in my original cut I had that a minute and a half or two minutes longer than it was in the final cut because I was thinking of the tense fight in Hitchcock's *Torn Curtain* (1966). [Paul Newman and Carolyn Conwell attempt to kill a spy but] he just won't die. He just won't go down. That's what I wanted. The guy just will not die. It's ugly, it's horrible, and Bond is thrown by it. It really affects him.

With Roger Moore's Bond—whom I enjoyed immeasurably—I never got a sense that he was doing it for king and country. I always felt that there was something about the job and the perks of the job that appealed to him. Bond's joy in his work was part of the appeal of Moore's Bond.
I enjoyed Moore's Bond movies, too. Sometimes the humor was so awful and on the nose, but I enjoyed the sheer comic-strip quality to them. They were less grounded. What's the one that goes up into space?

Moonraker **(1979).**
How ridiculous is it when you've got Jaws with the stainless-steel teeth and you've got Dolly [Jaws's girlfriend] with the bloody blonde hair done up in pigtails in the space station? Well, that just about tells you everything. It's entertaining as hell. I used to love [the more outlandish Bond films]; I used to thoroughly enjoy them.

What do you think motivates Brosnan's Bond? It's different than what motivates Craig's Bond; it's not the injustice.
For Pierce's Bond, I think it's probably more about king and country. It's about loyalty. It's about right and wrong. It's a strong sense of fair play. That's what motivates him more than anything. Pierce's Bond is a little more sophisticated than Roger Moore and perhaps the others, but I think it's more to do with king and country with him.

I hope when Craig is ready to hang up his holster you come back and reintroduce the world to one more Bond.
Well, we'll see.

Keep that in your back pocket.
[Laughs.] I will.

ROGER SPOTTISWOODE

Roger Spottiswoode directed Pierce Brosnan's second James Bond outing, *Tomorrow Never Dies* (1997), which starred Teri Hatcher as Bond's former flame Paris Carver, Michelle Yeoh as Chinese operative Wai Lin, and Jonathan Pryce as the evil media magnate Elliot Carver.

Spottiswoode has made a career directing both escapist entertainment, including *Shoot to Kill* (1988), a tense thriller starring Sidney Poitier and the futuristic actioner *The 6th Day* (2000) with Arnold Schwarzenegger, and socially conscious dramas, including *Under Fire* (1983) with Nick Nolte and Gene Hackman as war correspondents who become involved in the 1979 Nicaraguan revolution, *And the Band Played On* (1993), the Emmy Award–winning HBO docudrama that examined the early days of the AIDS epidemic, *The Matthew Shepard Story* (2002), which told the story of the twenty-one-year-old gay student who was beaten to death by two homophobes, and *Noriega: God's Favorite* (2000) with Bob Hoskins as the Panamanian dictator Manuel Noriega.

As an editor, Spottiswoode worked with maverick director and visual poet Sam Peckinpah on *Straw Dogs* (1971), *The Getaway* (1972), and *Pat Garrett & Billy the Kid* (1973) and with Karel Reisz on *The Gambler* (1975), starring James Caan.

How did you get involved with the Bond films?
Barbara Broccoli and Michael Wilson, who do things very much together, asked me if I was interested. They tend to come to people who are English but also have experience making films in Los Angeles. I fit that mold and they offered it to me.

We talked about what I liked about the Bond films and what I didn't like. Pretty much like everyone else, I like the Connery films. I had differing responses to some of the more recent ones. I thought *GoldenEye* was very good and I thought Pierce was very good in it. He is probably the best Bond since Connery. I thought some of the recent films strayed away from the original films too much. Some of them had too much action, but there's nothing you can do about that; the audience has an endless desire for action. So like everyone else, they're trapped into making films that rely heavily on it. The early Bond films were better because they had less action. They were more about suspense and the stories were stronger.

What else did you want to do with your Bond film?
I also wanted to have one strong ending instead of three or four endings. I thought Bond films might be better off with fewer endings. I also thought there was more creative casting to be done amongst the leading ladies. We wanted to find a leading lady who was good at the physical stuff but also seemed genuinely cerebral. We wanted to avoid the previous overly shapely ladies, who were all wonderful but

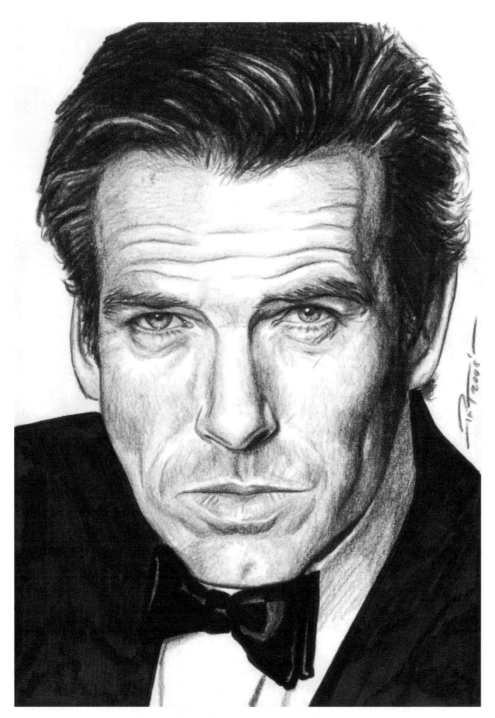

Pierce Brosnan as James Bond.

ILLUSTRATION BY PAT CARBAJAL

worked better for a different time. This thinking led to the casting of Michelle Yeoh. I thought Michelle would be a more contemporary and interesting casting against Bond. Michelle was a thoughtful leading lady who is up to date.

Were the Bond producers also thinking about going back to the early Bond style?
No, they felt that that would be nice but, in this contemporary world, one has to deliver a remarkable amount of action. That was certainly true of the studio. Not that the studio had the final word, but the studio did feel that strongly because whenever they suggested that the budget was getting rather higher than they wished, we would offer to remove one of the action scenes, because the only way you can do it is to take some big item out. They cost around anywhere between six and ten million dollars apiece. Of course, nobody wants to take any of them out.

I remember the old Aston Martin car chase in *Goldfinger* (1964), and I thought the previous Bond film *GoldenEye* had a wonderful tank chase. We couldn't do a better tank chase, but I thought we could have a good car chase. I also didn't want the Bond theme and score to get sidelined.

How about finding the right balance of humor?
I enjoyed the dry English humor and the irony of the Connery films, and I thought Pierce handled the humor really well. The Daniel Craig films are more consistently dark, so there's a little less room for that kind of humor.

How would you describe your relationship with Brosnan?
He and I were in sync on what he was doing, and he did it tremendously.

This is one of the first Bond films in which he has a personal stake in his mission. Bond had a past relationship with Teri Hatcher's character, but she gets killed while trying to help him.
Right. They're doing that more now. That was something that we all wanted to try to do and Barbara and Michael particularly wanted to try to do. And it seemed like a good idea. But it was a new approach to a Bond film. They've managed to develop it further in the Craig films.

Is there something you wanted to try but didn't have a chance to?
I thought that a Bond who had a more complex and perhaps more political view of the world might be interesting. I felt that the British secret service was evolving, was becoming more irrelevant in a way—just as England is somehow not quite at the center of things as it was fifty years ago. I thought one could make more of Bond being aware of how difficult it was to operate on the fringes of the

world and what a complicated relationship he has with both the United States and all these other emerging countries. To some extent they might be going in that direction, but there's a limit to what one can do. This is not a political film. I happen to have an interest in political films but that doesn't mean to say that Bond has to go that way.

The film looks great. There's a lot of gorgeous cinematography. Particularly in the party scene where a tuxedo-clad Bond sees Pamela Carver for the first time in years and where he first encounters Elliot Carver.
I do remember a lot about working with Robert Elswit who was a wonderful cameraman [and a longtime Paul Thomas Anderson collaborator, who would serve as the director of photography on films in the *Mission: Impossible* and *Jason Bourne* franchises.]. I was fortunate to have him with us. Robert has a clear knowledge of what to add to complement the set, so you could shoot in natural light and have an extremely controlled grip of what the camera was going to see. We could shoot in many directions, sometimes with multiple cameras, and always be within the same palette of light and color.

We also had a terrific production designer, Allan Cameron [*Highlander* (1986), *Willow* (1988), and *The Da Vinci Code* (2006)]. There were a lot of sets and a lot of different locations [including Southeast Asia, Mexico, and Germany]. Because the production is so complicated and it's easy to lose sight of the story, it's important to make sure the visuals convey the text and the subtext. Everyone was on the same page with that.

You use slow motion, which isn't all that common for a Bond film. Was that a holdover from your Peckinpah days?
I started with Sam who had a habit of shooting too much at ninety-six frames; he was a real pain in the neck about it. [Laughs.] It was beautiful at moments in *The Wild Bunch* (1969) but it was less useful in *The Getaway*. The use of slow motion back then was a subject of much debate and discussion with Sam in the cutting rooms, where we tried to figure out ways of using it. I like it but only a little bit. I'm wary of it. As a general rule, I prefer when style doesn't call attention to itself.

Can you talk about working with Barbara Broccoli and Michael Wilson?
It's their franchise, and they allow and encourage a lot of input and discussion, but at the end of the day, it has to be something that works for them. They're open to suggestions, but they are the guard. They're the producers and the owners. It's their cottage industry, and it's a big cottage. It's a profitable one that has survived for a long time because it's better than most and because it's been carefully looked after. Few family businesses survive as long as this one.

Besides the scope of it, was it a daunting task to direct a Bond film?
Yes, but that's also the muse. That's the interesting part. You want to see if you can change, alter, or at least further develop different facets of characters that are known by everyone. Many people are invested in Bond but often in different ways. That's a constant challenge. Working with Barbara and Michael, who continue to be so involved and know the films backwards, makes it an enjoyable ping-pong-like back and forth creative process—we can try this, we can try that. So many ideas have been explored in previous Bond films that it's difficult to find a new approach.

You don't do a Bond film unless there is a part of the history that intrigues you, and it certainly intrigued me. You have to make them with affection, otherwise it won't work. You have to try to find ways that look at it somewhat freshly while at the same time acknowledging that audiences come there for some of the same things. They come there for a Bond that fulfills certain sorts of fantasy elements of whatever one's idea of a perfect English spy might be and of a world that doesn't exist but that might exist as a similar version of the actual world. It's complicated. How much one can change the Bond films and reinvent them is intriguing. How one approaches the film reflects what you personally find interesting.

Some people find having an amused and ironic main character more appealing than having a darker one—just a different take on the way English characters should be portrayed and what one finds interesting in a character. You're also balancing how close to or far away from reality you are.

Would Bond still be Bond if he were not working for the secret service? Is his sense of duty to king and country essential for the character? Would he still be Bond if he were hired out by another agency?
That's a good question. If you're going to do that particular work, if you're going to have to live your entire life as a sort of fiction, as a lie, you can't tell anyone what you actually do. You need *something* to get you through it. You're not going to get paid a lot. You're not going to get support. I would think that you do have to believe in something. Whether it's queen and country or a set of ethics that, however fragile, you believe can protect and enhance the overall quality of life in your country.

I would think you probably need something. That's why there are presumably some good spies and there were some incredible traitors whose allegiance is firmly on the other side. The famous list of English traitors—Guy Burgess and Donald Maclean [two of the five students at the University of Cambridge who were recruited by the Soviet Union]—were absolutely locked in step with post-Stalinist Russia. So, I don't know, but it's an interesting question and one that must be relevant to some real-life spies.

Daniel Craig embraced the darker qualities of 007.

ILLUSTRATION BY PAT CARBAJAL

Bond is an isolated or closed-off figure who seems attracted to danger. Is that what makes the job perfect for his sensibilities?

Yes. I think so. It certainly attracts people with those qualities. Those are pre-requisites. There may be some other qualities as well—like an enduring sense that you can be a public servant in a rather exotic field. There are such things as being servants of the public, servants of the queen, servants of your country; it is a worth-while occupation. Spies are not people who would fit into the military. They're certainly not people who would fit into the police force. And I do think there are occupations that attract people who are temperamentally preselected; they select themselves.

If you take your kids on their school outings to any fire stations, as I did when we lived in California, you meet the same type of person. It's always the same group of people. And they're all versions of brave, tough, strong characters. They're loners who can work in teams. They have no interest in carrying weapons. They do not want to attack anyone. Instead, they will go out and do the most amazing things to save people's lives. They don't talk much about their work. They don't necessarily have college educations but they have educations of life and of humanity.

They're different from police or other professions where they carry weapons. I do think that there must be people in the secret world of espionage who possess certain qualities that attract them to it, and the service in every country finds them, and they're an unusual group of people.

A lot of times firemen and policemen are lumped together.

They're entirely different. In the same way that if you spend time with journalists or photojournalists. Now, they are also brave people. They go places that are extraordinarily dangerous and they never pick up a gun. They're not on either side of a conflict but they're often committed to strong ideals. Now, their hearts might be on one side, but they do their best to be independent and at the same time they are humanitarian, and yet they're recording more than anything. They're extraordinarily brave. They can kid about it and, at times be insensitive in certain areas, but they're fearless.

I met a lot of the wives who were at the screening for *Under Fire*. We had a screening for the wives of photojournalists, war photographers, and it was great. Of course, the husbands came, too. At the end of the screening, all the wives came over and were nice. "You got him exactly right." These are people who don't want to talk about what is really going on there. They'd rather change the subject and tell you about virtually anything else. They'll do anything not to talk about what they're really doing. Even though he's a spy, I always think of Bond in those terms.

Looking back on the whole Bond experience, what thoughts come to mind?

It was fascinating and challenging to make. There's no other film quite like them. You have to try and make it different and the same, at the same time. Bond is a great English movie character and there is an extraordinary passion for it both in England and around the world. Part of the passion is for the lingering notion of what the country thought it was going to be. Bits of its own history are wrapped up in it. I'm very glad I did it. It was a fascinating and terrific period—full of surprises.

Did you keep any mementos from the film?

No, I have some photographs and a lot of memories. Well, there's a watch they gave me. Then they gave me a second-anniversary watch. So, one gets a watch and a lot of very good memories.

JOHN GLEN

John Glen began his illustrious twenty-year association with the Bond franchise as both editor and second unit director of *On Her Majesty's Secret Service*, *The Spy Who Loved Me* (1977), and *Moonraker*.

Glen's ability to orchestrate tense action scenes led to his promotion as director of *For Your Eyes Only* (1981), *Octopussy* (1983), *A View to a Kill* (1985), *The Living Daylights* (1987), and *Licence to Kill* (1989).

The record-setting director of five consecutive Bond films, Glen shot some of the most iconic images in the series, including the dizzying ski jump that audaciously opens *The Spy Who Loved Me*. He also directed the most tonally differently films of the franchise, from Roger Moore's cheeky *Octopussy* to Timothy Dalton's gritty *Licence to Kill*.

Broccoli wanted to press the reset button after the space-themed *Moonraker*, which some criticized as being too over the top. For the follow-up film, *For Your Eyes Only*, the idea was not only to make a more serious picture but also to explore the possibility of casting a new Bond.
Absolutely, that's correct. The first instruction I got from Cubby Broccoli was, "We've got to find a new Bond." I traveled the world interviewing both experienced and inexperienced actors. However, I'm not sure how serious Cubby was. It could have been a ploy because Roger, who was out of contract by this time, was negotiating a new deal with Cubby. It could have had something to do with remuneration [and keeping Moore's asking price down]. Cubby was a pretty clever poker player and I think I was a bit of a pawn in the [power] play. Word got back to Roger that I was testing all kinds of people and I think Roger got a little upset. But, as I said, it was all part of a poker game.

The idea of finding a new Bond must have been overwhelming. Especially for a first-time director.
It was a challenge. It was difficult. I tested Pierce Brosnan. I tested him for three days and they were wonderful tests. We did love scenes from some of the earlier Bonds. We did the famous scene in the bedroom in *From Russia with Love*. It's the scene with Sean who is trying to get information from this girl, but he's being spied on by the Russians. That was one of the many things we tested Pierce Brosnan on because it's a great scene.

Pierce came through with flying colors but unfortunately, he was also under contract with Mary Tyler Moore [whose company MTM Enterprises produced *Remington Steele* (1982–1987). She had an option on him and when she heard Pierce was

Pierce Brosnan as Remington Steele, Brosnan's unofficial audition as Bond.

going to play Bond she took up the option. Straightaway Cubby said, "We can't have James Bond playing Remington Steele."

But it was probably for the best. When he was cast as Bond about ten years later, Brosnan was more mature and a better actor. He was a great success as Bond. I was sorry that I wasn't directing him.

He probably was too young when you were testing him.

That's a fair comment but we didn't think so at the time. We thought [his youth would enable him] to go on playing Bond for five or six more films. I was fortunate that Roger came back and did three Bonds with me because I'd had already worked with Roger on a number of films. [Glen is also the second unit director of three non-Bond Moore films: *Gold* (1974), *Shout at the Devil* (1976), and *The Wild Geese* (1978).]

On one occasion I turned up on the set and Moore said, "Am I in your contract or are you in my mine?" Roger's such a wonderful wit and such a great guy to have around. Very inventive. He directed [multiple episodes of *The Saint* (1962–1969) and *The Persuaders!* (1971–1972)] and he knows what a director goes through.

James Brolin also tested for Bond. Did you direct his screen test?

Yes, it was one of many we did. He was good but the idea of an American playing Bond just doesn't gel. Although it's perhaps more likely today than it was then. There are a few actors who have English qualities. One is Jon Hamm from *Mad Men* (2007–2015). He'd make a wonderful Bond. He's got a nice twinkle in his eye and he does humor well.

I don't think you necessarily have to be the greatest actor in the world to play Bond. You just have to have a certain personality. Roger had this fantastic star quality. You need an actor who is a bit of a throwback to the superstars of yesteryear.

When you were looking for a new Bond, did you have a specific type in mind?

No, I had an open mind. But I did know that it had to be an actor who could handle the humor. What's unique about Bond is the humor and how it occurs almost all the time, even during the action. It was easy to find the humor with Roger. With other actors, it isn't quite as easy. So you have to find another way to get to the humor. With the Bond films, you have to have tense and exciting scenes where the audience gets caught up in the action and then you had to have something funny happen at the *end* of the scene, which releases all that tension.

Roger Moore as James Bond.

ILLUSTRATION BY PAT CARBAJAL

In terms of finding the right balance with the humor, the joke has to be in the right place. Like the line at the end of the chase scene in *The Living Daylights*. Bond throws the cello over the guardrail and says, "We've nothing to declare." Otherwise, it undermines the tension.

Right. There's a scene in *Octopussy* where Bond has to hide in a circus train. I said to Roger, "We're going to hide you in the monkey suit there." He looked at me and said, "You're not serious are you, John?" He thought that was going too far. But I reasoned that Bond has to hide somewhere and it's the perfect place. It is pretty hokum but it's also fun. You can get away with that with Roger.

You pushed him to be a grittier Bond in *For Your Eyes Only*.

Yes, and that was probably the only time that we had kind of a serious disagreement. Roger was conscious of all the youngsters that watched Bond. He didn't think that pushing this bad guy over the edge of the cliff fit his personal take on the character. He preferred to throw the dove emblem at him, which would upset the car's balance and send the car over the edge.

I disagreed with him. I said, "No, this man has killed your friend. He deserves a more vicious ending." I'm looking at the clock and I haven't got time to argue too long so we shot it both ways. It certainly became an important turning point in the series as far as Roger's Bond was concerned.

How so?

From that moment, his Bond became a harder-edged person. Prior to that scene, Roger always took a softer view of Bond. You can imagine Sean killing someone in cold blood but it was difficult to imagine Roger doing that. It was difficult to see him as a hardened killer, which Bond is. Audiences had gotten used to him being a comedic actor.

But Moore also plays the action straight and makes sure you feel that he's in real danger; he doesn't always find the humor. To name just a few scenes in which Moore's Bond looks like he's in jeopardy: while trying to disarm the bomb in *The Spy Who Loved Me*, when he's trapped in the centrifuge chamber in *Moonraker*, and as he's climbing the cliff in *For Your Eyes Only*.

I think that's right. You have to be serious about the action and it has to frighten the audience. It has to put them on the edges of their seats. But once the scene is finished and the danger has passed, then you need the humor to come in and release the tension. That's a fundamental part of Bond movies.

Talk about the intro in the cemetery in *For Your Eyes Only*, where Bond visits the grave of his late wife Tracy. It was an effective way to maintain continuity with the previous Bond films.

I wrote that scene. I tended to invent all the pre-title sequences. Cubby would look at me and say, "We need a good pre-title sequence." I would look around at the writers and think, "Why is he looking at me?" I did quite a lot of them. I worked with Michael Wilson a lot. We did some unusual pre-titles like the free-fall sequence in *Moonraker* [in which Jaws throws Bond out of a plane without a parachute]. A free-fall sequence like that had never been done before in a movie.

I went out to California and worked on an airfield with young chaps who specialized in free falls. We filmed the free fall in sections. For each jump, we'd get enough for two seconds of usable film. Then we cut it together as we went along. It turned out to be an efficient operation. It was also fun.

But we were always looking for something new, something original. That's most essential with a Bond; Cubby would say, "Oh we can't do that. We did that already." We're always looking for something new, and we were often, often imitated but we felt we couldn't imitate anyone else.

Take the opening sequence [in *The Living Daylights*] where Bond is participating in a NATO exercise at the Rock of Gibraltar. I spent some time in Gibraltar and I was able to go to all the military establishments there. It's quite an amazing place. When you get inside the rock, you discover that it's honeycombed and hollowed out. It's an awe-inspiring piece of rock.

That sequence had to do double duty. It not only had to be exciting, but it also had to introduce Timothy Dalton as Bond to a new audience.

It's always a bit of a challenge to introduce a new Bond, and you try to do it in the most dramatic way. I was lucky with Dalton because he was so good at action. When you see him clinging to the roof of that jeep while it's speeding around those roads on the rock, he did that all himself. He was so fit, very good at action and keen to do as much stuff as he could.

It's a great intro. How did you find Dalton?

We were in a bit of a jam, to be honest. Pierce Brosnan, our first choice, had dropped out through no fault of his own and we were committed to making this film. Timothy Dalton had been considered many years before to play Bond, but he was on top of the world and he wasn't interested in playing a character like Bond. But life deals you different cards. Although he was a good theatrical actor who also did lots of films, his career hadn't taken off as he thought it might.

When Pierce dropped out, we approached Timothy again. We just knew he would be right and this time he was more receptive to our overtures. We met him in Michael Wilson's house in Hampstead and had a good meeting. He was keen to tell us his own impression of what the Fleming character should be. He wanted to have a much harder edge and we liked what we heard so we decided to go with him.

Is there a way to properly prepare an actor for what it's like to be Bond and how that changes everything in his life?
No, I doubt it. It's like winning the lottery. You say good-bye to your private life and that's tough. But Roger was good at handling it. Roger had a good attitude. I used to ask him, "How do you manage to keep your equilibrium when people want to take pictures of you in the middle of a meal?" He'd say, "They're my public. Without them, I'd be no one." He was good to his fans.

Pierce described it as being an ambassador to a small country.
He's right. Pierce handled it very well. I didn't direct him in any of the films. I directed him only in his tests. It's a shame; I would have loved to have directed Pierce in a Bond.

Who would your Pierce Brosnan's Bond be?
He would have been more similar to Roger. I don't think he would have been the Sean Connery type of Bond, with the harder edge. He would have played the dramatic scenes well but we probably would have had as much humor as Roger's Bond.

When you were casting Dalton, there were really only two Bonds in the public's eye. Lazenby was largely forgotten at the time.
I worked with Lazenby. I was the second unit director of *On Her Majesty's Secret Service*. I did some action scenes with him and he was an enthusiastic guy. He liked working with the stunt guys and he tried to do some of the ski scenes. It was a terrible responsibility for me because if he'd broken a leg on my watch I'd never have worked again. I had to keep monitoring all the time. "He mustn't do this; he mustn't do that." He wanted to do everything. I had to be the bad guy and say, "No, you can't do it."

It sounds like he threw himself into the part.
He was very enthusiastic. As you know, he was a successful model. He did a well-known advert for Fry's Chocolate where he was carrying this big crate of Fry's Chocolate and he's surrounded by beautiful women. He became a household name in England through this commercial. But he wasn't an actor. He was just a very good-looking guy who had all the physical attributes of Bond. Except for the acting

part. Peter Hunt, who directed the movie and is a very good editor, did all kinds of tricks with him to minimize the embarrassments.

Talk about finding and crafting his performance in the cutting room.
We knew that Lazenby was a bit wooden. You don't become an actor overnight. He had the confidence, the looks, the walk, he moved well, and was good in action. Where he probably let himself down was in the dialogue. Peter cunningly used George Baker, who played Sir Hilary Bray in the film, to re-voice George Lazenby's dialogue when Bond is impersonating Sir Hilary Bray.

That was discovered in postproduction?
That was improvised in the cutting room and happened in the latter stage of production.

Talk about shooting the pre-title sequence in *The Spy Who Loved Me*.
I did the ski parachute jump back in Ireland. Playing James Bond, Rick Sylvester skied off the cliff and the parachute opens. I shot that months before we even started shooting [principal photography on] the movie. That was a wonderful thing to have up our sleeves straightaway. It was great knowing that we've got this fantastic shot to go on the end of the pre-title sequence. Three months later when we started shooting the film, we shot the rest of the chase sequence. It just all cut together seamlessly.

The jump is one of the most iconic images of the entire series.
It encompasses everything that Bond stands for when you think about it. It has style, panache, patriotism, humor, and stunts.

You have to have nerves of steel to direct these sequences.
We use people who have got nerves of steel. It took a lot of nerve when Rick Sylvester went off that mountain.

In his memoir *James Bond, the Spy I Loved* (2006), screenwriter Christopher Wood said that in the original ending of the pre-title sequence, Bond would have jumped off the cliff, landed on the lake below, hitched himself to a speedboat, and water skied to safety. In both versions, the last image before the opening credits is that of the Union Jack.[4]
Because of tensions with Russia, I remember [director] Louis Gilbert saying that we'd start off the movie with the Union Jack and then we'd finish the film with the hammer and sickle. But it wasn't carried through somehow.

Bond films are unique. These ideas are not any *one* person's idea. In the end, it's a *collection* of ideas, which take on a life of their own. If they're executed properly and filmed properly, they become a wonderful sequence.

You start with the notion that Bond is forced to ski off the cliff. Then you have to reverse engineer it and come up with why he's there and who is chasing him.

Right and that gives birth to the idea of the Russian agent who is in bed with this beautiful girl [Barbara Bach as Anya Amasova]. It turns out the girl is a special agent and her boyfriend is an assassin who is ordered to killed Bond. But when Bond kills the boyfriend, the girl seeks revenge. That's the way the writers eventually worked it out, but it almost certainly started with the idea that Bond would escape off the cliff. You've got to go back and work out a reason for him to be there in the first place and that has to generate the story.

I get the sense that you're never off duty as a Bond director.

You're always trying to think of new [action sequences]. I went on holiday in France with my wife and her sister from Australia. Her sister was a bad backseat driver. She was a bit of a pain in the ass, quite honestly. We went into a car wash together and we all sat in the car while it was being washed. That's how I dreamt up the idea of Grace Jones killing Patrick Macnee in the car wash in *A View to a Kill*. That's where that idea came from.

Talk about Richard Maibaum, who wrote an impressive thirteen Bond films.

Dick's strong suit was story construction. We'd travel the world and find a fantastic location or come up with an incredible stunt and Dick would find a way to work it into the story. He was a good friend of mine and we have wonderful times writing some of these stories. We'd be in the office arguing the point about one scene or another. When he was first starting out, he used to be an actor. So he acted out the scene. He'd be on his hands and knees trying to sell the idea behind the scene. He was very funny. Oh dear, we had wonderful times writing those stories.

Can you describe the writing process?

We'd start off with a basic kind of storyline. Just three or four pages and then we'd start to expand it. Then we'd go and look at some locations and we'd get more ideas from the locations and then come back and work some more. Then after three or four months, you might throw the whole thing out. Cubby might come around and say, "Look, we're on the wrong track here. We have to bring in another writer." [Novelist] George MacDonald Fraser came in on *Octopussy*. I worked with him in Hollywood. I arrived on a Monday. At 9:00 am, George was in the office waiting to get to work. But nothing happened at 9:00. About 11:00, Cubby came in with his lawyer; they've got some problem with the legal aspects of Bond. There are always problems and they went straight into the inner sanctum. George MacDonald Fraser looked at me and said, "Well, what's going on?" I said, "Oh, be patient. Let's just throw a few ideas around among ourselves." We didn't do anything that day apart from talking among ourselves. Cubby and Michael were too busy with the lawyers. That happened quite a few days and George couldn't get used to that.

Licence to Kill was a much tougher Bond film than the public was accustomed to. It was also his first personal mission.
The idea was that Bond was on his own. He went to his old friend Leiter's wedding. Of course, it all goes wrong, and the drug barons come and they maim Leiter and kill his wife in the most horrible fashion. The whole tone of that film was far harder than any film we'd done. Leiter's maimed by a shark [an event taken from the novel *Live and Let Die*]. We had an awful lot of problems with the censor. Also the certificate we got excluded youngsters [under the age of fifteen] from seeing the film, which hurt the box office.

Did you try to cut back some of the violence to change the rating?
We did. We did all we could but we still had problems. We had problems when [villain Franz] Sanchez is on fire at the end. We kept chipping away at it but it only made the scene shorter and less effective. Cubby and I were ensconced with the censor in the cutting room. The censor took exception to it and he kept saying, "No, you've got to lose more of it." It was a dangerous stunt to perform and it hurt me to keep chipping away at it. Things change and now you can see scenes like that on films and on TV all the time. But, at the time, we had a hard time with the censor.

Quantum of Solace (2008) had a similar tone. In both movies, Bond seeks revenge on behalf of a loved one. As a whole, Daniel Craig's Bond films are similar to Licence to Kill in that his missions are often personal.
Yes, they are. *Licence to Kill* was before its time. I also think that Timothy was ahead of his time. If you look at his performance in *Licence to Kill*, it's not that different from Daniel Craig's movies. We suffered a little bit because the film was so hard [hard-edged]. But it's a very good film and I'm very proud of it.

By the way, the original title was *Licence Revoked*. But then we had a lot of hassle from America. They said people won't know what "revoked" means. I couldn't believe it.

For his debut in *The Living Daylights*, Timothy Dalton was marketed
as "The most dangerous Bond. Ever."

ILLUSTRATION BY PAT CARBAJAL

After *Licence to Kill*, legal troubles held up the franchise for years.
Yes, that seems to happen every now and again. Funny enough, when we were making *Octopussy* at Pinewood, the other Bond movie with Sean [*Never Say Never Again* (1983)] was shooting at the same time at Elstree [Studios]. One day their rushes [dailies] came to us by mistake. I promise you: I did not look at them. We even paid for the car to take them back to Elstree. All the guys who were editing that film were friends of mine anyway. We all got on well. I think Cubby had a financial interest in that film. He said to me, "I got a bit of a financial interest in it even though they are our competition."

Can you talk about some of the memorable supporting cast? Bernard Lee was a memorable M.

I worked on *The Third Man* (1949) when I was a young assistant editor. He played the paper sergeant in it who gets killed in the sewer chase. Bernard Lee was a fantastic actor and he was absolutely irreplaceable as M. He brought a lot of humanity to the part. Although he treated Bond harshly, you could tell that M had a great feeling for Bond. He mastered [those conflicting attitudes] beautifully.

What about Desmond Llewelyn who played Q?

Desmond Llewelyn was a great friend of mine. He was a prisoner of war for six years during World War II. For one of the Bond films, we went on the publicity tour to Germany and he was being interviewed on TV. The interviewer asked him if this was his first trip to Germany. He said, "Oh, no. I was a guest of your government for six years." He did it with a straight face.

He's a wonderful, wonderful man. But as he got older, he was finding it increasingly difficult to remember the lines because they were highly technical dialogue. They would be difficult for anyone to remember. On the first Dalton film, we were doing a scene where Desmond was demonstrating a nerve gas and while he did the experiment both he and Dalton were wearing gas masks. When he finished Dalton took his gas mask off and I said to Desmond, "Keep yours on, Desmond. Say anything you like and we can put the [actual] dialogue under when you loop." That's how we shot the scene.

Do you shoot different rhythms and deliveries of the line, "Bond, James Bond"?

You do a few takes but it's an actor's thing, isn't it? It's his timing, and, "My name is Bond." And there's a pause, "James Bond." It's fairly easy to do. You just have to have the confidence to do it.

When you include second unit work with Lazenby and the screen test with Brosnan, you've directed more Bond actors than anyone else.

That's right. I did the three-day test with Brosnan [when he was tapped to play Bond in *The Living Daylights*]. When it was time to recast Dalton, Broccoli wanted Brosnan to play the part. Years later, the new regime at the studio wanted to look at Brosnan playing Bond. Of course, he wasn't going to test again. So my son, who was the only one who knew where the tests were, went over to Pinewood, went into the vaults, and found the original tests. The tests that I shot ten years previously got him the job.

What is your most vivid memory of working on the Bond films?

My initial surprise when I was offered the job. That was quite an amazing time when Cubby turned around to me and said, "Would you like to direct the next Bond?" Then he said, "If you want time to think about it." I was stunned. The whole industry was surprised. But Cubby knew the work I'd done on action scenes and in the editing on three previous films and he obviously had great confidence in my abilities. But it was a surprise for everyone, Roger as well.

Did you instantly accept?

I recovered quite quickly and I said, "I don't need any time."

Why do you think he selected you?

It dates back to *The Spy Who Loved Me*. Harry Saltzman sold his share of the franchise to MGM and so Cubby was on his own and he came back to England after about three years. He was going to make a Bond film on his own and it had to be good. I think the fact that I went out and shot that pre-title sequence, which was such a success and a great start for the movie endeared me to Cubby and him to me. He obviously got his eyes on me as a future director but I didn't know that then.

What sort of producer was Cubby?

Cubby was a wonderful producer. He encouraged you to go out on a limb and do your own thing and he never interfered too much. He gave you plenty of rope. We succeeded pretty well doing that, and we certainly had a free hand.

Your films generally stayed away from Bond's personal life.

Yes, otherwise it becomes a different [kind of film]. We didn't go into his private life because Bond is always a man on the go. Bond has to be on a mission to be interesting. He has to be involved in the action. You mentioned the opening scene of *For Your Eyes Only* when Bond is at the grave of his [deceased] wife. He lays the flowers on her grave. I wrote that scene to introduce a new [actor playing] Bond. I wanted to remind people of the history of Bond. But it was such a good scene that, even when Roger decided he was going to do the film, we kept it in.

That scene peels a layer away from him but still retains the mystery.

Right. You show that he was married, and it helps people remember his past. Then a helicopter arrives and Bond gets in it. But Blofeld is operating the helicopter by remote control. I'll tell you how I came up with the idea. One Sunday I was walking around Pinewood with Cubby. One of the carpenters had brought his young son to work and the son was playing with a wireless controlled car. At the time, it was

James Bond (Timothy Dalton) is out for revenge in *Licence to Kill*.

ILLUSTRATION BY PAT CARBAJAL

brand new [technology]. I looked at this kid playing with this car and that's what gave me the idea for the remote-controlled helicopter. It's strange how these things happen.

You mentioned patriotism. Is that an important element for Bond?
Bond works for the queen. There's always a portrait of the queen in the office and there's always that feeling of patriotism. That feeling of patriotism was pervasive in England at the time, though I'm not sure it is today. In *The Spy Who Loved Me*, Bond's having a romance with a girl in a ski hut. He gets up to leave. She says, "Oh, James. Don't go." He says, "Sorry, my dear. England needs me." Although it's tongue-in-cheek, it is what Bond stands for.

If he wasn't doing it for queen and country, then something would be missing?
Oh, yes. It's something special. Even if you're not English, you still get that feeling he's doing it for queen and country. No matter where the film is shown in the world, it comes off.

One of the unplanned strengths of the series is that it's not American imperialism.
I'm not sure what makes it work. Everyone has their own theories. I'm not even sure Cubby knew exactly why it was such a success. Initially, [director] Terence Young was at the press screening of *Dr. No* and the press started to laugh. He got embarrassed and didn't stay until the end of the film. He left. Peter Hunt [who edited *Dr. No*] told me that he rang Terence and told him to go out and buy the evening papers and see the reviews. They were rave reviews about this new character and this new tongue-in-cheek humor. Terence said, "It's wonderful, Peter. But how are we going to repeat it?"

It's interesting that they didn't even know what they had.
We often discussed what it is that makes the films successful because it's a question everyone asks. If everyone knew what made it a success, they'd all be doing it. But it's a mystery. The rights to Bond were bandied around a long time before Cubby and Harry bought them. They formed the company Eon, which stands for everything or nothing, because it was the last of their money. They set out to make *Dr. No* and it was only through their friendship with the guy at United Artists that they ever made the film. They made it for $1 million. The original budget was $900,000 but when you include the contingency, it cost $1 million. I hate to think what the new ones cost. Probably about $250 million.

There were other popular characters they could have tried to serialize, and others they have tried. But none took hold like Bond.

Do you remember *Our Man Flint* (1966)?

Yes, with James Coburn as Derek Flint.

It had all the trappings of Bond. It was an American Bond but it didn't work. It didn't work because there's something unique about Fleming's Bond. It might have to do with class distinction. He's a man who defies all the boundaries of behavior. He's a guy who can play it rough or he can be the smoothest guy in the world. He's an expert on the best wine, the best food. He's very well educated. He's a man for everyone.

WRITING BOND MOVIES

BRUCE FEIRSTEIN

Bruce Feirstein wrote the screenplays for three of the four Pierce Brosnan films: *GoldenEye* with Jeffrey Caine and Michael France, *Tomorrow Never Dies*, and *The World Is Not Enough* (1999) with Neal Purvis and Robert Wade.

Feirstein also wrote the theme park attraction *James Bond 007: A License to Thrill* (1998), which featured filmed scenes with Judi Dench as M and Desmond Llewelyn as Q. He also wrote the video games *James Bond 007: Everything or Nothing* (2003) with Brosnan voicing Bond, *James Bond 007: From Russia with Love* (2005) with Connery voicing Bond, *James Bond 007: Blood Stone* (2010) with Daniel Craig voicing Bond, *GoldenEye 007* (2010) with writers Danny Bilson and Paul Demeo, which places Craig's Bond into the events of the Brosnan film of the same name, and *007: Legends* (2012), which expands on the conceit of *GoldenEye* and delectably places Craig into the storyline of Bond films from the previous era.

How do you write a Bond film? There are certain beats that the audience expects.
I always used to joke that every Bond movie has to contain the same five or six beats. It goes something like this: "We're sending you out on a unique mission, Mr. Bond. Pass me the shoe. It's not just about this diamond, Mr. Bond. Oh, James." God, I used to be able to riff it right off.

Can you break those down?
"We're sending you out on a unique mission, Mr. Bond" is the scene with M when he's given his mission. "Pass me the shoe" is shorthand for the gambling sequence, the tuxedo/casino sequence. "It's not just about this diamond, Mr. Bond" is about the reveal of the villain's super plan. And finally, the last beat is always, "Oh, James," which is the love interest. I used to be able to do it much faster than that.

I love that.
And if you do write this, say that I stumbled over it, because I haven't done it in so long. That's the basic arc of the movies.

Did you discover that prior to writing them?

No, as I went through them. Anybody who's watched the movies knows the basic arc of all the films, which is that Bond gets the mission, there's always a Bond woman involved, the mission never turns out what it appears to be in the beginning, the villain reveals the actual plan, which is never what it originally seemed to be, and then Bond ends up with a girl. Except in the case with *Casino Royale*, where the girl dies.

Bond screenwriter Richard Maibaum used to call the villain's evil plan a "caper" and he said that coming up with a fresh and original caper was the hardest part. Do you agree?

Yes, I remember working on *GoldenEye*, and working back and forth about the Lienz Cossacks [which was a part of Bond's friend-turned-adversary's lineage]. We knew what the caper was. We knew he wanted to set off an EMP [electromagnetic pulse] weapon. But there were all sorts of other questions like, "What does the villain *really* want?"

In the case of *Tomorrow Never Dies*, from the very beginning, it was going to be about a media mogul starting a war for his own ratings. It becomes harder and harder today to come up with new capers. You don't want to do the same old thing—global worldwide domination. But in some ways, the Daniel Craig movies are much more about Bond's character arc, as opposed to a caper. The movies have changed.

When *GoldenEye* was released in 1995, there hadn't been a Bond movie for many years.

Six years.

Licence to Kill, which was the previous one, wasn't as successful as Eon and MGM hoped, and some people were questioning whether we needed another Bond movie.

That was foremost in our mind.

Talk more about that self-doubt.

The last Dalton movie hadn't done as well as anyone had hoped. There was a new regime at MGM and they wondered if there was a demand for Bond. Today, we are living in a different world. Today, because of the internet, you can take the pulse of the audience and realize that there is a huge audience waiting for the next Spiderman or the next Batman. You can look at the internet and see that there are millions and millions and millions of people who still crave *Star Wars*. If, tomorrow morning, we were to announce that there's going to be a Star Trek convention in Los Angeles, fifty thousand people would show up, and you'd say, "Oh, my god, look at that demand. There's a huge audience." But back in 1995, you didn't have fan conventions. You didn't have fan sites. You didn't have this ability for communities to exist around intellectual property. Also, even in 1995, the idea of DVD sales and disc boxed sets, and things like that didn't exist. They had no benchmarks. So in 1995, operating in the dark, MGM wondered, "Is there still a market for Bond?" That would not be a question today.

When you were writing it, you had to figure out how much of the classic Bond to embrace and how much to modify for today's market.
Everyone was thinking about that. We knew there was a pent-up demand for Pierce as Bond. At the same time, it was, how do you make this thing new? Michael France, Jeffrey Caine, and I all addressed that problem in different ways. Michael France brought in the EMP weapon. Jeffrey Caine knitted in a lot of the fall of the Soviet Union. And I brought to it an idea that the world had changed but Bond hadn't.

When I worked on the script, every scene was changed to reflect that. Mind you, nothing I did could've been done without France and Caine. The question became, how do we show that the world has changed but Bond hasn't? Well, you make M a woman. Then you plant a flag on it and have M say, "You're a sexist, misogynist dinosaur." And because this was a period of analysts versus field agents, he says to her, "Yes, and you're the queen of numbers."

After the opening sequence, the first shot you see is of the Aston Martin DB5, which is to say to the audience, "We know where we came from. We know what our roots are." And then you're in a casino. The idea was to bridge the past, to acknowledge what Bond was, and then to move Bond into the post–Cold War era.

There's a scene in which Bond pulls a gun on Famke Janssen [who plays Xenia Onatopp] and she says, "You don't need the gun, Commander Bond." And Bond says, "Well, that depends on your definition of safe sex." This was a nod to the world that we were living in then. In 1995, AIDS was very much the zeitgeist. We wanted to acknowledge these things, while at the same time going back to the touchstones that made Bond.

At that point, did you know what kind of Bond Pierce would be?
No. So you go back to who your first Bond was. For me, it was Connery. As a child, Connery was my first Bond. That was the voice I heard. And then once Pierce came into the role, it was Pierce.

Before Pierce Brosnan, Bond's personal life isn't really explored.
Pierce was very much an advocate of that. Pierce kept saying, "I want to peel back the onion and see what makes him tick and why." And so we tried to touch on that. But the syntax and grammar [of what it means to be a hero] had changed at that

point. It was necessary and correct not to have him be a lone warrior out there trying to save England but to also to give explanations for who he is and to get underneath the skin of a guy with a license to kill.

What happened in his life that turned Bond into the man we know?
We went back to the books for that. We knew about him being an orphan. We wondered what it was like to be someone who travels with a tuxedo. We wondered what it was like to be a guy who kills people like that. I think I got it in *Tomorrow Never Dies*, when he meets Elliot Carver's wife, who he's had an affair with before. She slaps him, and Bond says, "Was it something I said?" She says, "Yeah, I'll be right back." And then she says, "You slept with a gun under your pillow." We were trying to show more of the character behind all this.

***Tomorrow Never Dies* was the second film in a row in which his personal life was relevant to the mission. In *GoldenEye*, he was avenging the death of his colleague and friend 006.**
Yes, in *GoldenEye*, it was his peer. In *Tomorrow Never Dies*, he had an affair with the villain's wife. I don't think we weaved anything into *The World Is Not Enough*. I did only three of them, and at that point Neil [Purvis] and Rob [Wade] took the ball and ran with it. [Purvis and Wade wrote *Die Another Day* and, along with other screenwriters, co-wrote all of the Daniel Craig films.]

In the pre-title sequence of *The World Is Not Enough*, Bond fails to capture the assassin and gets injured. His failure was a departure from the formula.
That was an enormously long pre-title sequence.

It's also an instance where Bond arguably fails in his mission. There are more departures from Roger Moore's Bond. He also shoots and kills his love interest Elektra later in that film.
Yeah, he kills her and says the line, "I never miss." That was also one of those things in which we were feeling that we needed to show more of the character. And Pierce was pushing to show more of the character.

Are you a big Richard Maibaum fan?
Maibaum is a god. We all stand on Maibaum's shoulders. I love when I read about people saying, "You've gotta go back to the books. You've gotta go back to the books." And yet one of the untold stories was that Fleming showed up on the set of, I think, *Goldfinger*, and Fleming told Maibaum that he liked Maibaum's Bond better than his own.

When you read the books, the wit is not there. Maibaum brought the wit. The Bond of *Dr. No*, "You've had your six" and then shoots the guy. Or the Bond in *Thunderball* (1965) who says that she's dead tired. Or Goldfinger's line, "Choose your next witticism very carefully, Mr. Bond. It may be your last." That stuff is Dick Maibaum. When you read back on the history of it, Maibaum found so much of it over the top that the only way it would be possible for us to accept a character running through this world of guys petting cats and hollowing out volcanoes and filling them with big-breasted women would be to *somehow* comment on it. So, Maibaum brought the wit to it.

He wrote so many.

I ended up talking to Maibaum's wife Sylvia about this endlessly because I wanted to know everything about what it was like and how he worked with those guys. Maibaum had been a journalist and a playwright; he brought a worldview to it. Though credit always goes to Connery, to Cubby, to the directors, and to Fleming, Maibaum never gets the acknowledgment that he deserves. I don't mean to diminish anyone here. What I'm saying is that if you're going to do the Mount Rushmore of Bond, you're going to have Cubby up there but you should also have Maibaum up there.

He wrote thirteen Bond films. It's incredible.

And he was always good at them, and he managed the shifts with the times. Having spent thousands of hours on the films and the games, you end up with certain theories. And one theory I have is that every Bond reflects the period that it was made. To Michael and Barbara's credit, to Cubby's credit, and to everyone else's credit, every Bond manages to reflect the period that it's part of.

Connery was the brilliant cold warrior. Taking out Lazenby for a second because he only did one, you go into Roger Moore. Imagine what Roger Moore was faced with. He's replacing a guy who's not only the sexiest man alive but he's taking over in the '70s, an era of bell-bottoms, and then he's in the Reagan era. These are weird times. But he was the great Bond for the Reagan era. Then you get into Tim Dalton, which is when the Berlin Wall falls. Pierce is post-USSR, and Daniel Craig is post-9/11. And each one of them reflects the ethos of the time. And the feelings of the time. Daniel Craig is the perfect Bond for right now. I don't think Roger Moore could do today's Bond. But I also don't think Daniel Craig would've worked in Roger's time.

Sean Connery as James Bond.
ILLUSTRATION BY PAT CARBAJAL

Before *GoldenEye*, there was only Connery and Moore. While Lazenby and Dalton both brought a lot to the part, they didn't take hold like Connery and Moore. For *GoldenEye*, a new Bond had to take over from those two giants.

Yeah, at that point it was the usual things you were reading about: Does the world need Bond today? Is there any interest in Bond? Is this your grandfather's Bond? Is anyone interested in this anymore? One of the things the American press didn't understand was how infused Bond is in popular culture.

When you begin to work on the series, on the franchise, because you're attuned to it, you can't believe how many times in an average week you will read that something is "Bond-like." Within the last twenty-four hours, I was reading some real estate site that was describing something as a "Bond-like villain's lair." It's ingrained into popular culture.

One of the funny things that I've always wanted to use in another movie—but not in a Bond movie—is that the third or fourth most popular password in the world is "007Bond." When you try to hack into an account, there are all sorts of things you try. But if you're doing a brute-force attack on someone's bank account, in the top tier of combinations you try, you append "007" to the name of the person whose account you want to break into. And if that doesn't work, then the first password you try is "Bond007" or "007Bond." Of course, when you're doing a brute-force attack, you're trying millions of combinations, but that's rather high up in the hierarchy.

For many men, Bond represents wish fulfillment. By channeling him, it helps to boost their self-confidence.

Everyone who's ever put on a tuxedo thinks he's James Bond. I spent a lot of time on the series and going around the world with this thing and I came to realize that Bond is an archetype that exists in every society. Going back to year zero, every culture has a myth in which the emperor sends out a lone warrior to save a vanquished nation. If you look at the [ninja] Japanese Koga stories, if you look at Japanese warrior stories, it's always there. When the empire's threatened, the emperor calls in the one warrior he can trust and sends the warrior out on a mission to save the nation. That same story exists in every culture. It exists in Greek mythology; it exists in Roman stories. It clearly exists in England, going back to *The Canterbury Tales*. It exists in the Mayan culture. This idea of the lone warrior out to save the nation. The one man who can do it.

You're already starting with something that is buried deep in our DNA. The same way to think of this is that—and this is slightly off on a different tangent—Americans think we invented the sensitive singer/songwriter girl who's been spurned and wants revenge. Whether it's Alanis Morissette, Taylor Swift, or Joni

Mitchell. Well, no. That character exists, that archetype exists in every culture. You can find that woman singer in Spain, in Greece, in Israel, and in China. There are these archetypes that Bond taps deeply into but on a subconscious level.

Though what I've always thought that made Bond work in a larger sense was that Bond was British and represented the end of colonialism. It became possible for this thing to travel in Malaysia, into Thailand, into China, Japan, all over the world, because it wasn't about American imperialism.

You're saying that Bond being English is critical to the success of the franchise.

Yes, it's totally necessary that he's English. It's why it works so well. In the history of the series, there's never been a scene in the prime minister's office. And yet every time you do an American movie, there's always a scene where you're in the Oval Office. Bond doesn't bring any of that baggage to it. Bond doesn't come with the trappings that an American character comes with. It's more palatable that you're not dealing with a superpower, and Bond is often at odds with his American counterparts.

In England, it became such a big thing on Christmas that everybody sat down and watched Bond. Or around the world, a father could take his son to see Bond, and it was the extraordinary toys, the women, the travelogue of it all, and it didn't bring the baggage of America, of Vietnam and B-52s.

I don't think this was a conscious choice. It's something you realize and you reflect on after your turn, and you think, "How did this work? How did this become so deeply embedded in worldwide culture? Part of it was that it was British, not American.

Part of it was that the archetype had already been buried deep in our psyche. And it all lined up. And you had the great looking women and the wit and all of those elements. Look at the rest of the franchises. *Bourne* and *Mission: Impossible* are nowhere near as beloved. None of them has its hooks as deep into the culture as Bond.

Where does class come into all this?

I don't think it's part of it in a premeditated way. There is the idea, due to the accent, that Brits are more sophisticated than the rest of us. And the fact that he was particular about what he drank and he drove a cool car. But I don't think class was at the forefront of it.

What were your thoughts on Tom Mankiewicz's Bond?

Mankiewicz was Hollywood royalty. When I talked to him, the fanboy in me came out. And it was, "What was it like?" When doing the Moore stuff, the jokes he made were fairly broad. And when we talked about it, he said it's a different era and he realized that some of that stuff doesn't work anymore. And I asked him about the line in *For Your Eyes Only* when Bond is about to kill Blofeld, who is bargaining for his life and offers to buy Bond a stainless-steel delicatessen. I just didn't get it and I asked him about it. He just rolled his eyes and said, "Let's talk about something else."

But I also think in a way that was the period and there were a lot of different writers. In the pre-credit scene in *Octopussy*, Moore is in this tiny little jet, and he flies through an airplane hangar and then runs out of gas. I remember talking to Cubby about that. I said, "Cubby, Bond doesn't run out of gas. What was that about?" Cubby kind of glared at me, and we went on to talk about something else. Looking back, I was stupid and impertinent. [*Note: Octopussy* was written by George MacDonald Fraser, Maibaum, and Michael Wilson. Christopher Wood, the writer of *The Spy Who Loved Me* and *Moonraker*, came up with the out-of-gas gag. In his autobiography *James Bond, the Spy I Loved* (2006), Wood reveals that he originally wrote the scene for *The Spy Who Loved Me* but Eon repurposed it two films later.]

But when you're doing *Octopussy*, which is kind of a superhero thing, you need for something to go wrong [for your hero]. Now, in my era, I would not have had that plane run out of gas. I would've done something else. I've never thought about what. But in that era, that was the right choice. And that's part of the real genius of the producers. Everyone said that you can't do Daniel Craig; it's never going to work. Well, guess what? They were wrong. It worked.

Credit goes to Cubby and then to Barbara and Michael in that they made movies that reflected the time and the feeling of the time and moved the series forward.

Fashion, as it reveals character, is also changing. John Glen had creative disagreements with Dalton about whether Bond could wear blue jeans. Bond didn't wear jeans in the Dalton era but does in Craig's era.
On one side, Brosnan never wore blue jeans, but Brosnan was always in situations where he wouldn't. But things change and Daniel Craig is in a different era. Connery is wearing a white dinner jacket in Las Vegas in *Diamonds Are Forever* (1971), and it looks ridiculous when you are looking at it today.

But in 1971 that would have been appropriate.
Yes. Although because the other guys are dressed like slobs you're wondering, why is he wearing a tuxedo? But that also could be looking at it from today's perspective.

How are Bond movies written differently from the way other movies are written?
In terms of practical screenwriting, all these movies start from a different place than any other project I've ever been involved with in Hollywood, which is that *we're making the movie*. It's a huge difference when you start from that point of view. Therefore, you don't have executives coming in and asking, "Is Bond is likable? And what's the

character arc? What's M's character arc? We need to know more about who M is." So all of the usual development nonsense is pushed to the side. All of the things that kill movies and screw up screenwriting are pushed away.

And it's replaced with what?
It's replaced with, "Okay, we're making a movie. We know this character. We know Moneypenny, we know M, and we know Bond. We know these are the players." You start from a place of, "What is the story we're going to tell this time?" You are not inventing characters, trying to convince a studio to make it. From the first block, you've already left 90 percent of Hollywood behind.

Let me give you just a quick example. I can't tell you the number of times I've turned in scripts, and somebody will say something stupid like, "What's this character's arc?" for a character the equivalent of Moneypenny. In other words, a third-tier supporting character. And you then do a rewrite to give that character a story, knowing full well that if you're actually going to make the movie, all that's going to get cut. With Bond, you just leap over all that. And you're into the nuts and bolts of what's going to be on the next 110 pages. What's the mission? Who's the villain? What's the personal story here?

Now, because you are dealing with a franchise that's fifty years old, Barbara, Michael, and Gregg Wilson and David Wilson, who are Michael's sons and Barbara's nephews, they know all the dead ends. They know what doesn't go anywhere.

If you were to bring in new writers, you find that they will try something immediately that won't work, like a scene in which Bond saves a little kid. No. There has never been a child in a Bond film. In the Bond universe, there are no children, and that's just one simple example. Barbara and Michael have a great sense of it. To quote them, "How much do you wanna take the piss out of Bond?" How much do you want to have someone remarking about how absurd what he's doing is?

When you begin working on a Bond film, you're starting off with a bible and a preexisting character, a preexisting notion of who he is and the world you're operating in, and more so than any other franchise I've worked on, the producers are in the room with you. Barbara and Michael are there in the boat, pulling on the oars with you. Sometimes you may not exactly agree on the same direction, but they're in the room with you. I found them always open to new ideas but with a strong sense of what was wrong and of what doesn't work in the franchise.

As we've discussed, you've written a couple of Bond films where the stakes were personal. But not every mission can be personal, right?
I have a reaction to that. Look at the early movies or the first fifteen of them. With the exception of the Lazenby movie, none of them had an overriding personal aspect. It was, here's your mission: There's this guy named Auric Goldfinger, go chase him

down. Or there's a guy, he's Dr. No. In *From Russia with Love*, it was about Bond being vulnerable to a woman but he had no personal connection with her beforehand. Or he faced Red Grant but again there was no personal connection there.

If you think of them as TV shows, they were each closed-ended stories. And Dalton's were closed-ending stories. Pierce's were closed-ending stories. Robbie Coltrane reappeared [as KGB agent turned Russian Mafia boss Valentin Zukovsky], but there was no personal arc, no long arc. Now we're into the Craig era, when it is much more personal.

It reflects the period we're in. I don't believe that [the long-form telling of] *The Sopranos* (1999–2007) has had any direct effect at all on Bond. But we all live in the same pop culture soup, where they explore the larger story of a character's journey, which we see in *Breaking Bad* (2008–2013), *The Sopranos*, and in many other shows. Because it's in the air, it has clearly had some effect, so it's natural that Bond is part of that. But now Bond reflects that as much as it causes it. None of these things moves along in complete isolation. And we're in a world where people want these longer stories and want to know more about the characters.

James Chapman, who wrote a book called *License to Thrill* (2008), describes the evolution of Bond films as being about continuity and change.
I call it going forward and back, but that's right. The first example of going back I made in *GoldenEye* was to bring back the Aston Martin DB5. The DB5 was not originally in the script and I remember going to [director] Martin Campbell and saying, "We need to make this the DB5 to signal to the audience that we know who it [Bond] is." And what was funny was that the transport department pushed back and didn't want to use it, because they said the car's a piece of shit and it keeps breaking down. Martin rolled his eyes and gave it to me. Martin was a big Bond fan, and Martin also knew about those touchstones and the need to go forward and back.

The casting of Judi Dench as M was a great way to go forward.
I was in the studio at 6:30 one morning, and we were talking about how to fix the scenes with M. And Martin looked at me and said, "Why don't you try it as a woman?" While what you see on the screen is what I wrote, the idea came from Martin. Martin felt that we needed to push it forward there.

There is a Bond-M arc over the course of the Brosnan movies. She barely tolerates him in *GoldenEye*, but over the course of a few films, they come to respect each other tremendously.
Totally unplanned. That just came about fortuitously.

Bond's relationship with Q is different in Pierce's movies than it is in the earlier movies, where Q is eternally frustrated with Connery and Moore. Q seems to have affection for Pierce's Bond.

I'll explain how that happened. I became great friends with Desmond. And Desmond explained that on his first Bond, he was not sure how to play it and the director said to him, "Everyone in the movie likes Bond, but you can't stand him."

It's interesting to think that at one time Desmond Llewelyn would have had any trouble playing Q.

He didn't know how to play him because the words on the page are [extremely technical]. Desmond asked, "What's my relationship to Bond?" Terence Young said, "Bond thinks he's better than your equipment. So you don't like Bond." So now this comes all the way forward, and by the time Desmond is in *GoldenEye*, there's more than a generation between Bond and Q. I also think there was a real affinity between Pierce and Desmond.

In the first one [*GoldenEye*], there was obviously a certain amount of warmth between the two of them but there was still an edge to it. At the end of the scene Bond points to a sandwich and says, "What's that?" And Q says, "Don't touch that, that's my lunch."

I didn't plan it or anything, but then in the second one [*Tomorrow Never Dies*], there was irony about their relationship. For instance, Bond shows up at the airport to rent a car. And then Q appears and says, "Will you need damage, personal injury?"

Then in the third one [*The World Is Not Enough*], Desmond knew he wanted to be written out. He and I talked about it. Barbara talked about it. Michael had talked about it. We all talked about it. Barbara always said to him, "I refuse to deal with this. We're not going to talk about writing him out of the series. It's not going to happen." But we all knew that sooner or later it was.

I went back that night to think about it and really try to figure out the relationship between these guys. And then it just came to me—and this is going back to *The Sword and the Stone*—that Desmond was Merlin to Bond's Arthur. That's where the relationship ended up. And that's one of those [emotionally resonant] scenes that I don't think you could've seen thirty years earlier.

Q's exit is a surprisingly touching and tender moment between the two of them.

Yes, Desmond was beloved.

Was your office at Pinewood?

We worked at Pinewood, and we also had offices at Piccadilly.

What's a Bond writer room look like?
It's just a regular office. No, there are no Bond girls running through it.

Any remnants of Bond in the offices?
There are some posters. But there's nothing that would say to you that this is where this stuff comes from. If you're wondering if there are props and things like that, the answer is no.

It's Universal Exports [the nondescript office, which acts as cover for MI6].
Yeah, it is Universal Exports.

In addition to your three Brosnan films, you also wrote Bond video games. It seems unlikely but Connery came back as Bond in a video game.
He came back and did *From Russia with Love* as a video game. He did it because his grandchildren liked video games, so he wanted to be a part of it. Meeting him was truly one of the most amazing moments for me. It's the kind of moment when I'm sitting there and suddenly I think, "Fuck, I'm talking to Sean Connery. How did I get here?" I think back to when I was a little kid in Maplewood, New Jersey, looking up at the screen at *Goldfinger*, and you just go, "How did this happen?" He was incredibly kind to me. The funny thing is that I've never met anyone who worked on the franchise who did not immediately embrace you.

You're all brothers?
In some way. If you've been inside this circus, and you've been inside of this machine that's so big, in some way you have to be brothers. When you meet Sean Connery, you're not going to ask stupid questions. Because you've both been in that branch of the army, you're not going to ask, "So what was it like?" Yes, you may get to the point of gossiping. You might ask, "Did you have this same problem that I did?"

I remember once being in London and introducing [former Bond women] Maryam d'Abo to Denise Richards. I watched as they fell on each other like long-lost sisters. Because I don't think it's possible for you or me to know what it's like to be a Bond girl. And it's like a small fraternity of people who have done this. And you all treat each other as if you've been through the wars together.

What were Connery's concerns about the video game? Did he have any?
No. No, he was a gent. He just showed up and did the work. He understood what it was and understood what we had to do. I don't recall any notes from him.

Sean Connery's Bond is gunning for trouble.
ILLUSTRATION BY PAT CARBAJAL

Tell me about that encounter.

I had met him in Los Angeles before that. I knew that he was doing it, and it was a social event. And it was, Oh, I know who you are, and you know who I am, and it's good to meet you, and let's gossip a little about this or that and the next thing. And Connery joked, "I hope you're getting paid." I said, "Yeah, I hope you're getting paid." He talked about how much he looked forward to doing the game.

I spoke with one of the game producers, and he indicated that Connery was not only great to work with but fondly reminisced about his time as Bond.

I cannot speak for him but he probably has great affection for the character. I've heard the stories of him being somewhat prickly about Bond. I can imagine where that comes from. In my own life, if I get introduced to somebody and they start in with Bond stuff, I smile and say, "Okay, you got three questions. And then we're going to talk about you."

A dinner party must be hell for you.

No, because nobody does it anymore and you learn how to deal with it. You trot out one great story and then you just say, "Come on, I don't wanna talk about that. Let's talk about you." But you don't want to be the guy sitting at a dinner party trotting out stories about your days playing college basketball or college football. I can only imagine what it was like for Connery. Here's a guy who whenever he went into a bar anywhere in the world, somebody probably thought it was cute to send over a vodka martini. But we didn't start from that point. We didn't start there.

You also were a writer on the *007 Legends* game. It takes Daniel Craig and puts him in non–Daniel Craig movies. It's a great idea.

Well, that was Barbara and Michael. And David Wilson supervised that. It was never a question that it was going to be anybody but Daniel Craig because Daniel Craig was Bond at that particular time. And they wanted to do it for the fiftieth anniversary, and so it was a question of, can you do this to reflect the current Bond? And the writing had to follow. Let me give you an example. With Pierce, I would write more witticisms, more wry remarks. But that's not Daniel's character, so you don't write that in. In fact, it was a learning curve as I was doing it. Because Daniel is a man of fewer words than Pierce, I had to adjust the writing.

What did you have to do to make Craig's Bond into Connery's, or were they closer?

No, that one was closer. This was just keeping the dialogue short. And it turned out, in the end, Daniel didn't do the voices for that game.

I didn't know that until after I played it. I thought it was Craig until I started researching this book. [*Note*: Timothy Watson performed a pitch-perfect imitation of Craig.]

No, it was a sound-alike, because Craig was busy making the movie.

The Daniel Craig Bond films delved into the spy's psyche.

ILLUSTRATION BY PAT CARBAJAL

Bond games introduced me to the world of gaming.

Probably *GoldenEye* [the acclaimed video game].

No, it was *Blood Stone*.

It's funny you played *Blood Stone*. *Blood Stone* is my favorite of all the games.

What do you like about it?

Well, I liked it because it's a Bond adventure. It's entirely new. There was nothing in it that had been used before. And I liked the female character [Nicole Hunter]. I thought about her as an ex-supermodel, kind of like Jerry Hall, who was married to Mick Jagger. I thought of her as a Jerry Hall-ish character, a former "It girl" who was in this situation. She was a jewelry designer, and I loved the character. I thought it was great to have a former "It girl" who had fallen into this spy world. I liked that part of it, and I thought it was a great story. Gregg Wilson and David Wilson worked on the story, and I just thought it was a fun romp.

Teaming up with a jewelry designer isn't a mission that they would use in an actual Bond movie. It's almost a spinoff mission. But the game felt like an actual Bond movie and it hit all the beats you want in a Bond film.

Yes, but we weren't adapting a Bond movie. We got to make up everything. It begins with an attack on the Acropolis. It felt fresh. We weren't working from anything. It was just, Go have a good time and tell us a Bond story.

Do the games take a long time to develop and write?

The Bond games took a lot of time, particularly *Legends*. That one was the most fun to work on. *From Russia with Love* was just a straight adaptation, taking out things that didn't make sense today and updating it. It was interesting because it was the first time I realized that there had been an entire generation of kids who fell in love with Bond through the [original 1997 version of] *GoldenEye* game, which I did not work on. I would've never expected that.

You made some structural changes to the *From Russia with Love* game. In the movie, Red Grant is killed about halfway through. In the game, his death is moved to the end.

Yes. Because there was no bigger baddie.

Do you know why *From Russia with* Love was chosen and not another title?

No, I don't. Certain decisions take place above your pay grade. It's funny though. I remember reading some of the online criticisms in the fan community about the game, about why they didn't get this actor, why they didn't get that actor. "Surely this actress would've just been delighted to have been part of this. These people clearly would've worked for free." No, they wouldn't have worked for free. It's a billion-dollar franchise and the actor and the agent and everyone else wants a piece of it. They're not doing this out of the goodness of their hearts for the fan community.

Shocking, positively shocking.

Yeah, shocking, exactly. Again, that's Maibaum. There's a perfect example of his contribution. That line doesn't appear in the book *Goldfinger* (1959).

Your point is that people should go back to Maibaum, not the books. His papers and screenplays are preserved at the University of Iowa. Even then, you never know whose ideas are reflected in the various drafts of the script.

Yeah, you never know. Only the writer knows. Let me give you an example. There's a scene in *GoldenEye* where Pierce is on the beach with Izabella Scorupco [who plays Bond girl Natalya Simonova.] Natalya asks, "How can you be so cold?" Bond says, "It's what keeps me alive." She says, "No, it's what keeps you alone." That scene came about because Izabella and Pierce separately went to Martin Campbell and said that they felt there wasn't enough of their relationship. Martin Campbell agreed, and he called me and said, "Come to London and write this scene on the beach. Write a scene." And that's where that "boys with toys" thing came from. [When Natalya finally has had it with the verbal jousting between Bond and his interrogator, Defense Minister Dimitri Mishkin, she cries out, "Oh, stop it, both of you! Stop it! You're like . . . boys with toys!"]

Now I don't know this for certain but I'm pretty sure that Barbara and Michael are probably somewhere in the gears of all of that. I can't say that it came from Izabella. I can't say that it came from Pierce. I can't say that it came from Martin. It came from the five of them. It's interlocking.

There are a lot of people with a lot of different ideas, and the writer needs to find a valid reason to include something in the script.

Yeah, and so stuff comes from many different places. Clearly, a lot of it comes from the writers. But I remember in *GoldenEye* that the Zukovsky character, who was Robbie Coltrane, had not really been written. There was a character named Zukovsky who was a former KGB agent but it wasn't fully developed yet. I remember sitting in our offices at Leavesden, which is now Warner Brothers London, and a former Rolls-Royce jet engine manufacturing plant. I had met Robbie Coltrane once before when he was making the movie *Nuns on the Run* (1990), so I kind of knew him, but not really.

Martin walked into my office with Coltrane and said, "He's going to play Zukovsky." And Robbie made fun of me and said, "You better write a good role for me." Of course, it was already written, but you better [flesh it out]. And I thought, "Who do I steal from? What am I going to do here?" I thought back to *Casablanca* (1942) and took the Sydney Greenstreet character. Sydney Greenstreet is doing all sorts of illegal things in Casablanca. So then it became an homage to that character. His first lines are, "The free-market economy. I swear it will be the end of me." That's very much Sydney Greenstreet-ish. But Robbie made the character his own.

And there's a hilarious line, which is completely ad-libbed and is not in the script. Robbie's character is complaining about his knee, which Bond had shot in an earlier episode. And Robbie goes, "My knee hurts every day, Mr. Bond. It hurts in the winters, and it hurts in the cold, and the winters are long here." And he turns to somebody in the back and he goes, "How long are the winters?" And the guy just goes, "It depends." That line was completely ad-libbed.

IMDb trivia made a connection about that scene. In *The World Is Not Enough*, Bond is tied up and Robbie Coltrane shoots him free with his cane. If Bond hadn't shot Coltrane in an earlier episode, which is referenced in *GoldenEye*, Coltrane wouldn't have been able to save Bond in *The World Is Not Enough*, because he wouldn't have had a cane that shoots bullets.
Exactly. It was all fortuitous. And then you take stuff from real life. I was getting per-diem money in London. Every Friday they would give me this wad of cash, which I would then hand to my wife. And there's a line in *The World Is Not Enough* where Bond holds out a wad of cash and says, "Here, take an inch." That had to do with my per diem.

What is your proudest Bond moment?
Desmond's good-bye.

What else comes to mind?
When you walk onto a Bond set, you're working on something that's much larger than life. You feel lucky to be a part of it. Everyone is part of it for a short period of time. And in the years that followed, how wonderfully gracious and loyal Barbara and Michael have been. And how incredibly lucky I am to have gotten a chance to be part of what is the largest franchise in motion picture history.

TOM MANKIEWICZ

Tom Mankiewicz was a widely respected craftsman whose wit was the trademark of his writing. Mankiewicz wrote the screenplay to Sean Connery's last Eon-produced Bond film, *Diamonds Are Forever*, with Richard Maibaum. Cubby Broccoli and Harry Saltzman were so impressed by the work he did on *Diamonds Are Forever* that they hired him to pen the next Bond film, *Live and Let Die*, while *Diamonds* was still in production. For *Live and Let Die*, Mankiewicz met another challenge: he tailored the script to accommodate the flair for playing light comedy of the new James Bond actor, Roger Moore.

For *The Man with the Golden Gun*, Moore's second Bond film, Mankiewicz devised Roger Moore's favorite one-liner. As Bond trains a rifle at the crotch of a hostile weapons maker from whom he has to extract information, he demands, "Speak now or forever hold your piece."

The celebrated screenwriter also performed uncredited work on the next two Bond movies. Mankiewicz rewrote *The Spy Who Loved Me*[5] and wrote an early treatment for *Moonraker*.[6] He also co-wrote the screenplays for *Superman* (1978) and *Superman II* (1980).

Mankiewicz died at the age of sixty-eight on July 31, 2010. His father was writer-director Joseph Mankiewicz (*All About Eve*) and his uncle was screenwriter Herman Mankiewicz (*Citizen Kane*).

When people go see a Bond film, they go because they personally like the character and want to spend some time with him. The plot is almost irrelevant to them.

Absolutely. You're absolutely right. It's the character of Bond that makes the movie. After George Lazenby played Bond in *On Her Majesty's Secret Service*, Sean came back with *Diamonds Are Forever*. One night he said to me, "I couldn't understand the fucking script. Could you? You wrote it." And I said, "Sean, all I know is at the beginning Harry Saltzman said to me, 'What's Blofeld's ultimate threat?' I said, 'Harry, he's going to destroy the world.'" I swear to God, Harry said, "It's not big enough."

But when you look at the rules—and start with the rules—who are you writing? You're writing a guy who every man wants to be and every woman wants to fuck. No woman wants to marry James Bond. I'm sorry—even though it's a heartbreaking thing in *On Her Majesty's Secret Service* when the Diana Rigg character dies. Every woman who goes to see Bond thinks about spending a weekend with him. How would you like to go to Rio with Bond? How would you like to go to the Bahamas with Bond? You don't want to stay too long. He's every woman's one-nighter, two-nighter, three-nighter fantasy.

Once you know that, Bond can be as cruel as you want him to be. I don't mean actively cruel, but that wonderful line in *Thunderball* when Luciana Paluzzi is shot in the back when he's dancing with her and he says, "Do you mind if my date sits this one out? She's just dead." Then he puts her down at a table full of people and the audience laughs. Because you've established that character so well. If a normal character did that onscreen, you'd think, "What a despicable, horrible human being." But it's James Bond.

During my time writing Bond, Bond was becoming more like a Disney picture. That car in *Goldfinger* changed James Bond forever. The ejector seat, the squirting of the oil, the machine guns. The audience just loved it. So the pressure was on to get more and more stuff, but Bond should have remained the same. Bond should have been a smoker, although they outlawed it. Sean smoked for the first five or six movies. There was a limit to how much he could drink onscreen. It became more of a family movie. Bond's original character got a little softer toward the end of Roger's run, and with Timothy Dalton, they tried to bring back the tougher guy.

Do you think the audience should see only a limited amount of his personal life?

His personal life is never really dealt with in the books except in *On Her Majesty's Secret Service* (1963). By the way, the novels are a lot of fun to read. In terms of his private life, it's always been verboten to get into that. Bond's personal life is a cipher to me. I don't see that he has a personal life. He's always on the move. He's always checking into a hotel suite. He's always got the good girl and the bad girl. Usually two bad girls. There's the bad girl that he turns around and makes a good girl. The bad girl who tries to kill him that he winds up killing, but essentially it's Bond faces the world as opposed to Bond sits at home.

Bond shouldn't be an introspective or self-reflective person?

I don't think he can be introspective or self-reflective. Also, he cannot be involved in a serious relationship with a woman whom he truly loves and continue to be James Bond because it's totally irresponsible. Here's a guy who gets caught inside coffins and thrown out windows. You couldn't say, "This is my wife and I love her," or, "This is my wife and kids," and continue to put yourself in harm's way as James Bond always does.

I had said to Sean back then, "If you want to do a completely original film"—and I talked to Cubby about it—"we should do a James Bond where you are in the Caribbean or wherever and you're on the heels of an assassin, and you are one step slower. You realize that your time is up. He outmaneuvers you. It's only through your wits that you finally kill him. During the film, you fall in love and we'd cast a big movie star." I was thinking of Sophia Loren back then, who would be about Sean's age, and

Timothy Dalton deepened the character of James Bond.
ILLUSTRATION BY PAT CARBAJAL

they'd sail off into the sunset. Cubby said, "That's great except there'd be no more fucking Bond movies and I want to keep making them."

By the way, Sean once came to me to write his unofficial Bond movie, *Never Say Never Again*. I was very close to the Broccolis and I said, "I can't do that." Then after the picture was made and they had to reshoot, he asked me to come see it and to give him suggestions. I called Cubby and said, "Is that all right with you?" Cubby said, "Oh, absolutely. Absolutely." He said, "By the way, it would have been alright with me if you had written it." I never asked him because I didn't want to put Cubby in that position.

In addition to your three Bond films, you also wrote two Superman movies. Christopher Reeve had concerns about being typecast as Superman.

It's amazing that he was thinking about it at the time because the film had not come out and he had been in only one other movie in a supporting part. His first concern was—and it's a young actor's concern—"Am I going to be Superman for the rest of my life?" He wanted me to get him in touch with Sean Connery because I had done *Diamonds Are Forever* with Sean and I knew him pretty well. He said, "Sean Connery will know about typecasting because he doesn't play Bond anymore. I've got to talk to him." He was so earnest.

One night there was a party. I knew Sean wouldn't want to talk to him about it in that way. Sean could be a prickly guy, too. Well, we were there, and there was Sean. Chris said, "Oh, please. I've got to talk to him." I went up to Sean and said, "The kid playing Superman is over there and he wants to talk to you about typecasting." Sean said, "Ahh, geez, Boy-o." Sean used to call me "Boy-o." I was only twenty-seven when I wrote *Diamonds Are Forever*, so I was "Boy-o" to him, but I persisted, "Do me a favor and just talk to him." He agreed finally and then he said to Chris, "In the first place, if Boy-o wrote the script, it's probably not going to be a fucking hit." He loved to take the Mickey out of me. He said, "So you don't have to worry about that. Now, if it is a hit, then find yourself something completely different to do right away." Which I guess was why Chris did *Somewhere in Time* (1980), a love story [with Bond woman Jane Seymour]. Then Sean added, "By the way, if it is a big hit, get yourself the best fucking lawyer in the world and stick it to them." Then, the favor granted, he walked away. I said to Chris, "Well, there's your advice."

What is the difference between writing for Sean Connery and Roger Moore?

As a writer, I always said the difference between Sean and Roger is that Sean used to throw away the throwaway lines, and Roger, because of his RADA [Royal Academy of Dramatic Arts] upbringing, *played* them. So I wrote dialogue for Roger to really play those quips. The difference is you can put Sean at a nightclub table with a beautiful girl opposite him, and he could just as easily lean across the table and kiss her or use his steak knife under the table to stick it in her gut and then say, "Excuse me, waiter. I have nothing to cut my meat with." The audience will accept him doing either one. Roger can kiss the girl but if he tries the knife thing, he would look nasty. Roger looks like a nice guy. Sean can look like a bastard, meaning that there's a twinkle of violence in Sean's eye that just isn't there in Roger's.

In *The Man with the Golden Gun*, Moore as Bond slaps a woman. Do you think it wasn't that successful for the reasons you described?

Yeah, that's right. First of all, they were trying to make Roger more physical. In the beginning of *Live and Let Die*—and Roger's just a wonderful, wonderful man and has become a great friend—in the first scene we filmed, he was running for the double-decker bus that eventually gets shaved off during his car chase. Guy Hamilton said, "When we start, Roger, you run for the bus and hop on." Roger said, "There's something you oughta know about me, Guy. I can't run." Guy said, "Can't run?" Roger said, "I look like a twit when I run. I have such long legs." He said, "Watch." And he ran and he looked like Bambi. So you had to adjust. Guy said, "Right then. Roger, walk briskly towards the bus and get on." Of course, every actor has his strengths and weaknesses. [*Note:* As usual, Moore might have been unnecessarily hard on himself about his running abilities. In *The 007 Diaries*, Moore's 1973 account of filming *Live and Let Die*, the actor revealed that on the first day of principal photography he injured his leg while performing a stunt.[7]]

It was a huge deal for Roger to take over for Sean. When he did, we were down in Jamaica, where there was an enormous press conference. Someone said, "Why are you doing this?" Roger said, "When I was a young actor at RADA, Noel Coward was in the audience one night. He said to me after the play, "Young man, with your devastating good looks and your disastrous lack of talent, you should take any job ever offered you. In the event that you're offered two jobs simultaneously, take the one that offers the most money." Roger said, "Here I am." He's wonderful. He's a terrific guy.

When Roger Moore told the Noel Coward story, he was obviously being self-deprecating. He brought a lot to the role.

Oh, absolutely. Roger is very smart. Besides his natural modesty, he was self-deprecating because he understood that people love Sean and that Sean is a legend. It was exactly the right thing, the graceful thing to do. Especially at that particular press conference, since there wasn't a foot of film yet with him as James Bond.

He got a bit of a bum rap over the years.

Of course he has. It's because he followed such a big act. Sean was the *only* guy at the time—as George Lazenby found out—that people would accept in that part. The fact that Roger stayed on for so many of them is a real tribute to him, and he did it really well.

In *Moonraker*, outer space belonged to Roger Moore's James Bond.

ILLUSTRATION BY PAT CARBAJAL

Do you recall any other script notes that Connery gave you?

Sean wanted to have a meeting when he arrived in Vegas to do *Diamonds Are Forever*. I was so pleasantly surprised that about half of his notes were for other characters. He would say, "Are you sure she should say this here? Wouldn't it be stronger if she did something?" I thought, "Good for him. He's really read the script and he's thinking about everybody in it." I'm sure he thought, "Don't worry about me, I've played this part before." He would say, "Can I get something funnier here?" When Lana Wood appears at the crap table and says, "Hi, I'm Plenty." Bond says, "Why of course you are." She says, "Plenty O'Toole." He asked me if he could respond, 'Named after your father perhaps?'" I said, "It's a great line."

But the very fact that he asked me—I was only twenty-seven-years-old—shows you the way he goes about his work. He's totally professional. Any other actor would just have tried it right in the take. I was amazed. It's a good line. It's *his* line.

Do you think that the character of Bond in *Diamonds Are Forever* is consistent with his character in *Live and Let Die*?

No. Roger's character in *Live and Let Die* is a much more urbane Bond. I played to his strength. For instance, one of my favorite lines in there occurs when he's taking the little old lady for the flying lesson and, because they're being chased, they fly around in the plane, half-destroying the airport. The little old lady is so frightened by the end of the chase that she nearly passes out. He looks at her and says, "Same time tomorrow, Mrs. Bell?" Now, Sean wouldn't have played that well. I would have found another line for him, but Roger had this urbane kind of cheeriness about him that you can do that. It's just an instinct. You know who you're writing for.

You spoke earlier about Connery's uneasy relationship with the part. How did Moore feel about playing Bond? Moore seemed more comfortable with it, a little more at ease.

Roger is very comfortable in his own skin. He really is. And that shows. So when you give him a part to play that suits him, he is just awfully good at it. He's a real pro. That's a wonderful quality for an actor to possess, especially when you know that you're playing something that you are absolutely right for. If you cast Roger as a crazed killer because you thought, "Boy, this is gonna be great because you're casting Roger against type," you'd probably be disappointed. I don't know if Roger plays that very well. I suspect he'd be uncomfortable playing so dark a character.

Do you have a favorite one-liner?

Maybe the best Bond quip that I ever wrote—and I wrote hundreds of them—was cut out of *The Spy Who Loved Me*. It's when Roger meets Barbara Bach at the bar. He knows that she's a Soviet major, and she knows he's 007. Anyway, he says, "I must say, you're prettier than your pictures, Major." She responds, "The only picture I've seen of you, Mr. Bond, was taken in bed with one of our agents—a Miss Tatiana Romanova." She's the girl in *From Russia with Love*. Roger then said, "Was she smiling?" And Barbara Bach answers, "As I recall, her mouth was not immediately visible." Roger retorts, "Then I was smiling."

DICK CLEMENT AND IAN LA FRENAIS

The writing team of Dick Clement and Ian La Frenais performed an uncredited rewrite on Lorenzo Semple Jr.'s *Never Say Never Again* script while the non-Eon-produced film was in production.

Clement and La Frenais wrote the Beatles jukebox musical *Across the Universe* (2007) with director Julie Taymor and the heist film *The Bank Job* (2008). They have scripted many beloved British television shows, including Bob Hoskins's career-launching sitcom *Thick As Thieves* (1974) and the Ian McShane caper *Lovejoy* (1986–1994). Writing partners for more than five decades, Clement and La Frenais are known for their carefully drawn characters and their witty dialogue.

Irvin Kershner (*The Empire Strikes Back*) directed Sean Connery in *Never Say Never Again*, his seventh and final filmed performance as Bond. Connery effortlessly plays the debonair spy with a welcoming twinkle in his eye and the confidence of an actor who is clearly at ease in his own skin. Rounding out the cast is an eclectic ensemble, including Klaus Maria Brandauer as an idiosyncratic and unhinged mega-lomaniac Maximilian Largo, Edward Fox as a stuffy M, Max Von Sydow as an imperial Blofeld, a wide-eyed Kim Basinger as the too-trusting Domino Petachi, Bernie Cassie as the first African American Felix Leiter, and Barbara Carrera as the black widow SPECTRE operative Fatima Blush.

The movie begins with a frustrated Bond, wasting his time by playing war games and squandering his skills by teaching would-be agents the art of spycraft, and ends with him eschewing his traditional five o'clock martini and speciously vowing retirement. Along the way, Bond seduces multiple women, dances the tango, plays a deadly video game, kills a beautiful assassin with a pen gun, battles enemies underwater, and thwarts an extortion plot involving two stolen nuclear warheads. In other words, it's business as usual for a weathered Bond who, despite the mileage, still hasn't lost his mojo.

How did you become involved with *Never Say Never Again*?
Dick Clement: We were making a television series called *Auf Wiedersehen, Pet* [1983–2004] in England and we bumped into Irvin Kershner in the commissary in Elstree. We already knew him, so we said, "Oh, you're doing this Bond film, do you need a rewrite?" He replied, "Yes, I probably do." We thought that'd be great. We went back home to California and didn't hear anything. So after a little while, we called our agent and asked, "Do they still need a rewrite on the Bond film?" He called back and said, "Yes, can you go to Nice [France]?" We were in the middle of writing a very boring TV pilot and we couldn't wait to get out of that. So we hopped on a plane and went to Nice.

The first thing we did when we got to Nice was to look at what they had already shot. They had been shooting for about three weeks, and it was clear to us that there were a lot of problems. We could see that Klaus Maria Brandauer, who was playing the villain, was going through all sorts of tricks that actors do when they don't trust the script. Things like that were going on and the scenes were very long-winded. Then we started to do some work and one of the things we noticed was that Bond goes to the Bahamas and there was no explanation as to why he went. Kersh [Kershner] just looked at this and said, "Well, you better find a reason because there's a unit shooting underwater there now." So we did at least try to piece that together. [*Note:* In the finished film, Bond travels to the Bahamas because he learns that Largo is a resident of the island.]

It was a curious situation because there was a lot of paranoia around the set because they were terrified of being sued by Broccoli. At one time we were told that we could shoot only the dialogue that's in the original novel. Obviously, you cannot make a movie in which you can use only the dialogue from a novel. The insurance company was also paranoid about being sued. Everybody was very jittery. This made Sean somewhat bad tempered because he had hoped that all these problems had been sorted out before he started shooting. We were kind of in the middle of all that.

Ian La Frenais: The problem was not the script; we're not badmouthing the previous writer [Lorenzo Semple Jr., who also wrote the conspiracy thrillers *The Parallax View* (1974) and *Three Days of the Condor* (1975) as well as the television series *Batman* (1966–1968)]. But for whatever reason, they started shooting before they were ready and the film was definitely not ready to shoot. We were in the position of plumbers fixing a bad leak. We had to be aware of the logistics and the politics as well as the writing. But all the problems stemmed from the behind-the-scenes financing and insurance issues, all the logistical things. They were not prepared to start when they did.

Clement: We did about a week's work in Nice and we're at the airport ready to fly back to London because they finished shooting the Nice section. I remember going up to Kershner and saying, "Do you like your opening sequence?" He looked at me and said, "Not especially, why?" I said, "In the current script, it's a jousting tournament sequence. But it was also a fake-out because you don't know whether you're back in the Middle Ages or it's the present." It turns out to be a jousting tournament for a modern audience between a knight wearing black armor and a knight in white armor. The knights bash the crap out of each other. Eventually, one of them wins, takes off his helmet, and he's revealed to be James Bond. We said, "Here's the thing: the key asset you've got in making this movie is Sean Connery whom a lot of people regard as *the* James Bond. You've got him and they [Eon, which was shooting *Octopussy* at the same time] haven't. It's a huge asset. Why don't you show him from the word go?" We got back to London, checked into a hotel, and then in the middle of the night we got a call saying, "Can you possibly be on a plane to the Bahamas in the morning?"

As a result of that conversation at the Nice airport, we suddenly found ourselves continuing with the film when we hadn't thought that was going to happen. It was delightful and great fun. We then wrote a good bit more in the Bahamas, including creating a new character, Nigel Small-Fawcett, that we suggested. We got Rowan Atkinson to play the part. That was entirely our thought. We thought we needed a little bit of humor in the middle of the film.

La Frenais: We replaced the jousting sequence with the training exercise, which is a fake out [for the audience, which thinks Bond is stabbed while conducting a dangerous mission]. M tells Bond that he would have been dead if he was on an actual mission.

Clement: Halfway through shooting the movie, they showed the sequence to the crew to encourage them and say, "Hey, we've got some good stuff here." After watching it, the crew applauded it and thought it was a great sequence. It was a great introduction.

La Frenais: It was supposed to be a tense and exciting sequence with a ticking clock.

Clement: But they made a decision late in postproduction, to put a [jazzy pop] song over it and that killed the tension.

La Frenais: The song killed all excitement. It should have been at the end credits.

Clement: Or over a separate credit sequence.

La Frenais: It was just so counterproductive to what we'd written. Anyhow, from the Bahamas we then went back to work on it in Elstree in London.

How long were you in the Bahamas?
La Frenais: We were in the Bahamas for about ten days.

Clement: We shot a sequence with Kim Basinger; we shot another sequence with Barbara Carrera.

La Frenais: By now, we were aware of the politics and the schism between [producer] Jack Schwartzman's people, which included [executive producer] Kevin McClory and Sean and his agent. Irvin was in the middle but he also needed to get on with it, to look for locations and direct the film. Schwartzman gave us his view, and Sean gave us his view. We tried to remain neutral. But one time we were in the hotel suite with both parties. At the end of the meeting, Sean remarked that this is a Mickey Mouse outfit. Then he turned to Dick and me and said, "Right, let's go for dinner."

Clement: We only met McClory once; he seemed slightly secretive. There were introductions and nothing much more. We were then told the whole backstory of his involvement with *Thunderball*, which is fascinating. He'd come up with the original plot and Eon said, "We'll give you the remake rights to the Bond film" and everyone laughed as if that's ever going to happen.

Where did you do the writing?
Clement: In hotel rooms. Then we'd go out to the set for a little break and usually lunch, and then we'd go back to the hotel room, and then we'd have a game of tennis before they all wrapped. Then it was back on Elstree to be in the cutting room with Kersh, where we were looking for solutions to problems. Sometimes we needed a line to explain something. We kept trying to fix things.

La Frenais: We spent hours in the cutting room with Kersh. A lot of it was boring, the action was underwater and Kersh was exhausted and sick of it. So he was glad when we'd pop in for a few hours.

Clement: [Dryly] We don't do underwater.

La Frenais: We'd say, "You can cut that; you don't need that." Both of us loved being in the editing room, so it was no drag. Barbra Streisand was next door cutting *Yentl* (1983). One day she sent Kershner and me a bottle of red wine. That was when I became a fan of hers. I'd been indifferent to Streisand before that.

When you're rewriting on location, with production already underway—and since you have to work within the existing framework of the script—are you primarily adjusting the dialogue and finding more character moments?
Clement: Right. On this occasion, in addition to fixing dialogue, we suggested whole new scenes. Like the opening scene, for example, and the scenes with Nigel Small-Fawcett. We suggested and wrote those scenes, and then they found the locations for them. So it was unusual, but we felt we made quite a significant contribution.

La Frenais: It's a lot of fun because as writers you spend so many hours writing things that don't get produced. Or you can spend two years writing something before it gets produced and then you just wait for that day when you get your call sheet. When you're writing on location, you're in a building with sets, diagrams on the walls, and costumes. You have to deliver because everything is going on around you, so that's exciting. It's an adrenaline fix.

Judging by his performance, Connery seemed invested in the picture and wasn't merely coasting through it. What was your impression of Connery's feelings about returning to Bond?
La Frenais: Because he'd never made his fair piece of the pie on the previous Bond films, this was a chance to be compensated properly for being the iconic Double-O-Seven.

Clement: I think that had a lot to do with it.

La Frenais: Yes, the financial [incentive] had a lot to do with it. Not that he would've taken it on if he didn't think he could convince people that he could play the part.

Clement: I remember watching the dailies of the scene where Bond is being confronted by Barbara Carrera in the garage and she's about to kill him. The camera was on Sean while she was doing her lines. It wasn't even Bond speaking but I remember being incredibly impressed by how alive Sean looked. There was never a moment when he went flat or dead or went on automatic pilot. There was something happening in his face the whole time, even when it was the offscreen lines, and that impressed me. I thought, boy, he really does know what he's doing. It was there. I was very impressed with that.

Ian, what do you remember about watching Connery in the dailies?
La Frenais: I thought, oh my god, the governor's back. I've never ever been disappointed by anything Connery's done; I don't think he's capable of strolling through a film. It was exciting for me.

Clement: I remember saying to him about the script, "Bond is still Bond. He gets up, has a bonk, goes underwater, fights sharks, comes up, and has a bonk. That proves *something*." Sean says, "It proves it's a movie."

What was your take on Bond's character and his motivation?
Clement: We inherited Bond and we're going along with what's already there so we can't claim to have had a fresh vision of Bond. But the main thing was he was a little older but he's still the quintessential Bond. We weren't trying to reinvent him at all.

We thought that just having Sean was enough. When somebody's already played the part several times, you don't come along and say, "Here's a new way of doing it." Everybody wanted to re-create what he had already done successfully. The masculinity of Sean is so strong and his charm is there. He looks like a lady's man who also likes a fine life. He created that.

La Frenais: Every time a new actor is cast to play Bond, they're fairly young. But, of course, that wasn't the case with this movie. This is a Bond who'd already been established in the 1960s and Bond was returning twenty years later. This is an older Bond. We never wrote anything to establish that he'd come out of retirement, but our idea of the training program was to see if he was still up to snuff. We faced the issue of his age head-on when Edward says, "You're not in the best of shape. You're two seconds slower than you should be." We're acknowledging his age.

La Frenais: I don't think age ever has had any impact on Connery's sexual attractiveness or potency. I remember Dick and I were at a party years ago at a restaurant in LA called The Dome. It was in its heyday. Elton John was there, maybe Rod Stewart. There were a lot of people there and Sean came in. Sean was in his late fifties, nearly sixty, and every woman's eye in the room went to him. It's a sexual magnetism that I know is too late for me ever to acquire.

There's a lot of wit in the movie.
Clement: We always try to make sure that whatever we do—however serious it is—that there is always some humor because there is always humor in life.

La Frenais: We said, "Let's acknowledge this is an older Bond and that things have changed." We gave a line to Q, "Now you're back Mr. Bond, I hope we can have some more gratuitous sex and violence." They weren't sure about that line at all and we begged them to use it.

I remember that line was frequently quoted in reviews for the film. Speaking of that same scene, that Q dynamic was wonderful and a different dynamic than Desmond Llewelyn's Q, who barely tolerates Bond. This Q seems to have affection for Bond.
La Frenais: Yes, it was Alec McCowen who played Q, and he was very good. Yes, it was a different way to play that relationship. It's nice hearing that that line resonated so much. That definitely was one of ours.

Sean Connery set the template for 007.

ILLUSTRATION BY PAT CARBAJAL

La Frenais: I'll tell you, we had one funny reward. The props people in films are meticulous. Dick and I wrote a scene and we specified the vintage of champagnes and wines. We wrote a line quite intentionally where Bond's suitcase contains the 1964 [Château] Cheval Blanc.

Clement: It was one of the sixes; I forget whether it was 1964 or 1963.

La Frenais: Well, Dick and I chose a fantastic wine, and we knew that props were just going to get it for £2,000 at Berry Brothers [& Rudd, a liquor store].

Clement: I remember the prop guy came up to us and said, "I couldn't get the 1964 Cheval Blanc. Will the 1963 do? We said, "Yeah, yeah, that'll be fine." But he was concerned with the authenticity of it.

La Frenais: We said to Sean, "As soon as that scene is wrapped, you grab the [unopened] bottle so the three of us can have it." He said, "I'll give it to you two." They shot the scene, cut, and to his credit, Sean grabbed the bottle. Later, Dick and I were doing rewrites in a service flat in London and we looked at Sean and said, "Well, we might as well open it. It wasn't quite as good as the 1964."

I understood that there were problems with production that Connery found frustrating. But did you get any sense that he enjoyed revisiting the role with his additional experience and maturity as an actor?

Clement: I think he did. He is a great professional and he was impatient with the lack of professionalism from other people. He said to us he experienced it before on *Cuba* (1979), where the script hadn't been right before they went on the floor, and he always swore that he was never going to do it again. To some extent, he found that this was a similar situation. But once the camera was rolling, he certainly played the part that he knew well, and I always got the feeling that he was enjoying that part of it.

La Frenais: Once he'd seen some new scenes that we'd written, and once he knew we'd given him some funny lines, and once all the narrative problems were sorted, he was so much more relaxed. Having dinner with him and Kersh in London, we would talk about work that needed to be done on upcoming scenes. But it was a different kind of writing—we were talking about how to tweak it, how to improve it, how to have fun with it. The stress of all the other shit had been removed. And yes, he loved being Bond.

The humor is tricky in a Bond movie. It has to be witty, but it should never go over the line into mockery or camp.

Clement: Yes, it is tricky. When I first saw the tango scene, I thought it might have crossed the line—seeing Bond do the tango. I thought Sean definitely did get away with it, but I was nervous about it. Were you, Ian?

La Frenais: Yes, but it was even worse because [other than the scene where he poses as a masseur], this was the first time he'd met [and could talk privately with] Kim Bassinger's character. He had to break the news to her that her brother had been killed [at Largo's behest]. In the original dailies, he takes her on the dance floor, twirls her around, and his opening line is, "Your brother's dead." We couldn't believe it. We thought, hello?, you might want to ease into that a bit. It couldn't be reshot so we had to rewrite that scene so that our lines could be used while you're looking at the other character's face. Sean's newly added lines are on Kim Bassinger's face and Kim's lines are on Sean's face. All that was done in the editing room.

Clement: We wrote a line that Bond says: "Try not to react when I tell you what I'm about to tell you. Your brother's dead." I thought it was in the film until I saw that clip a little while ago when it was on cable. The line is not in there but that was our intention. Otherwise, it seems brutal.

"Your brother's dead. Keep dancing."

Clement: Could I have this dance, please? Oh, your brother's dead.

La Frenais: It's a good line but it's not gonna get you laid.

Do you have any other favorite lines from the movie?

Clement: There was quite an amusing scene early on with Edward Fox about free radicals. [M warns Bond, "Too many free radicals, that's your problem . . . caused by eating too much red meat and white bread and too many dry martinis. Bond sensibly replies, "Then I shall cut out the white bread, sir."] At the health retreat, a nurse says, "I need a urine sample," and he says, "From here?" We had used that line in a television series [*Porridge* (1974–1977)] and we shamelessly recycled it.

La Frenais: Interestingly enough, at the beginning, we were shooting a television series called *Auf Wiedersehen, Pet*, which had just been voted the most popular series ever on British commercial television [in a survey consisting of English TV critics and five thousand members of the public]. When we originally bumped into Irv, we were shuttling between the *Auf Wiedersehen, Pet* set and the Bond film, and so was

Pat Roach, one of our actors. Pat Roach played the big guy [Lippe] who has the fight with Connery in the health spa with the weights. We went over across the set and there was Pat Roach.

Your urine sample joke pays off in the fight scene. Bond throws it at Pat Roach, who recoils, inadvertently impales himself on a shelf full of glass bottles, and then falls over, dead.
La Frenais: [With mock seriousness] Yes, so you see the urine joke wasn't gratuitous.

It was an important element of the plot.
La Frenais: [Not breaking the gag] Absolutely, all of us planned it that way.

There's a wonderful line in the movie. Wearing a wet bathing suit, Barbara Carrera falls on Bond and apologizes, "How reckless of me. I made you wet." Bond responds, "Yes, but my martini's still dry."
La Frenais: Barbara Carrera on her water skis. We watched that being shot.

Clement: We thought she was great. She was a fantastic presence and villainess. She had wonderful energy.

La Frenais: But once they're in Klaus Maria Brandauer's desert lair, it suddenly becomes a different kind of film.

Clement: We had much less to do with the last third of the film. Once you get into the action—the underwater sequence—that had very little to do with us.

What did you think about the completed film?
La Frenais: I couldn't get over them putting that song on the beginning over the training exercise. That got us off on the wrong foot. We said that to the Schwartzman and to Irv, but Irv said the studio wanted it. I enjoyed the film and I never enjoy the first screening of any of our films.

Clement: The first time you see something you've written all you see is what's *not* there. That's true even on the ones that you come to love later.

La Frenais: We did uncredited rewrites on *The Rock* [the 1996 film, which starred Sean Connery and Nicolas Cage]. I thought *The Rock* was great when I first saw it. We went on *The Rock* because of Sean. He said to the producers, I want Dick and Ian because of the Bond film.

Clement: But the historical truth of it is that Sean did not sign on to do *The Rock* until he'd read some pages that we wrote. [Producer] Jerry Bruckheimer was always extremely grateful to us for nailing Sean for that role; Sean didn't sign until we had written some stuff. Again, it was an uncredited rewrite, but it did us a lot of good in the business; the business tends to know.

What do you remember about your time working on *Moonraker*?

La Frenais: We got a phone call, "Would you like to do some work on a Bond film?" We said, "Wow, yes." We were sent the script and we did some work. I remember we wrote an amusing sequence that took place in a brothel in Rio. In those days [the late 1970s] people would say, can you be in Paris tomorrow? And you got a first-class ticket and stayed in a five-star hotel, the Rafael. I arrived before Dick and was taken out to dinner that night by Broccoli with Roger Moore and about six beautiful girls. I just thought this was a great life. Broccoli said, "We had a logistical switch and we won't be able to go to South America. So we won't be able to use any of that stuff that you guys have done." I thought he could've called us in LA and told us this rather than fly us over. We said, "Oh well, we're still here."

Do you remember anything about that sequence?

La Frenais: No, I don't remember. Then we were there for [additional] lines and we wrote something when Lois Chiles went to a Venetian glassworks.

Clement: In the end, I'm not sure if they used anything we wrote.

Do you still have the pages?

La Frenais: No, because it was pre-computer, pre-laptop.

Clement: That's disappeared without a trace. We've got an awful lot of stuff but not that.

La Frenais: I just remember that the action sequence took place in a Rio brothel. It wasn't based on personal experience.

When you write for Connery's Bond versus Roger Moore's Bond, are you writing the same Bond?

La Frenais: Yes, we try. Though it's different because we weren't on *Moonraker* much. But our approach is, this is Bond. We're not thinking of Roger's raised eyebrow or Sean's approach. You've just got to write what's best for the *character*.

Clement: Although if we were asked to do a Daniel Craig Bond, that would be a different approach. He has certainly reinvented Bond to a great extent. It's a different Bond, more muscular.

La Frenais: In a nice bit of symmetry, years ago we were doing a film [*Archangel* (2005)] in Latvia with Daniel Craig, right before he was Bond. This was not a rewrite. Daniel was working out a lot. We would wrap and we'd say, "We'll meet for dinner," and he'd say, "I'm going to the gym first." He knew what the rest of us didn't; he was going to be the next Bond.

Do you know what you would do with a Daniel Craig Bond?
Clement: He's been vocal about the fact that [certain aspects of Bond's character] have passed their sell-by date and need to be rethought. At the same time, the audience wants a muscular hero who can handle himself. You can't go away from the archetype too much.

La Frenais: Bond was established by Sean Connery. Connery's Bond liked being Bond but he had a job to do. Moore *loved* being Bond. "I'm James Bond; I can have everyone." Then, Timothy Dalton said no, I'm a more *serious* Bond. I'm James Bond but I have a job to do, then Pierce Brosnan was almost back to, I *love* being Bond. With Daniel, it's I *despise* being Bond; I'm a lonely, fucked-up person. But he was a Bond for the millennium.

Clement: I believe that Daniel's Bond could look after himself. I found Daniel very believable.

La Frenais: If you're flippant or casual about a precarious situation, then you remove the threat. So for me, if Bond is not afraid, then I'm not going to be afraid in my cinema seat. Daniel Craig makes us feel scared shitless about some of the situations he's in. I also like Timothy Dalton as Bond.

What is the Bond archetype?
La Frenais: Daniel has reinvented Bond definitely. He's right out of the up-to-date espionage, counterterrorism of contemporary movies. He's from the breed of people in the series *Spooks* [(2002-2011) retitled *MI-5* in the United States]; it's hardnosed, it's realistic, it's dealing with a world of terror, and Daniel fits that bill. The original Bond was a more glamorous figure. It was nightclubs, it was casinos, it was gambling, and it was also patriotism and the glamor of being a secret agent. But it's a half a century difference.

Clement: Bond's a maverick.

La Frenais: Who breaks all the rules.

La Frenais: Today, *all* the cinema heroes have that.

Clement: [imitating M] "Bond, this is the last time you'll ever do this."

La Frenais: [imitating M] "I don't like your attitude."

Why do you think that a shift occurred from the glamorous Bond to the hard-edged, more serious one of Craig's version?
La Frenais: The idea of a glamorous hero is dated. The world is dangerous and Bond has to reflect that. I don't think you can believe in him or his world if it's sex- and alcohol-centric basically. Every hero has to reflect the world he lives in, and Craig does. I'm still surprised they put Bond in a white tuxedo in *Spectre*. That looked ludicrous on Daniel Craig. Maybe they thought that's an homage to the past but we're living in a less glamorous world. If you look at contemporary cinematic heroes and compare them with cinematic heroes from the past, they're a long way removed. If you look at Clark Gable, David Niven, or the Hollywood heroes of the '50s, they all look good in a tuxedo, holding a martini glass.

Clement: I saw a film from the '50s the other day where it was a butch-looking leading man and he was holding his jacket by one finger, draped over one shoulder. I thought that was a '50s thing to do. I can't imagine anybody doing that now.

La Frenais: The next time we go to a cocktail party, we'll try it. Bond was not a '60s person; he was a '50s person. But Bond broke in the '60s. Because of that whole transformation in the '60s and what was going on in London—miniskirts, pop music, and the [birth control] pill—audiences expected more sex and more references to sex. They wanted to see a more amoral, if not immoral, lifestyle. That was just part of the zeitgeist. But Bond, by his look and his chauvinism, wasn't what you'd call a '60s person.

Was working on Bond just another working gig of many or was it special to you?
La Frenais: No, it wasn't just a writing gig. We were both aware, fuck, it's James Bond and the expectation and anticipation of it. It's Sean Connery back as Bond. That was quite a bit of pressure.

Clement: Oh, we wanted the job; no question.

Bond fans have heard about a three-hour cut of the film. But a long rough cut is not uncommon, and especially with underwater scenes, which are slow by their nature. Do you recall any important scenes that didn't make the final cut?

La Frenais: No. I think it was mostly underwater stuff.

Clement: And Klaus Maria Brandauer's pauses.

La Frenais: Yeah, that added a bit.

When is the last time you've seen the film?

Clement: Oh gosh, I have not seen it from beginning to end for probably twenty years.

La Frenais: But we've seen bits of it because we do some lecture gigs and because we were trying to choose two clips from it. So we did a bit of fast-forwarding while watching it fairly recently.

Which clips did you select?

La Frenais: A scene with Bond and Barbara Carrera and the urine joke. It'll be interesting now that we've done this talk with you; I want to go and watch it again.

It's a tricky film to discuss. It stars the original Bond but it's also outside the official canon.

La Frenais: It *is* interesting because the film wasn't leading to another Bond film starring Connery. It was: Here is Connery's return as Bond, but now he's done with the role, never to be seen again 007, and then it was back to the regular Bond series. The audience didn't quite know what to make of it.

WRITING BOND SONGS

LESLIE BRICUSSE

"Goldfinger" is for many Bond fans the gold standard of Bond theme songs, if you'll forgive the unfortunate pun. Sung with full-throated passion by Shirley Bassey, the jazz and rock-infused melody pulsates with thrusting, irresistible energy, as the lurid seduction demonstrates that Bond's adversary is a sinister and malevolent force. Leslie Bricusse wrote the lyrics to the memorable song with singer, songwriter, and actor Anthony Newley. John Barry composed the music.

In addition to "Goldfinger" and the sumptuous and haunting "You Only Live Twice," (1967) Bricusse also wrote the lyrics for "Mr. Kiss Kiss, Bang Bang," a witty but unused track for *Thunderball*, which describes Bond as a "shark" who "looks for trouble" and as a "knife" who "cuts thro' life."

Bricusse's virtuosity in the two official tracks is displayed in his ingenious dual imagery. In "Goldfinger" he juxtaposes images of gold with spider images; in "You Only Live Twice" he blurs the line between the rewards and dangers of living life daringly with the allure of a dream life: "One life for yourself and one for your dreams." These striking and unexpected contrasts give the theme songs uncommon texture and force.

He has written or cowritten many other memorable songs for films, among them "Talk to the Animals" for *Doctor Dolittle* (1967), "Pure Imagination" and "Candy Man" for *Willy Wonka and the Chocolate Factory* (1971), "Can You Read My Mind" for *Superman* (1978), "Somewhere in My Memory" for *Home Alone* (1990), and "Christmas at Hogwarts" for *Harry Potter and the Philosopher's Stone* (2001).[8]

Bricusse, a longtime friend of Roger Moore, also has a successful career as a songwriter for theatrical musicals, including *Stop the World—I Want to Get Off* (1961), which features the song "What Kind of Fool Am I"; *The Roar of the Greasepaint—The Smell of the Crowd* (1964), which includes the song "Who Can I Turn To?"; *Sherlock Holmes: The Musical* (1989); *Jekyll and Hyde* (1990); *Scrooge* (1992); and *Victor, Victoria* (1995), an adaptation of Blake Edwards's comedy.

What are the essential elements of a Bond song?

It needs to be composed by John Barry. Unfortunately, he ran out of time. [Barry passed away in 2011 at the age of seventy-seven.] He is the essence of what Bond music should be. Also, Shirley Bassey should sing all of them because of the combination of her voice and her delivery. She delivered it with great impact and she made sense out of a totally ludicrous lyric. But the song works mainly because the music was so wonderful.

How would you describe Barry's Bond music? Lush seems to come to mind.

Look at all John's scores and you'll see that he captured the *passion* of all the films. Look at *Out of Africa* [1985], *Born Free* [1966], and *The Lion in Winter* [1968] with Peter O'Toole and Katharine Hepburn. He captured the essence of the passion that was the underlying feeling of the film of all those films. Take the plane ride in *Out of Africa*. His music captured the whole essence of the relationship between Robert Redford and Meryl Streep's character and the awe she experienced when seeing something she'd not seen before. John had a rare gift.

What do you think is the essence of a Bond song?

It varies. Take two of the songs I did. "Goldfinger" is as ludicrous a title for a song as you could possibly find. "You Only Live Twice" has a kind of metaphysical mystery behind it. What does the song mean? Ian Fleming used to take phrases and turn them around on themselves. For example, he turned "live and let *live*" into *Live and Let Die* [1954]. He turned "you only live *once*" into *You Only Live Twice* [1964]. He twisted the phrases into titles, which made it more difficult to make lyrics out of them.

Talk about having to include the title in the song.

You have to write the title of the song as the title of the film. But the third song that John and I wrote was called "Mr. Kiss Kiss, Bang Bang" and it was intended for the movie *Thunderball*. I regard it as the best of our three Bond songs. "Mr. Kiss Kiss, Bang Bang" was the nickname Bond had in Japan, which was a big market for the films. After we'd written it, Shirley Bassey and [then] Dionne Warwick recorded it.[9] The producers decided that they wanted to stay with the title of the film. But *Thunderball* is a daft title.

I was in California at the time and I couldn't do it, so somebody else [Don Black] did it. It's impossible to do well because while you can rhyme "ball," it is not a good word to end a song on. With the word "Goldfinger," the stress was on the first syllable, as opposed to "Thunderball," where the stress was on the *last*. Where you put the stress can have a great effect on the lyric.

There was a rule with Cubby and Harry that the title of the song had to be the title of the film. It wasn't the case with "Nobody Does It Better" but Carole Bayer Sager, who wrote the lyrics, used the title *The Spy Who Loved Me* in the bridge of the song. They got away with it. She and Marvin [Hamlisch, who composed the music] wrote one of the better—if not the best—Bond songs of all with that one.

Many would give that distinction to "Goldfinger."
We were lucky because it was one of John's great melodies. It was so dramatic. While it was the third film, it was only the second Bond song because *Dr. No* didn't have a theme song. Lionel Bart, who wrote the music and lyrics for "From Russia with Love," got taken away with the idea of love. The song should've been more dramatic. If John had written it, it would have been more dramatic. I don't know how he would've done it, but it's an interesting thought, and it would've been a totally different song.

In "Mr. Kiss Kiss, Bang Bang" you referred to Bond's code number "007." You wrote, "And like the shark, he looks for trouble. That's why the zero is double." Did you first think, "I have to rhyme "Double-O-Seven." So what rhymes with seven? There's "heaven" and "eleven." Then perhaps it occurred to you that the idea of referring to "Double-O" might be more interesting."
No. I thought, "like a shark, he looks for trouble," so you've then got to find a rhyme for trouble. That's how I got there.

And then you realized that "trouble" rhymes with "double" as in "Double-O-Seven" and you could do something with that?
Right, because people don't say "O-O-Seven," they always say "Double-O."

How did you and John Barry work together?
We got off to a bad start. Tony Newley and I wrote "Goldfinger" together and we were in John's apartment. When John played the first three notes, which were, "da, da, da," Newley and I, without looking at each other, both sang, "Wider than a mile" [from the Henry Mancini song "Moon River"], which was what the melody said to us.

"Goldfinger" was quite easy to do, although it may not have appeared to be, because the first thing I thought of was: "The man with the Midas touch." Then it followed from there. That was the second line of the song. It guided it, so you knew what you had to do and you had to get the feeling of the girl who's going to be painted gold. The line had to say, "Beware of this man, he's dangerous."

I wasn't with John at all on the third one, "You Only Live Twice." That was an interesting moment. I wrote "You Only Live Twice" in Kirk Douglas's house in Palm

Leslie Bricusse and Roger Moore on the right, Luisa Mattioli (Moore's wife at the time) and Yvonne Romain (Bricusse's wife) on the left, 1969.

PHOTOFEST

Springs. I thought, *this is pretty good; I'm in Spartacus's living room writing for James Bond. How good can it get?*

Were you given the script or did you see scenes?
No, but I had previously read the book.

There are a couple of visual images in the song "Goldfinger." First, as you just said, there's gold and Midas touch, but then you take a turn and refer to a "spider's touch."
I had to use "spiders" because that was the only rhyme that existed with "Midas."

I guess that's what Stephen Sondheim might call a "near rhyme?"
Yes, and it shows that he's a creepy, crawly man that you want to avoid. Spiders create those same bad feelings among people. So, while he's got the Midas touch, he's also got the spider's touch. He's not someone you'd touch easily.

Once you've got a spider as a second image, the "web of sin" is a natural progression.
The lyrics just flowed. When you write lyrics, you automatically hear rhymes and other uses [of words]. It becomes part of the mechanism of the mind when you're composing.

It's a short song but you have two strong and distinct images.
You don't have that much room to do it all, because you've got to go on and develop the thought. If you're going into the "web of sin," then you've got to say who you're warning. So you're warning the girl about Goldfinger, and you think of Shirley Eaton, the girl who was painted gold.

Although both songs are roughly the same length, there are twice as many lyrics in "Goldfinger" as there are in "You Only Live Twice." [Both songs run about 2:48.]
The lyric is as long as the melody; the melody comes first. There are more syllables to a bar in the word Goldfinger. [Humming both songs] *Da, da, da, da, da, da, da, da*, as opposed to *da, da, da, da, da*. There are more syllables, and so it will affect the length of the lyric on the printed page.

How did you start writing "You Only Live Twice?"
I have to put my mind in a kind of animated suspension. "You Only Live Twice" is a fairly oblique idea. You have to ask, "What's the second life?" So I thought, "So one life for yourself and one for your dreams." That became the image and then I had to deal with that second image of dreams. I deal with that in the second stanza, which takes you to the word "love," which takes you to the "dangers" of love.

Before you settled on "dreams" as the second "life," did you consider other options?
I got lucky with that one because that was the first thing I thought of and I went with it. "Dreams" gives you the rhyme that you need for "or so it seems" and that carries you on. A lyric unfolds itself as you go; you develop one thought to the next and see how it unfolds. Sometimes it doesn't work, so you have to do it all again.

What do you remember about writing the line: "And love is a stranger who beckons you on. Don't think of the danger or the stranger is gone?"
It works, doesn't it? When I got the bridge of the song, when I got that, I knew I had the song, so you have to then take it back to the beginning in the last stanza, but it doesn't mean anything. You understand that the song is about a man of action. The

Japanese-style melody reflects that the movie was set in the Orient, but the meaning alters depending on your mood.

And are you writing these down on paper with a pencil?
Yes. Writing a lyric is not unlike doing a crossword puzzle. You have to find the right word that fits in a crossword puzzle and it's basically the same thing in the lyric, but instead of little black squares, you've got the music controlling the shape of it. You have to make it fit and appear effortless so that you're not clunking your way through it.

I'm thinking about your crossword puzzle analogy. Sometimes when you're doing a crossword puzzle you think you've written the correct words for the first three clues going down. But when you get to the fourth clue, which goes across, you then realize you have it all wrong. Then you have to start over.
Yes, the same thing can happen in a lyric. I used to make up crossword puzzles, not solve them, but I used to create them. It's a stepping-stone in the mysteries of lyric writing. You have to make the words fit and it's exactly the same mental process as lyric writing.

Do you think you could write a Bond song that's from Bond's point of view, using *I* rather than *he* to express his thoughts?
That's very interesting. Yes, that would be good. The lyrics to "Kiss Kiss, Bang Bang" are about the way Bond sees *himself*. "He's suave and he's smooth. And he can soothe you like vanilla." It's a vain song. But we have to be objective because we're describing the man: so it has to be, *he's* this, *he's* that and *he's* the guy. It's the same thing as in "Goldfinger": "*He's* the man, the man with the Midas touch." [Using the first person] wouldn't be quite the same because I don't think he'd say it about himself. He'd *think* it about himself, so that's why we described the total image of the man.

It seems that determining the character's point of view is a critical step in writing a song.
When you sit, think about it, condense the whole idea of the character, you've got to ask yourself, who's singing it and what's his point of view?

How long does it take? Is it weeks?
I wrote "You Only Live Twice" on a Sunday morning in Kirk's living room, so that was three or four hours, and "Goldfinger" was about the same.

That's very quick.

I had an advantage because I've got the title, the context, and the idea of what the content of the lyric will be. It's much easier to write a musical than to write one song where you have to dream up an idea. It's the reason I write musicals as opposed to individual songs. I write musicals and so I have a huge advantage of knowing the story. I know the character who is going to sing the song and I know the context in which he's got to sing it. It narrows down the search enormously because I know what the song has to say. Whatever the next line of dialogue would be is the song.

The process of writing a lyric is no different for a Bond song than any other theme song. You have a set of requirements but that's not a problem. I love writing film songs because there's a context and you know what you have to achieve from it. If you're given a title, you just find a way to do it.

I've heard Stephen Sondheim say that he's not able to write a generic love song. But if you ask him to write a song about a woman sitting alone at a bar wearing a red hat, then he can do it.

Yes, because it's got a context. I agree with Steve. He's a brilliant man of the theater. We're old friends and he writes a particular kind of lyric and a particular kind of music, sort of jagged-edge music that somehow fits the lyric.

Do you think about how the song has to market a movie and play over the credits and be used as the logo in the film?

You don't think about that. If you get the song right, then those things automatically happen. When Tony [Newley] and I wrote "Goldfinger," we were doing a show on Broadway, *Stop the World—I Want to Get Off.* We were so involved in the show that we didn't know that Shirley Bassey had recorded "Goldfinger." We didn't know it was a number-one song that knocked the Beatles [and their album *A Hard Day's Night* (1964)] off the top of the charts.[10] We only found out about it when United Artists Music called us and said, "We've got some gold records here for you. Do you want to come by and pick them up?" That's the first we knew. Funny enough, I'm looking at that record right this minute. It's hanging on the wall here.

Should a Bond song work beyond the movie?

"Goldfinger" couldn't work beyond the movie. It can't. Anytime you hear "Goldfinger" you associate it with the movie. "You Only Live Twice" doesn't make any sense outside of the movie because it means that Bond has nine lives.

Ian Fleming, whose enduring hero has been adapted into movies, graphic novels, video games, radio dramas, and a television series.

I completely agree with that. With one exception: *Mad Men* used "You Only Live Twice" in its season five finale "The Phantom." It's the only time I've heard a Bond song used outside the movie that successfully took on a different meaning.

It could work because it doesn't refer to anything specific. "You Only Live Twice" is a general statement, which you can pick out of the air. You wouldn't have been able to use "Goldfinger" in *Mad Men* because it's too specific. "You Only Live Twice" is just a random thought, which obviously the writer of the show thought was appropriate to include. I didn't know about it until you just told me. That's fascinating.

What's interesting about it is that the TV show is about people living double lives.
Yes, that's lovely, that's a good use of a song. And there are shades of Bond in Jon Hamm's character [Don Draper], aren't there? That's interesting, very interesting.

Were you a Bond fan?
I was an Ian Fleming fan. I bought the books as they came out. I still have a complete set of James Bond first editions, which everybody connected with the films have signed for me over the years. There are hundreds of autographs in the books. It's a unique set; I bet nobody else has got anything like it.

What did you like about Bond as a character?
Oh, they were so readable. All the Bond books were quite short and were something you could read in a day if you had nothing else to do. They became fashionable and everybody read them. But just to show you how long it takes for a book to become that famous, there was a complete set of Bond books, perfect first editions for sale at the Covent Garden Bookshop. They were £20 each. Everybody thought they were very expensive because they would cost around 15 shillings when they came out. Everybody said, "My god, that's ten times the price." But now they're worth around £5,000 each.

I'm looking at a list of your songs. Not just Bond, but all of them. Whenever I hear one of your songs it takes me back, not just to the movie, but also to a specific moment in my life and it anchors that moment.
That's very interesting, very interesting. Yes, people do associate certain songs with certain moments that apply to them.

It must be nice to have a song like "Pure Imagination," which you wrote in 1971, continue to find new audiences today.
Yes, it happens particularly with the *Willy Wonka* songs; people respond to them. It's lovely to have my songs have a continuing life and through your own life. It's very flattering.

DON BLACK

Don Black has written more Bond theme songs than any other lyricist. With bravado, flair, and economy of language, Black crafted the lyrics to composer John Barry's music for "Thunderball," "Diamonds Are Forever," and "The Man with the Golden Gun" and to David Arnold's compositions for "Surrender" from *Tomorrow Never Dies* and "The World Is Not Enough." A diverse group of singers—Tom Jones, Shirley Bassey, Lulu, Garbage and k.d. lang—have interpreted his often-risqué lyrics.

Black won the Oscar for best song for *Born Free* (1966) and was nominated four other times: for his work on *True Grit* (1969), the Michael Jackson tune *Ben* (1972), *Gold* (1974), and *The Pink Panther Strikes Again* (1976). For the theater, Black wrote the book and lyrics for the Broadway productions of *Sunset Boulevard* (1994) and *Dracula, the Musical* (2004). He also wrote the lyrics for *Bonnie & Clyde* (2011) and contributed lyrics for Neil Simon's *The Goodbye Girl* (1997) and *Dance of the Vampires* (2002).[11]

What does a Bond song need to do?
A Bond song should be provocative and seductive. It should have the allure of the forbidden and a whiff of the boudoir. It should be sexy. It should draw you in. It should get you hooked on the adventure that's about to start.

You have to construct your lyrics around the movie's title.
That's true but it never bothered me. In addition to the Bond movies, I've had some luck with song titles. I did *Born Free* and *To Sir, with Love* (1967). You write in a different way when you know the song title in advance. It helps get your mind around the song and it points you in a direction.

I always assumed that it would be limiting to have to use the title. But you find it helpful to not start with a blank slate.
Right. In some ways, it's easier. Unless you got a lousy title like *Octopussy*. Then you say, hang on a second. You gotta draw a line somewhere. [Laughs.]

Let's start with your first Bond song, "Thunderball." How did that job come to you?
[Eleven-time Bond composer] John Barry was a friend of mine. I wrote the lyrics to a couple of hit songs in England that were recorded by Matt Monroe that he liked. [Monroe sang "From Russia with Love," the first Bond theme song.] John said to me, "Do you fancy having a go at this thing called *Thunderball*?" I said, okay. It was as simple as that.

Then I looked up "Thunderball," and it wasn't in the dictionary. It doesn't mean *anything*. I just thought, what kind of man is Bond and how do you get that title so that it falls effortlessly? Then I thought of the lyrics, "He always runs while others walk." I thought, hey, that's good. That's Bond. Then you go from there.

Because John wrote a muscular tune, I thought the song should have a muscular voice like Tom Jones. That's how it started. I just instinctively do these things. I always remind myself of what Paul McCartney said when someone asked him about how he wrote "Yesterday." He said, "It was just a good day at the office." When you write all the time you have good days and bad days.

For "Thunderball," you were given the music first?
With John Barry, I'm always given the music first.

Do you also get the script?
Yes, I do, but I'm never worried about that. I don't have to pour over a script and have endless discussions about it. I much prefer someone telling me about the movie over the phone. I just asked John, "What's it about?" He'll tell me in a sentence or two. When writing a song, you don't have to stick that closely to the narrative of the movie. Most people say to me, "You must be sitting down with that script racking your brains." But I don't. I just think of a nice way of getting the title into the lyrics. I also want to create an exciting scenario.

There has been a playful debate among Bond fans about who the subject of the song is. It could be about either Bond or the bad guy. You're saying it was about Bond?
Yes, it was.

You wrote the lyric, "So he strikes, like Thunderball." The line makes sense emotionally. However, as you found out, the word "Thunderball" doesn't mean anything.
Right. In my mind, I used it as a kind of code word for the mission. But it just sang so well.

What about the creation of "Diamonds Are Forever?"
John Barry took a long time to write the music to these tunes. By the time he eventually phones and says, "I've got something," I know he's honed it. He's been through it so many times in his head that when he finally plays it to you it's like an unveiling of a finished song and not a work in progress. Once I have his melody, I just have to make the words hug the contours of the melody. I have to get some bite into the lyrics. Bond songs have to have bite.

Is the character in "Diamonds Are Forever" a Bond woman?

To tell you the truth, it didn't matter that much to me. As a songwriter, I thought it had to start with the lyric, "Diamonds are forever." I thought it has to be a girl singing it. You want to make it alluring and sexy. In fact, Harry Saltzman thought it was too sexy. There's a lyric: "Touch it, stroke it, and undress it." Saltzman said, "You can't say that." But Albert Broccoli loved it and Shirley Bassey loved it. John Barry wouldn't dream of changing it. I thought it was such lovely imagery: "Touch it, stroke it and undress it." I also thought Maurice Binder, who created all those title sequences, would love it and he did love it. But there was some trouble getting those lyrics through because of all the sexual innuendo.

Bond songs seem to be sung by and about different characters from the movies. "Diamonds Are Forever" is sung by a Bond woman. "The Man with the Golden Gun" is about a villain. "Thunderball" was about Bond.

Yeah, it doesn't matter who the character in the song is as long as it sounds attractive. "He always runs while others walk. He acts while others just talk." You want to meet this guy. You know that he's a special guy. The music is so exciting, and when you hear: "He strikes like Thunderball," you think, *we're in for a hell of a ride tonight.* It's as simple as that.

Talk about your writing process.

I stare out of windows a lot. Just thinking. I also walk around the park and then I come back and just sit down and write it. It doesn't take a long time. I think about it for three or four days before writing, and the whole song is written in under a week.

Bond songs have to serve many masters. They have to play over the credits, they are sometimes woven through the movie itself, and they are also ambassadors for the movie. They are played on the radio and they help sell tickets.

Everyone wants a hit record. Every time the song is played, it's three minutes of advertising for the movie. That's the reason they like the title of the song to be the title of the film. I was the second writer on *Thunderball*. They first wrote a song called "Mr. Kiss Kiss, Bang Bang" and Dionne Warwick recorded it. Then they had a meeting saying, "We've got to call the song 'Thunderball.'" That's when John Barry called me and said, "Don, let's do it." It is valuable to have the title of the song. I'm pleased that no one asked me to write for *Chainsaw Massacre*.

With "The Man with the Golden Gun," you integrated the plot into the song: "Love is required whenever he's hired."

That's true. I thought those details were exciting. With John's music, you have to hook them right away and get on with it. "He has a powerful weapon. He charges a million a shot." It's a good tale and it's going to unfold right now. I always go with my gut instinct. It has to sing well and it has to tell a story. But more important than that, it has to chronicle emotions and not waste any syllables. I eliminate the unnecessary and make every bloody syllable count.

You have a fun line, "Lurking in some darkened doorway or crouched on a rooftop somewhere. In the next room or *this very one*, the man with the golden gun." You're suggesting that he could be in the same room where we are listening to the song.
That's right. It's kind of a scary line. It's slightly chilling. He could be right next to you.

You said you always like to be a little bit naughty. You write, "His eye may be on you or me. Who will he bang? We shall see." That's a double entendre.
Yes, it is. I plead guilty there. That's not a bad thing.

The songs need to be as exciting, witty, and sexy as the films themselves. That's a tall order for a short song.
Yes, but it's fun to write. It's the only franchise where you can have some fun with the lyrics.

"One golden shot means another poor victim has come to a glittering end." You're painting pictures with your words.
"Glittering end" is very Bondian. But don't ask me how I did it. I haven't got a clue. I get John's music and while I'm writing I become immersed in that Bond landscape. I just have some fun with the words.

After "Golden Gun," the next one you did was "Surrender" from *Tomorrow Never Dies*.
Yes. That's one of my favorites.

"Surrender" is told from the point of view of the villain.
"Your life is a story I've already written." It explains what the film is all about. It's about a guy who runs newspapers and other forms of media. [Five-time Bond composer] David Arnold came up with that melody; k.d. lang did a lovely job and it was going to be the opening title theme but we were unlucky. Sheryl Crow came in at the last minute with a new song and they went with that. We had high hopes for

"Surrender." Many fans have told me that they think it's one of the best of the Bond songs.

Why do you think they went with Sheryl Crow's song instead of yours?
Probably for commercial reasons. Sheryl Crow was hot and whoever's hot usually sings that movie's Bond song. That's what happens. When John and I started, first you wrote the song and then you got the singer.

So you were not writing "Surrender" specifically for k.d. lang?
No, when we finished it we knew it was a song for a woman. But it was David Arnold's idea to get k.d. lang.

I can easily imagine Shirley Bassey interpreting these lyrics, "I'll tease and tantalize with every line. Till you are mine." That's a Shirley Bassey lyric.
It is a Shirley Bassey lyric. "The World Is Not Enough" is also a Shirley Bassey lyric. "The World Is Not Enough" would've been a bigger song if Shirley Bassey had recorded it. [Bassey, who recorded the theme songs to *Goldfinger*, *Diamonds Are Forever*, and *Moonraker*, sings for the rafters and makes a meal out of a song title.] They went with Garbage because it was contemporary but it was a mistake. Garbage is a terrific band but they're not Bond. Shirley Bassey is Bond. She's someone with an incredible identity. She is a good storyteller. Like an actress singing a song. Shirley Bassey should sing them all.

You wrote the lyric "Tomorrow never dies, surrender." You added the word "surrender" after the movie's title. It's a wonderful but unexpected counterpoint to the rest of the lyric.
It is an unusual word to follow it, I admit it. But it sang beautifully. I wrote it because there were an additional three notes that were there after the title. [Singing] "Tomorrow never dies, da, da dum." So I added the [three-syllable] word "surrender."

You needed another word to fill the space of music?
Right, the music was there and it was good. Everyone liked the tune so I didn't want to mess around with the music.

Instead of calling the song "Tomorrow Never Dies" it became "Surrender."
David Arnold called and said, "Listen, we can't call this song 'Tomorrow Never Dies' because Sheryl's got 'Tomorrow Never Dies.'" So I said, we'll call it "Surrender."

Next came "The World Is Not Enough." You used a line from the script in your song, "No one ever died from wanting too much."[12] How did the song come about?

Normally, I'd spend an hour on the phone talking with David Arnold [the film's composer]. He's lived with the film and I said, "Talk me through it, David." He would give me a summary of what the film is about. He may have said a couple of lines that stuck with me. That's the way it works for me. With *Born Free*, I asked, "What is the film about?" He replied, "It's about a lion who should be free. Then he goes wild." I said, "Okay, thanks." That's it. You don't need to know a lot to write it.

The character in the song "The World Is Not Enough" is a Bond woman but the lyrics could also apply to Bond. "I know how to hurt. I know how to heal. I know what to show. And what to conceal."

It does apply. It's very provocative. It's alluring and dangerous. You wonder, what's going on here? There's a mystery about it all and that's what I like to get in a Bond song.

"Thunderball" is one of the instances where there's a male voice and it works very well with Tom Jones. But do you think it's generally better to have a woman?

There's something about a woman opening up her heart and her mind. It gets to you more than a man. It's more acceptable somehow.

Do you think you could write a song from Bond's point of view? He's not an emotional character. But could you write a Bond song in the first person?

With Bond singing?

Yes, with a male singer.[13]

No. I would never do a Bond song in the first person. "I'm Bond." It would take away the mystique. I don't want to put it in your face or lay it on the line. You want [the listener to ask], what is it all about? It should feel like a prelude to some great adventure.

Do you keep your notebooks?

No, I don't. But the other day I did come across the original lyrics to "Diamonds Are Forever" in my handwriting from years ago. It was interesting because there was a verse that wasn't used in the film. But I've never been one to look back on these things.

What were the unused lyrics?

"Diamonds are forever. I can taste the satisfaction. Flawless physical attraction. Bitter cold, icy fresh, till they rest on the flesh they crave for."

It's quite an accomplishment to have written five Bond songs over the course of four decades.

It is. It's quite extraordinary. I've written more than anyone else. I'm delighted to be associated with it. I've had a full career—writing songs, themes for movies, musical theater, and shows on Broadway. Yet people always say, "I can't believe you wrote 'Thunderball.'" It's that Bond association. There is a glittering sparkle when you are involved in the world of James Bond. Every generation knows Bond and there is always a Bond film on television. Most films come and go but Bond is always around. So these songs are always around. The songs are perpetuated by the popularity of Bond.

PART II

BOND IN
PRINT

WRITING BOND NOVELS

ANTHONY HOROWITZ

Novelist Raymond Benson observed, "More people have been on the moon than have written James Bond novels."[1] Anthony Horowitz joined Benson in the exclusive club when he was chosen by Ian Fleming Publications to be the eighth author to write a Bond continuation novel.

Horowitz follows in the footsteps of Kingsley Amis (who wrote one Bond novel), John Pearson ("authorized biography"), Christopher Wood (two film adaptions), John Gardner (sixteen novels, including two film adaptations), Benson (nine novels, including three film adaptions and three short stories), Sebastian Faulks (one), Jeffrey Deaver (one), and William Boyd (one). The exploits of teenage Bond were explored in five novels and one short story by Charlie Higson and four novels by Steve Cole. Samantha Weinberg has written three novels and a pair of short stories about M's private secretary Miss Moneypenny, whose first name we learn is Jane. Taken together, the Bond books have sold more than a staggering one hundred million copies.[2]

Set after the events of Fleming's *Goldfinger*, Horowitz's *Trigger Mortis* (2015) features the return of gang leader–turned-Bond-ally Pussy Galore and introduces Jai Seung Sing, a sadistic villain who perversely uses a deck of illustrated Korean playing cards to determine the manner of death of his enemies. Enticingly, the novel includes original material written by Fleming, set in the world of Grand Prix, for an episode of an unrealized Bond television series.

Horowitz's second Bond novel *Forever and a Day* (2018), a prequel to Fleming's first Bond adventure *Casino Royale*, begins with M delivering the eye-catching and arresting line of dialogue, "So, 007 is dead."[3] But fans didn't have to mourn Bond for long. Before the first chapter concludes, Horowitz reveals that the fallen agent isn't James Bond but another spy who has been assigned the now-familiar code name. M tasks Bond with finding out who killed the former 007.

Horowitz is also the author of the successful young adult spy series Alex Rider, whose surname is a variation on Bond woman Honey Ryder, and two mysteries inspired by the work of Arthur Conan Doyle: *The House of Silk: A Sherlock Holmes Novel* (2011) and *Moriarty* (2014).

How did you prepare to write *Trigger Mortis*? Did you start by rereading Fleming?

Yes, I had to reread the whole lot. I had previously read Fleming's books many times throughout my life. They've been part of my genetic makeup for as long as I can remember. But in order to do the job, I had to read them in a different way than I had before. I had to read them *technically*. I had to look at how Fleming achieved what he did. I had to see what Fleming's mannerisms and tropes were so that I could exactly imitate what he had done before.

Were you also looking for any characters or plots that you could use for your novel—a launching point?

Unlike the other franchise writers who had come before me, I was given an original short story by Fleming called "Murder on Wheels." It was a treatment for a television series, which I used as a springboard to leap into this world. While reading "Murder on Wheels" and the novels, I was looking for clues that reveal what makes Fleming's writing so idiosyncratic and special. I had to ask myself why this character has survived so long, why the books are so good, and what clues and secrets are inside of them. I wanted to isolate those secrets and then imitate them. It could be phrases, a couple of words that hinted to me how he wrote, or products that Fleming references.

I have my notebook in front of me now as I'm sitting here, and I'm looking at all the different things that I wrote down.

Would you mind sharing them?

In no particular order: "The herb garden . . . smiled up at him," which is a line out of *Thunderball* (1961). Fleming takes inanimate objects and animates them. He makes them seem real and he makes them seem like participants in the story. He does it all the time. Above that [and also from *Thunderball*], I've got "a room-shaped room with furniture-shaped furniture." That's classic Fleming writing. It's absolute deadpan but there's a smile in there somewhere. It's cold-blooded and yet somehow so exactly right.

"Do you want to drink solid or soft?" someone says. That's Fleming. Here's another one, "The men laughed various kinds of laughs." That is out of *Thunderball*. It's that same trick he used with the furniture and it's so Fleming. There are lots and lots of them in my notebook. About fifty or sixty. That's how I began.

You were soaking up his style and the way he uses language.

His language, his style, and the little tropes that he uses time and time again.

What about his sentence length?

Absolutely. If you read the books carefully, you'll see that the modulation of the sentences is cleverly done. If you look at the opening of *Casino Royale* or *Goldfinger*, the sentences are considered to be *Weltschmerz* [world ache], which is a part of Fleming's style, this tiredness with the world. The sentences are long but they're well-modulated. They're slightly elegant.

Look at the opening sentence to *Trigger Mortis*: "It was that moment in the day when the world has had enough." You got into that *Weltschmerz* feeling. The world incidentally being personalized just as I showed you in that example I gave you a moment ago. That's one of his styles.

Then there's a second style, which is his action style, which I kept in mind while writing the car chase in my book. When I wrote that section, I went to the nearest chase scene I could find in Fleming, which was the sleigh run in *On Her Majesty's Secret Service*. It's fast and it's speedy. Suddenly, the sentences become incredibly short. Sometimes just a few words and they jump around. Instead of getting narrative flow forward, you're going in and out of Bond's head, you're going where he is. The camera is outside him when he's speeding down the hill but then suddenly you're right in his thoughts thinking, *Hang on, damn you. Don't let go.* It's staccato, punctuated writing that adds to the tension and excitement.

Did you look to the novels to help answer the question, where do we find Bond? How do I reintroduce Bond in this book, what should his opening scene be?

They vary. Some of the books open straight with the action. Sometimes it's the blubbery arms of the good life that wrap themselves around him, and he's in a stasis and waiting for something to happen. In my case, it was clear that the book was going to start two weeks after *Goldfinger*, and, therefore, I knew exactly where I was going to be both within the canon and within his life. Between missions, it seemed like the best place to begin. But some of Fleming's books take you into the action faster.

When did you come up with that idea?

As soon as I got the job I decided that for me and for my Bond it had to be within Fleming's world. It had to be within the canon of the books. For me, the best James Bond novels are the early ones: *Live and Let Die* (1954), *Moonraker* (1955), *Diamonds Are Forever* (1956), *From Russia, with Love* (1957), *Dr. No* (1958), and *Goldfinger* (1959). They are the golden period of about 1954 to 1959. Then after that, you get short stories and the novels *Thunderball* (1961) and *The Spy Who Loved Me* (1962), which even Fleming himself said was a mistake.

I love all the books. I'm not criticizing them, but for me, the great ones are the first six or seven, which is what you'd expect. It seemed to me critical that any new

Bond novel should take place within those parameters and in that time period. I just simply looked at when he might have had a rest.

I'm looking at my notebook now. *Goldfinger* takes place in April to June 1957 and then there's a little gap and we don't know what he's up to until May 1958, which is when [the short story] "From a View to a Kill" (1959) takes place. So there you've got the time period for Bond to have another mission.

That moment in time also immediately allowed me to think, "What happened to the girl from the last novel?" By and large, when the books end, the relationships ends. But in *From Russia, with Love*, Tiffany Case is referred to as having had an affair with Bond that lasted a little bit longer than in the previous book *Diamonds Are Forever* and that it ended unhappily. It seemed an interesting thing to look at that first and to see what happened next.

We know that Bond's going to eventually end the relationship from the previous novel. But how would he do it and, more importantly, what would he be feeling?
Well, yes and no. One has to be careful when you use that word *feeling* and ask, what is Bond feeling? By and large, Fleming doesn't give us the soft center of Bond's emotions. One of the chapters in *Trigger Mortis* was criticized in which I wrote that Bond attacks a young man and decides not to kill him. I have a moment where Bond thinks, this is just a young guy trying to earn a living. But that isn't part of Bond's makeup and there's a danger in over-humanizing him.

The reason he has survived as long as he has is that he is slightly on the edge of humanity. He's not somebody you want to sit down to have dinner with. He's not somebody whom you will ever truly know. In that respect, he's a little bit like Sherlock Holmes. [In *The James Bond Dossier* (1965), a study of the Bond novels,] Kingsley Amis famously pointed out that Bond has few hobbies. He doesn't read literature, he doesn't go to the cinema, and he doesn't have any particular cultural awareness. He is a man with limited capacity in terms of his humanity. There's a danger in trying to humanize Bond too much.

If I had written sequences in which he and Pussy Galore had been at each other's throats, it would've been a mistake. The way that the relationship ends is carefully controlled. It's ennui. He likes her more when she's in danger in America and when she's a gangster. When he comes back home and they're just going out to dinners, to the theater, or doing tourist things, that's not him.

You couldn't get too far into his emotional life, but was there anything that you figured that you could reveal about his character?
I thought to myself, for Fleming, where does Bond come from? He comes from two places. The first is World War II. Special executive and military intelligence, a

world of secrecy. It's a world where nobody really knows anybody, where everybody observes fine lines of both rank and of "need to know." It's quite a cold and highly focused world. If you're in the SOE (special operations executive) like Fleming was, you're not spending your time chatting about what you did the night before. That focus is very much a part of Bond.

I also think Bond harkens back to the nineteenth century to that type of Englishman who Kingsley Amis has identified as the Byronic hero [Romantic hero]. In modern terms, it's like Clint Eastwood in the Sergio Leone westerns. He's that same figure who comes from nowhere, who is going nowhere, but who affects everybody and saves everybody while he's in the room. And Bond is in the tradition of that character. Holmes would be equivalent; he's the only other British character in fiction who has had the same impact as Bond has, and it's much the same thing. You don't know about their parents, you don't know about their childhood, their friends, or anything like that. They are what they are. They come and they go.

That opaque character is well suited for the movies because you could read into their faces whatever you want to.
You could also add to that that each movie incarnation brings the spirit of his age to that part. That's what's been so clever about the franchise. Sean Connery, along with Daniel Craig, was closest to Ian Fleming's original Bond. But when you get into the '70s, everything is getting a little bit softer and larkier. Roger Moore takes over, and there's suddenly a completely different Bond. You're getting more jokes, more double entendres, and the action is a little bit more camp. Then you get a reaction against that in the late '80s with Timothy Dalton trying to go back to the harder incarnation. However, the truth of the matter is that Bond always reflects the current society in which he operates. That's one of the clever things about the franchise: it keeps redefining itself. It hasn't stuck to the '50s and Cold War Bond or Byronic hero Bond. It has done a Bond for each age.

But you deliberately went back to the time period where you wanted to be within Fleming's canon. You're going against the grain of what you just said has made the franchise so successful. Were you at all worried about not being reflective of our time?
Well, it's a good question and the answer is that my job was to write an Ian Fleming pastiche, to write a homage to Ian Fleming. As far as I was concerned, it was to be set entirely in Ian Fleming's world.

Having said that, I could make a few little poststructural nudges toward the modern age. For example, there's a reference that smoking can give you cancer. I had to put that in because I'm a children's author and I don't normally write books in which characters smoke. I also give Bond an openly homosexual friend named

Ian Fleming and his creation, an extension of the author's experience and vivid imagination.

ILLUSTRATION BY PAT CARBAJAL

Charlie Duggan. I did that in order to tease out the latent homophobia in some of the books. There's also a slight feminist smile there in both the creation of Jeopardy Lane and in the way Pussy Galore treats him. [*Note:* Galore leaves Bond for another woman.] In fact, all three women treat him quite roughly. [The third woman who treats Bond roughly is Logan Fairfax, a race car driver, who M appoints to train 007 in professional auto racing. Upon meeting Bond, Fairfax sizes him up as a "stupid sort of policeman."[4]]

These are all nodding to a modern audience who will not put up with some of the attitudes of the '50s. But outside of that, my job as I saw it had nothing to do with the films. The films and the books are two separate things. The films remain a huge global event. They are probably one of the most significant cultural events of our times. *Spectre* made god knows how many billions of pounds, and when it came out, it felt like that was the only film people were talking about. That's true all over the world.

The books, however, are nestling in an oasis, in a remote place. I'm not sure how many people now go back and read the books and have an understanding of what Fleming created. What I've found is that the audience of people who wish to read a James Bond novel—either the originals or one of mine or someone else's—is minute compared to the number of people who are going to see the films. It never occurred to me to try to modernize, make it relevant, or make it cinematic. My job was to live in the world of the books, as if the films had never been made.

I discovered Fleming after the films. Like many, I liked the movies so I read his books. The Bond of the films has eclipsed the Bond of the novels. Why isn't there more interest in going back to the source material?
It's because we no longer live in a particularly literary world. The ratio of people who read compared to the number of people who play computer games, watch television, and go to the cinema or whatever is small. *Trigger Mortis* did well; it sold I think about a hundred and twenty thousand copies in hardcover and in e-format. Everyone is happy with the result of it. But the fact is that in audience terms [compared with the movies], that's relatively tiny. But I knew that before writing it. Even the decision to do the book as authentically as I tried to was not a commercial decision. Having said that, Jeffrey Deaver tried to move Bond into the modern period with *Carte Blanche* (2011). I'm not saying he failed, but I'm not sure that he satisfied either side of the equation.

Kingsley Amis wrote *Colonel Sun* (1968), the first continuation novel. Then John Gardner picked up the torch.
I've read them all, of course. I know the Gardner novels.

When I first started reading Gardner, I didn't truly understand what a continuation novel was. Bond belonged to Fleming and I didn't originally understand how another novelist could continue where Fleming left off. As much as I wanted to read more Bond novels, the notion of a continuation novel seemed foreign to me. These days, the idea has permeated throughout pop culture.

You're right, the whole word "continuation novel" has probably only entered the lexicon in the last ten years. It isn't just Bond, of course. It's a huge industry. From Jane Austin to Jeeves and Wooster to Agatha Christie, etcetera. I have always feared that there was a certain cynicism at the heart of this exercise. A mixture of slightly nervous publishers desperate for an instant bestseller and in some cases—not with Fleming—an estate that might be trying to rekindle interest or value from a trademark.

I have to emphasize that has not been the case with the Fleming estate. They have very good motives for wanting to continue with the books. But it is a modern phenomenon, that's for sure. It was one that I had to think about twice before I accepted doing it. There were only two characters I would've ever done: Sherlock Holmes and James Bond. Holmes was the first one I did with *House of Silk* and *Moriarty*. I was reading Sherlock Holmes when I was in my late teens, and he was very much a part of my life. I did Bond because there was no way I was going to turn it down.

Could you talk about working with the Fleming estate? Did they ever say Bond wouldn't do that or you shouldn't do that? I don't ask that in an authoritarian context where they're trying to arbitrarily limit your creative approach to the project. My question comes from an assumption of their love of the character and wanting to see him being treated in line with Fleming's conception.

On the other side of that equation is you have a writer who will not kowtow. I'm old and experienced enough to be quite arrogant in the way that I write. Generally speaking, I write what I want and I don't like being told what to do. When I entered into this agreement, I was quite nervous to be honest with you. I knew that the Fleming estate is quite powerful and certainly would have the last say on matters. They could basically fire me. I did have great nerves.

When I wrote the Sherlock Holmes books, I made it a condition of writing that I would not meet the Doyle ancestors and I would take no notes from them. That was the condition on which I would do it. That did not hold true for Fleming because I wouldn't have got the job if I had asked for it. But I met with them and I was quite nervous. I thought it was going to be a bad experience, that I would get a lot of notes that would cause arguments. However, they were terrific to work with, they were very smart and very sympathetic to what I wanted to do. We did have discussions, but they had great notes.

One of the members of the family was concerned about the title, *Trigger Mortis*, being too jokey and also that it might not translate. In retrospect, that was quite a good note and maybe I chose the wrong title. The title of a James Bond novel is, without any question, the hardest thing to get right.

We discussed at some length whether Pussy Galore could come back; there were some members of the family who didn't think it was a good idea. I had to hold my own on that one and say, "Look, this is what I want to do." They voted on it and the vote went my way. To give them that credit, they said, "Fine, okay, go ahead."

There were other things in the books that I got wrong. I'll give you a good example of that. The origin of the name Jeopardy Lane was going to be that her parents had watched the television show *Jeopardy!* day in and day out; they liked it so much they named their daughter after it. The estate pointed out to me that the program *Jeopardy!* started in the mid-'60s and my book is set in 1957. So that wouldn't work.

Another example of a correction was in the original manuscript. I had Bond getting out of bed with Pussy Galore and going into the bathroom naked. I made a big point of the fact that Bond slept naked. They pointed out that Bond doesn't sleep naked; he wears what is called a bed jacket [or "pyjama-coat," as is established in the novel *Casino Royale*]. Now, a bed jacket is probably the least sexy piece of clothing a man could put on. It's sort of a pajama jacket that comes down to the knees. I had to smile and take out the naked section because that wasn't accurate and it wasn't true to Fleming. But I didn't specifically mention what he was wearing because he would have seemed ridiculous.[5]

That was the sort of thing we discussed when they got the first draft of the manuscript. I think they gave me about ten big notes and twenty small ones. I corrected about two-thirds of those notes and the other third I argued and won.

That seems like a good give-and-take, a healthy collaboration.
It was a collaboration. They were also in charge. They could've said no. They could've said, "Do this or you're off the job," but they never did. They never threatened me; they were always reasonable. They're smart.

I learned from the *James Bond Radio* podcast that when Raymond Benson took over from John Gardner, he had to come up with an outline on spec.[6] Then he had to write the first four chapters on spec before they officially hired him. He had to jump through a lot of hoops.
I didn't have that same experience. I produced an outline and the outline was what I wrote. It ran about five or six pages. I went to my first meeting with them with the outline. Before they had even asked for one, I had done it. The plot for the novel came quickly. Normally, plots take me a while, but for the Bond novel, it fell into my lap almost at once.

Can you talk more about that meeting?

I had lunch with Corrine Turner, who works for the estate [as a managing director], and she gave me the once-over. I started talking ideas with her. I came to the meeting with that treatment and a photograph. I submitted a photograph of a train station in New York, which is underneath the United Nations. It's a disused station, an art deco station, and it's beautiful. The American transit authority must be crazy not to open it to the public but maybe there's a security issue. I was going to set the climax there, but as things turned out, it wasn't possible to that. But that was how I presented the original idea. I was thinking visually. Although the book has nothing to do with the films, nonetheless, the book has to have a modern pace and it has to be visual. It has to be written for a modern audience.

We were talking about the interior life of the character and you said that you don't want to get too deep. In a movie, the audience will impose their thoughts on what a character is thinking and feeling. The silent hero works particularly well. But in a book, we expect to get inside a character's mind.

I don't think you do expect to go inside Bond's mind, because where in the Fleming novels does that happen? Where do you ever see doubt, insecurity, anything but the occasional anger, self-anger, determination, ruthlessness, snobbery, and carnal desire? Where do you see: Am I doing the right thing?; his doubts or uncertainty? The rule was only to do what Fleming did and to do nothing that he didn't. With Bond, that works.

It works in the same way as it does with Holmes. I could write a Sherlock Holmes novel in which he bemoans his lack of sexual activity and that there are no women in his life. However, that would be anathema to anybody who loves these books. That's where I begin; I begin on the side of the überfan. I'm not that interested in the public at large; I'm not interested in publishers. I tell you I am interested in the estate because they are the überfans of all überfans. I'm beginning with the purists.

Although I have taken exception to one or two things in some of the [other continuation] books and in one or two of the films, that's only as a purist. That is not to say that the books aren't wonderful and the films aren't brilliant. It's just that as somebody who is attached intellectually, emotionally, and psychologically to this character I was reading in my formative years, nothing should break the rules, nothing should break the spell.

The way you ended *Trigger Mortis* gave a sense that though Bond survived this mission, his luck will inevitably run out and his mortality will catch up with him. Not today, but eventually.

When I pitched to the estate, that paragraph was in my pitch; that last paragraph and those last three words, "But not today," were included. That sense of nothing is forever is so Bond. It's an existential ending. That whole hard-edged, rain coming down, another dead body, the endlessness of it. It felt right for the book. The end of *Moonraker* is a fairly bleak ending, as he and Gala Brand go their own way. The books don't always end with a smile. They sometimes end in a gray area, which is what I was aiming for.

What surprised you most about the experience?

I was unprepared for the way that being involved in James Bond puts you in a strange place. Things that you say innocently and trying to be helpful, as I am with you now, are misinterpreted. It can sometimes seem as if everybody is looking to hurt you. It was quite a painful experience in some ways. I was embroiled in rows that were certainly not intentionally of my own making and I upset people. But while I've been talking to you, I've been careful to say nothing that can be misconstrued. When you go back over this tape you'll see that I have not criticized anybody and would not dream of it. But to give you an example, if I were to compare James Bond film A with James Bond film B and say I preferred B, a journalist might run a story about how much I disliked A and try and make something of it. That happened over and over again and I was hounded. It was not a happy experience.

The experience of writing the book—of working with the estate, of doing serious interviews like this one—and of the response to the book, the critical response certainly, and, more importantly still, the response from the überfans has all been 100 percent positive. But in terms of what it did to me as a writer, it made me realize that there is a world out there that I don't necessarily want to be too much a part of. I'm happier with my head below the parapet, just writing quietly, not in the bright spotlight. That was the worst of it.

I found myself at a signing with [Bond continuation authors] William Boyd and Sebastian Faulks. I'm not quoting them, but they said they had experienced much the same thing. I apologized to them because somebody had written a piece that suggested I had criticized their books, which I had never done. I've been talking to you about how Bond should be this, should be that, but I've carefully said, "That's as far as I'm concerned." But I'm not judging others. They said, "There's nothing to apologize for, because we know, we've been there, we've been through this fiery hoop and we know what it's like."

You're now part of a small club of authors who have written Bond continuation novels.

Correct and I'm hugely proud to be part of that. I'm proud of everything I've done. I'm proud of Alex Rider, which came out of my love for Bond. But to be one of a small group of people in the world who has written a James Bond novel is a fantastic thing. Going back over the whole experience, although I might have been a little more circumspect and more careful when it came to publicity, there's nothing else I would have changed. I've heard writers say that this is the book I was born to write. It always sounds a little saccharine and horrible when I've heard it. But this is the book I was born to write and I've written it.

ILLUSTRATING BOND COMIC STRIPS

JOHN MCLUSKY

As told by his son Graham McLusky

The first adaptation of Fleming's superspy did not appear onscreen in the 1962 film *Dr. No*. It occurred four years earlier when the *Daily Express* published *Casino Royale* in 1958 as a daily comic strip. *Casino Royale*, illustrated by John McLusky and written by Anthony Hern, sticks closely to the plot of the 1953 novel. However, because only a few panels were published each weekday, the complex story took five months to unfold.

McLusky drew twelve more Fleming titles for the newspaper from December 1958 to January 1966. He worked with Henry Gammidge, who adapted eleven stories including the Fleming short story *Risico*, and Peter O'Donnell, who adapted *Dr. No*.

His bold, sharp, vividly expressively black-and-white illustrations are thick with atmosphere. McLusky's panels were film noir—newspaper noir, if you will—his men were square-jawed and ruggedly handsome, the women perfectly coiffed, sultry, and scantily clad, and the villains menacing and slightly grotesque.

McLusky was replaced by Yaroslav Horak, who illustrated thirty-three adapted and original Bond stories from 1966 until 1979. When Horak left the series, Harry North created the artwork for 1981's *Doomcrack*, an original story by Jim Lawrence. McLusky returned to drawing duties from 1981 to 1983 for five original Bond adventures: *The Paradise Plot*, *Deathmask*, *Flittermouse*, *Polestar*, and *The Scent of Danger*, which were all written by Lawrence. Lawrence and Horak were paired for the final two *Daily Express* strips *Snake Goddess* (1983) and *Double Eagle* (1984).

In this interview, John McLusky's son Graham McLusky remembers his father, who died in 2006 at the age of eighty-three.

How did John McLusky settle on the look of his Bond?

Dad took Fleming's description and then made more of a man out of the character. He saw Bond as a rugged, handsome fella and developed this his own way, which Fleming liked.

John McLusky's portrait of James Bond.

Ian Fleming commissioned an unknown artist to illustrate James Bond. Your father's Bond was quite different from the original interpretation, which had angular features.

I have the actual artist's impression, which Fleming commissioned; it looks very "Sherlock Holmes" or "Sexton Blake" [the British detective] rather "po-faced" [serious]. Dad's version is perhaps more like the way Fleming would have liked to be, had Fleming been the spy he always wanted to be. Dad decided that Bond should be more rugged and good looking.

What was a typical workday for your father?

He always started early and didn't allow any distractions. He worked from a studio in our garden. We lived in the middle of the countryside and it was the perfect surroundings, being so quiet. He took breaks and meals and then a long walk after work. A strict routine.

In terms of nuts and bolts, what was the process of drawing a Bond comic strip?

Dad would receive a plain typed script from the writer, in stages. Perhaps just half a page at a time. He would then interpret the story and develop it into three or four frames. This happened every day. He would sketch in pencil, straight onto the board and work the sketches in a fluid manner until he saw what he wanted. Then he would "ink in" the lines, add body and texture, shadows and tone, using Zip Tone—a plastic dot screen film with various tonal qualities, ideal for the printing process. He would then touch out errors and loose ends with a thick white ink. This was before White-Out or Tippex. Then he would wrap the board and send it by train to the parcels office in London, from which the *Daily Express* would collect it each day. No pressure then.

The average strip contains three or four panels. How long did it take him to draw them?

One per day.

What did his studio look like?

The studio was built from the ruins of three old cottages, which were at the far end of our garden. The only salvageable parts were the brick chimney gables. A studio was built on the upper level with some stone stairs leading up. Inside it was wood paneled in a light pine, with lots of huge windows and skylights. He had a desk, a drawing board, and some other furniture. There were lots of paints and inks, pencils, etcetera, and pictures on the walls. It was a relaxed and perfect environment.

John McLusky.

What are your most vivid memories of your dad working?
He used to wear a green transparent eyeshade and worked with such concentration.
He didn't want disturbances but would always welcome his kids into the studio, as
we were always curious.

What insights did he give you about his approach to drawing Bond?
I'm not sure if he ever did. The process of drawing Bond on a daily basis didn't allow much time to think. He had to put down his first thoughts, which in most cases were perfect. He did, however, do the most meticulous research, using references he compiled. For instance, for *Casino Royale*, he took the family to France, took many photos of the French buildings, a casino, people etcetera, etcetera. He even had a Walther PPK and a firearms license so that he could draw Bond's gun properly.

Did your father have any contact with Ian Fleming?
I don't know if Dad met Fleming but I do have a letter from Fleming's secretary stating that Mr. Fleming is pleased with Dad's interpretation and was happy to proceed [with the strip and with McLusky as the illustrator].

What are the hallmarks of a John McLusky Bond strip? How would you characterize his drawings?
Meticulous detail in every way. Slick, with each panel a work of art.

In 1966, the *Daily Express* hired Yaroslav Horak to draw Bond. Do you know why?
I really don't know why but I think that the newspaper wanted a change. I don't think dad was happy about it at all, but he never really spoke about it.

About fifteen years later, your dad drew five more original Bond stories from 1981 to 1983. What did it mean to him to return to Bond?
I remember Dad was finding it rather awkward as Bond became a more violent man and Dad disagreed somewhat with the way it was going. However, some of Dad's later work became some of the slickest he ever did. His drawings were always full of life.

There are about 311 panels in the *From Russia with Love* strip. Drawing a strip seems like demanding work. What toll did it take on your father?
One a day. It was relentless. He had to take regular exercise, walks, and get his mind off it regularly, too. He was a clever fella and had a wonderful mind and a fabulous sense of humor. He was used to drawing boards, bad posture [from being hunched over his drawing table for extended periods], and getting on with things.

What became of his original artwork?
My brother and I have some of it.

Did drawing Bond hold a special place in your father's heart or was it just another job?

I think that over the years it became quite consuming and Dad got to know Bond very well. It was a job indeed and it was his way of supporting his family.

What place does John McLusky have in the Bond legacy?

I think it was giving a great deal of pleasure to a huge number of *Daily Express* readers. However, the fact is that Dad developed the face of Bond. No other face existed and that's the man we all grew up with. [Four] years after the first strip cartoon, the first film was made. The man chosen to play Bond looked uncannily like the image Dad developed beforehand. Also, note the resemblance of parts of the film to some of Dad's panels. They were used as the storyboard.

WRITING AND ILLUSTRATING BOND GRAPHIC NOVELS

MIKE GRELL

Mike Grell adapted the film *Licence to Kill* for the comic book (with writer Richard Ashford and artists Chuck Austen, Tom Yeates, and Stan Woch), and he wrote and illustrated the original three-part sprawling graphic novel *Permission to Die* (1989–1991). Bond's assignment in *Permission to Die* is to extract an eccentric physicist's niece from behind the Iron Curtain, in exchange for the scientist's plans for an advanced, low-cost satellite launch system.

How did you adapt *Licence to Kill* into a comic book?
I was given the shooting script and a ton of on-set photographs. I was responsible for constructing a story out of that. If you know anything about how hard it is to adapt a novel into a screenplay, then you know there's so much that has to be thrown out. Compound that with trying to cram a two-hour-plus film into forty-odd pages of comic book. It's difficult. There's a lot that gets lost by the wayside. Also, the script I was working from didn't contain all the material from the finished film. For instance, a prominent sequence, which featured Wayne Newton and his religious group, was not in the working script that I was given.

Anything else?
The other thing that was missing from the adaptation was the scene in which they're fighting in the factory. James Bond and Dario, one of the villains played by Benicio Del Toro, are fighting in the factory that's grinding so much cocaine into powder that there's white dust in the air the entire time. Those guys would have overdosed.

The Bond in the comic book doesn't look like Timothy Dalton. I understand that you weren't permitted to portray Dalton and you were instructed to create a composite Bond.[7]

I think it was based on the universal image of Bond that people kind of had in their mind. By the time it got translated from layouts into the finished form, the rendering became quite similar to the depiction in the newspaper strip. And it's different by far from what I had portrayed that same year in *Permission to Die*. For what it's worth, the reason that I didn't illustrate *Licence to Kill* was because I was already working on *Permission to Die*.

How did you get the job to write *Permission to Die*?

I was the hot ticket at the time. I had just had a massive success with *Green Arrow: The Longbow Hunters* (1987), and I was well known for my series *Jon Sable Freelance* (1983–1988), which has certain aspects of international intrigue and kind of James Bond–type action. It was a combination of the two that did it.

Did they suggest certain story elements?

No, it was all mine.

How did you craft that story?

Simple. Take your basic elements of James Bond: exotic locations, beautiful girls, dastardly villains, and a plot that could either destroy or possibly save the world. I threw in a twist—you think the scientist is creating a technology to save the world but his ultimate goal is to destroy it.

I picked up *Permission to Die* basically more or less where *On Our Majesty's Secret Service* left off. I incorporated some of the elements that were current at the time. In the John Gardner novels, Bond had been given a new gun, the ASP 9 millimeter, which is a great gun. But it's not likely to be the type of weapon that a spy would use. But the Walther was popular for its concealability. The ASP was a larger caliber, and graphically it's a beautiful gun to draw. At that time, we didn't have compact 9 millimeters like we do today, and it was a handmade custom type gun. It was a modification of a Smith & Wesson. I added all those elements.

The story itself contains a number of elements from the movies. There are references to *Dr. No*, *From Russia with Love*, *Goldfinger*, *Thunderball*, and *You Only Live Twice*. I referred to the death of Tracy, Bond's wife, and set him in the time and emotional state that he would've been after *On Her Majesty's Secret Service*. I didn't refute everything that had gone on after that. But I didn't refer to *Licence to Kill* at all.

The only restriction that I was given was that I was not allowed to use characters that had been created specifically for the films. Anything that Fleming had created was pretty much carte blanche. But I couldn't use Q, for instance, so I used Major Boothroyd. That didn't hinder me.

You had Bond driving his famous Aston Martin.
Right. At the time, Bond's car in the novel was a Saab, which is ridiculous. John Gardner put him in a Saab [for several of his Bond novels, including *License Renewed* (1981), *For Special Services* (1982), *Icebreaker* (1983), *Nobody Lives Forever* (1986), *Never Send Flowers* (1993), and *SeaFire* (1994)],[8] but I went back to the Aston Martin DB5 because nothing else says Bond like the Aston Martin.

How long did it take to write the treatment for the three comic books?
The treatment probably took somewhere between two and four weeks. That's my average working speed. Then it went through several passes back and forth between me, Eclipse [the publishers] and Glidrose Publications [the rights holder, which has subsequently changed its name to Ian Fleming Publications].

How do you write your treatments?
I write my story treatments the same way you would write a screen treatment, which is everything is written present tense. Bond leaps from the car, rolls to the ground, and comes up firing. It has complete information, background information, and everything that goes in the scenes—the background of the story, information about the characters. Then I do a complete finished script.

How many pages is a finished script for something like this?
It runs on average of one page of script to one-and-a-half pages per finished page of artwork.

Sounds like a hefty document.
It is a fairly hefty document. I write sparsely, but I also know that I have to show the editor exactly what I'm going to do. In this case, I had to get approval from a lot of different parties, including Glidrose.

What feedback did they give you?
I learned that people outside the comic industry who are doing a cold read don't necessarily understand that the scene descriptions are not going to wind up in print. [Laughs.] It's just to establish the visual.

I also learned that there are language differences between English and American [English]. The funniest example was this scene where, in order to get Bond away from a casino, where they're under the watchful eye of the bad guys, this beautiful girl [Mary Chase] spills her foo-foo drink all over Bond's suit, and drags him into the

Mike Grell's portrait of James Bond for the graphic novel *Permission to Die*.
COURTESY OF MIKE GRELL

men's room to get him cleaned up. The accident is just her ploy to get Bond alone. In the bathroom, she bends over to check under the doors of the stalls to make sure that there's nobody there. In my scene description, I wrote: "She bends over. Bond eyes her fanny appreciatively." But the people at Glidrose had a fit. They pointed out that that was unacceptable because, in England, the word fanny refers to a particular part of the female anatomy, which is why they don't call it a fanny pack. They call it a belt pack. Even though the word fanny was never going to appear in the book, to get the script approved, I had to eliminate it. [The finished comic shows Bond admiring Mary Chase's derrière without any written characterization.]

Any notes about how you handled the character of Bond?
Actually, no. They pretty much left me alone. I had read all the Bond books, all the Bond stories, including *Colonel Sun* [by Kingsley Amis]. I had read everything that Fleming ever wrote, multiple times, and I was something of an expert on Bond myself. I also had Raymond Benson's *The James Bond Bedside Companion* (1984).

It's a fantastic resource.
Yeah, Raymond Benson's *James Bond Bedside Companion* is on my nightstand. It was literally my bedside companion. Even before I was ever associated with James Bond, I had two copies. I kept one on my nightstand and one in my studio.

To add authenticity, I made contact with the British embassy, and it was cooperative. A gentleman there gave me a lot of background information that I used in little bits and pieces. For instance, as a cartoonist, there are a lot of things that you have to know. When somebody writes: "The setting is New York City, a squad car comes rolling down the street," you have to know that. When I wrote the scene that involved police cars, I had to find out. They're white in the middle with a red stripe all around them. Because they look like two pieces of white bread with jelly in the middle, they are colloquially called a jelly sandwich. Today, the information is readily available on the internet. But, in those days, you had to be more resourceful.

It has to be a formidable task to plot a Bond story.
The only really daunting part for me was making sure that I lived up to the audience's expectations of who and what James Bond is. I wanted to provide all the dramatic and romantic and high-action elements, the high-tech goodies and wonderful toys that Bond has at his disposal but ultimately strip it down as the best James Bond stories do. Even though he's got all these gadgets at his disposal, ultimately it comes down to the man.

Fancy tools don't do you any good if there isn't just a hell of a person behind it to wield those weapons and those gadgets. That was foremost in my mind. I wanted to include all the elements in that story that I wanted to see in a James Bond story.

The basic plot is that there is a scientist [Erik Widziadlo] who is working on a new system that could possibly be a weapon. Or it could possibly be for the betterment of mankind. And the only kicker is that he's a refugee from behind the Iron Curtain, and he has left his niece [Edáine Gayla] behind, and Widziadlo wants her brought out before he'll turn over his information to the secret service. The first two issues have to do with Bond fulfilling that mission.

It harkens back to *From Russia with Love*. I wrote a similar scene in a gypsy camp—just because in the movie, it was such a cool bit, right? I've got Bond in a knife fight with a gypsy, challenging him for the beautiful girl. I've got the beautiful girl fighting for Bond. I've got the shoot 'em up, bang-bang action. I added a clever little helicopter that ran on hydrogen peroxide–powered motors, the same way that the jetpack works. They were actually selling it through Sharper Image. But it was something that could be transported in for short flights, and that was the whole point of it.

Then I have the pursuit where Bond and Edáine Gayla are running from the deadly killer who is after them. Now, the killer has already proven that he can kill from a great long distance, and he's basically just a presence in the background whom you never get to know any more than you got to know the Red Grant character in *From Russia with Love*. The killer is more of an entity than a person. Then after Bond finally succeeds in delivering the girl, he comes to find out in the last issue that all is not as was expected in the first place. The first twist is that Edáine Gayla is not the scientist's niece; she's his lover. The second twist is that Erik Widziadlo's invention is not for the betterment of mankind; instead, he intends to shake up the world to make everyone wake up to the dangers that exist.

I based Dr. Erik Widziadlo on Captain Nemo [and his look and penchant for playing the piano] are based on the *Phantom of the Opera*. Widziadlo wears a mask that covers half of his face. He's an elegant-looking gentleman who lives in an underground cavern, which overlooks a huge lake in northern Idaho. He has a submarine system that's bringing in all of his supplies, and he's building a full-size operational model of a smaller rocket system that was being developed at the University of Washington at the time, which, using a tube, enables you to fire projectiles of an oxygen-methane mixture into space. As the projectile goes forward, sealed off by various membranes, it sucks the combustible material in at the front and ignites it out the back. It's reusable and it's economical.

Most interestingly of all, the launch system has absolutely no weapons value, because it has to be built on a permanent location, like on the side of a mountain, which means you could aim it only up into space and not at another country. You can't reposition it. There were launchers being built back in the day that could throw projectiles more than one hundred miles. This was designed to put projectiles into orbit. It would have only peaceful application. Well, that's not exactly what he has in mind. Instead, he's planning not to launch a projectile into orbit; he's going to launch a nuclear device, and his target is Victoria, British Columbia, which is on Vancouver Island, on the northwest coast. In his mind, targeting Victoria would limit the number of casualties, because despite being the capital of British Columbia, it is not a particularly large city. But it would send a hell of a message. This guy's intent is to wake up the world and end the Cold War. The Cold War was still going on when I drew the story and turned it in.

But that [third and final] book sat in the publisher's drawer for more than six months, possibly a year, before it was published [two years after the first two issues]. In the meantime, the Soviet Union collapsed and the Iron Curtain came down, and my story looked a little out of date and kind of a moot point at that stage. It was a different world. It had changed in a hurry. We included a blurb in a newspaper about the wall coming down and the collapse of the Iron Curtain. We gave Bond a closing line that had something to do with the change in the world. [Bond says, "Who knows, it might have worked. . . . And I'd be out of a job."[9]] The story worked all right, but it would've been that much better if it had come out when it was supposed to.

Why were the second and third issues published two years apart?[10]
The publisher was having financial difficulties. They couldn't find a printer that would print the book if they didn't have the money to pay for it up front.

How did you arrive at the Bond that you selected, the composite Bond?
This is *my* Bond. But my Bond is actually Ian Fleming's Bond. If you look at the frontispiece of the comic, James Bond has the Walther PPK in his hand, and he is leaning on something. I took that from a photograph of Hoagy Carmichael leaning on a piano. All I did was I took about half an inch off Carmichael's nose because he was a bit too long in the face and too angular to suit me.

I changed his hairstyle ever so slightly to give him the traditional James Bond look and the black comma [Fleming likens the way that Bond's hair rests on his forehead to a black comma in several novels, including *Casino Royale*, *Live and Let Die*, *Moonraker*, and *Goldfinger*.] I also added a scar, which I modified from Fleming's description because frankly, a spy who's walking around with a three-inch scar on his right cheek is going to be pretty darn easy to spot. But if you're like me, growing up, we were rough-and-tumble kids, and every kid I knew had a scar on their eyebrow from taking a bad fall. I also knew a young lady who had an interesting scar in her eyebrow, and I said, "If you enhanced that and just brought it down to your cheek, it would be stunning," She was a pretty girl to begin with but that scar through the eyebrow made it distinctive. That was what I had in mind when I did James Bond.

Mike Grell, like Ian Fleming, based Bond's look on composer,
singer, and pianist Hoagy Carmichael.

I drew the scar coming down through his eyebrow, missing the eye, and then just catching a portion of his cheekbone so that overall the length is three inches. But it's actually two small scars that are less noticeable. This way somebody can't say, "Keep your eye out for a guy with a three-inch scar on his right cheek." The reality is, even back then, plastic surgery would've covered that up.

Was there a lot of trial and error in drawing Bond?
Oh, hell no. I just did one preliminary sketch and sent it to them, and they liked it. That was it.

The character was waiting inside you.
Oh, absolutely.

Have you seen the Ian Fleming–commissioned drawing of Bond?
Yes, yes.

It's almost too elegant.
It's not that it doesn't work. That commission is also very much Hoagy Carmichael plus a scar on the cheek. I changed it but it's all subjective.

You said that it was important to show Bond's weaknesses in your story.
Bond is a guy who is carrying ghosts with him. I mentioned that I picked up pretty much where *On Her Majesty's Secret Service* left off. I wanted to let the reader know that this was the guy who was still healing from the death of his wife. He had not fully recovered from that yet. Everything that he does is geared in that direction.

He's a bit reckless. At that stage in his life, Bond would've had a bit of a death wish. That's why Boothroyd tells Bond, "You're licensed to kill. No one gave you permission to die." That brings Bond back to who and what he is. He's a military guy. He's got orders. He's going to obey his orders, and no one has given him permission to die.

Was *Permission to Die* your title all along?
Yes. I knew that they were going to be doing *Licence to Kill*, and I was looking for something that sounded very James Bond. I still think it does.

It's the flip side to *Licence to Kill*.
Right. Raymond Benson paid me one of the biggest compliments I ever had. He told me that he thought my book, *Permission to Die*, was the best James Bond *movie* that he had ever *read*.

How long did it take to draw all these books and pages?
It was probably about a year-long process.

Bond comics aren't always good. Is Bond difficult to write as a comic?
No. [Comic book writer] Cary Bates, whom I worked with on *Superboy and the Legion of Super-Heroes*, was a huge James Bond fan. I remember saying to Cary that I thought it was silly that James Bond hadn't been turned into a [monthly] comic book. He said, "It's all a question of the visuals and the action." I said, "What do you mean?" Cary said, "Take the scene in *The Man with the Golden Gun* where James Bond jumps

the car, ramp to ramp, over that broken-down bridge. It rotates, spirals 360 degrees in midair, lands on its wheels, and drives off. In the movie, that's spectacular. In a comic book, it's three panels. Who gives a shit?" And he's right. Cary's right. At that point, the thrust of Bond films seemed to be more emphasis on the action and the gadgets and less emphasis on the character, which is a huge mistake.

For me, this story is more about the character, and that's why the critical reaction that I got to *Permission to Die* was as good as it was. It was because I tried to give all the characters in the book something important—an arc, a personal backstory. The villain, who is about to blow up a major city and kill a whole bunch of people, is in a great deal of personal turmoil over the act that he's about to commit. Widziadlo sees this as a sacrifice that he is about to make; he is about to be branded the worst terrorist criminal ever to exist. In his mind, Widziadlo is willing to do that because he thinks that in doing so, he'll be saving the world. Right? It's the logic of his own twisted psyche; he's a damaged character.

Widziadlo may be insane, but his insanity doesn't take the form of being a sociopath or a psychopath. It's something that happened to him that scarred him. My revelation is at the end of the story. When Widziadlo and his girlfriend Edáine Gayla are embracing, she reaches up and removes the mask that he's wearing. Everybody's expecting him to have horrific scars. Widziadlo's not scarred at all. All the scars are on the inside. Just like James Bond, all the scars are on the inside, except for the one.

When writing a Bond comic, do you have to make sure to somehow include fans who only watch the movies and aren't familiar with the books?
You have to. I come from an era when you were more likely to read the book before you saw the movie. Today people are not interested in reading books at all, or for the most part, few of them are. They're more likely to have their first experience regarding Bond from a movie. Fortunately, the old films hold up extremely well. The newer ones, not always so much.

The biggest disparity between the literary Bond and the film Bond came during Roger Moore's tenure as James Bond. I'm not saying anything against Moore, because he's a terrific actor. I really like the guy. He's got a terrific sense of humor. But there was a point where there was little difference between James Bond and Maxwell Smart. Bond was played goofy, played more for laughs than it was for serious. In the middle of that, he made a couple that were pretty darn good. *For Your Eyes Only* was the best of the bunch that he made. *The Spy Who Loved Me* was pretty good, too. But the other ones were sort of goofball, broad comedies. That didn't suit my image of Bond at all.

What are the best comic strip or comic book Bonds?
You have to put the newspaper comic strip, the original one in the *Daily Express*, right at the top. And, for my money, all the rest of us are wannabes.

What made the *Daily Express* comics so good? They were faithful to Fleming, took their time. . . .
It was the combination of all of that. The characters were true to the Fleming stories. The comic strips took a good deal of time to tell the story that they wanted to tell. The artwork was just terrific. In the strips, all they had was black and white. But they were stunning—rich texture, bold blacks, and you had no trouble at all reading it, even though it reproduced at a microscopic size by the fastest publishing method known to man on the crappiest paper available.

The two major illustrators on the original Bond comic strip were John McLusky and Yaroslav Horak. What were their stylistic differences?
Horak already had a well-known, rather distinctive style, whereas McLusky seemed to be more of the old-school illustrator, at least in my view. McLusky's Bond resembled Sean Connery a bit closer than Horak's did. Horak's characters have a particular stamp to them, a particular way he has of drawing eyes, for instance. Horak's women had a particular look about them. It's like the difference between Neil Adams and Jack Kirby. One is more illustrative, the other is more stylized and perhaps a bit more dynamic.

Horak is Neil Adams in that example?
Right.

Kirby's work is bold and dynamic, while Adams is more realistic.
Right.

Out of Horak and McLusky, which is more realistic?
Yeah, that's gonna get my head handed to me. You get stylized images more frequently from McLusky, and a more illustrative kind from Horak. Take for instance their portrayal of James Bond. I prefer Horak's James Bond to McLusky's. But McLusky's rendering and his old-school style appeals to me. Maybe it's nostalgia. Let's face it, when we're talking about cartoonists and comic books or comic strips, you're always going to have a soft spot in your heart for the one that attracted your attention first.

You said McLusky was an old-school illustrator. Can you elaborate?

Cartoonists tend to use shorthand. We draw things that we know and that look a certain way. A good guy looks a certain way. A pretty girl looks a certain way. We draw types, stereotypes, because a lot of times we don't have a lot of time or space to establish whether somebody's a good guy. If you want somebody who'll be recognized as a good guy, you'll draw him with softer features and nicer eyes. And bad guys look a little more stern around the edges. It seems to me that the guys who have that ability to draw different characters, different styles of characters realistically, without resorting to stereotypes are kind of few and far between, even today.

What does a good Bond comic capture that a novel or film can't?

That's interesting. As an artist, when I look at a page, I'm not just looking at the people on the page and what they're doing. I'm looking at the world that they live in. And at a glance, you can absorb the world of James Bond in a comic book, whereas in a novel, it has to be described. Sometimes at length, and sometimes ad nauseam. Fleming was guilty of spending page after page describing a game of golf or page after page describing a dinner. Now it's all stuff that was interesting to Fleming, which adheres to what Agatha Christie said: when you read a book, you get 10 percent plot, 20 percent characterization, and 70 percent of whatever the writer knows best. That holds true with Bond. It's the texture that can be missing unless you're willing to wade through all those pages.

Reality and good storytelling don't necessarily always mix. You can do something that can be a ripsnorter, a great action yarn, a terrific action scene, and have little to do with reality. But if it's entertaining and the audience buys it, that's all that counts. Denny O'Neal, who was my editor on the Warlord and Green Lantern/ Green Arrow comics, used to say, "Yes, it's bullshit science, but it's our bullshit science." And that holds true with James Bond. You have to just accept that, even though the world of modern-day spies is a little closer to John le Carré's George Smiley than it is to Bond. They've established the world that Bond lives in, and you go to Bond for that reason.

Is there a panel that best encapsulates what you were trying to do with Bond?

Oh, lord. That would presume that I remember the frames because I sure don't have a copy of the book. My favorite page of the book is probably in the first issue, when we introduce Bond and he's basically gotten out of bed with a young lady, and he's staring out the window. There's a flashback to a number of iconic Bond moments. I included moments from *Dr. No*, *From Russia with Love*, *Goldfinger*, and *Thunderball*. As many as I could, on up to *On Her Majesty's Secret Service* and that crucial moment when the camera pans to Tracy in the car with the bullet hole. That spread basically encompasses everything that I thought was important about Bond.

Grell depicts memorable moments from *Dr. No*, *Goldfinger*, *Thunderball*,
and *On Her Majesty's Secret Service* in *Permission to Die*.

You don't have a copy of your book? Or it's not in front of you?
Yes, it's in storage someplace. Someplace. If you said, "I will give you $1,000 if you
could mail me copies tomorrow," I would have to go to eBay and buy copies to send
to you. I've had to do that more often than not. One day I will come across those
books, and that'll be great. But the likelihood of finding them anytime soon is slim
to none.

Where's the artwork?

In the '90s, there was a collapse of the comic industry, starting about 1993, when Marvel Comics went bankrupt. When I started in the business in the early '70s, the cancellation point for a book at DC Comics was 33,333. If you did 33,334, you were just over the line into the black. If you dropped into the red, the book was canceled. In the '90s, sales of books typically were three hundred thousand. And could go as high as three million. That's because of what collectors were doing: People were buying comics not one and two copies; they were buying ten, twenty, or fifty copies and putting them away, hoping to resell them a year later for more than they paid for them.

But all that ended the first time some kid walked in, tried to sell his dozen copies of whatever back to the comic book dealer. The dealer probably reached under the counter and pulled out a giant long box packed to the brim and said, "Kid, I got all you want for a quarter apiece." That big booming sound that you heard all around the world was the collectibles market collapsing. And the comic business went down with it.

It collapsed as exponentially as it expanded. You went from having a book that was selling half a million copies one month to one selling a quarter of a million the next month. The next month you'd be selling maybe eighty to one hundred thousand copies. The next month after that, you'd have about fifty thousand. Before you know it, even well-known titles like *Batman* were down to selling eight thousand copies a month. *Eight thousand.* Right now, even though the industry has rebounded considerably, there are few titles that have recovered to the levels that we were selling in the '70s. Few comics are selling thirty-thousand copies a month.

Given that context, where's your artwork?

I *sold* it. I had rent to pay, a mortgage to pay, food to buy. I sold *everything*. I sold everything to stay alive, and I'm still on the green side of the sod. Where the artwork is, I have no idea.

Did you keep any art?

I didn't keep anything to commemorate my time. I have a couple of pieces that were stashed away in storage and avoided the mass sell-off. But I don't have anything of my own hanging on my walls right now. I'm at the stage where I'm not interested in leaving something behind for somebody else to sell. At the moment I'm in the market for a new car, so everything's for sale.

PART III

BEING
BOND

ROGER MOORE IS JAMES BOND

Talking to Roger Moore when he's wearing a tuxedo is like trying to hold a conversation with Leonard Nimoy when he's wearing Spock ears. Your rational mind knows you're talking with an actor but your fan instinct can almost trick you into thinking that you're talking to the real James Bond.

Moore and I met at a gala dinner where he was invited to talk about his work for UNICEF, a charity that provides aid to needy children. Moore became a goodwill ambassador for UNICEF, and from 1991 until his death in 2017, he traveled the world meeting ill and impoverished children and raising money and awareness for the organization.

At the gala, diners listened politely as Moore spoke about his ties to the charity. However, I suspect that many of them, like me, were there less to see and admire Roger Moore the philanthropist than to rub shoulders with James Bond. After Moore's speech, the moderator opened the floor to questions. Moore responded to all of them knowledgeably and passionately, but it wasn't until I asked Moore about his work as the superspy that the gathering turn festive. Moore knew his audience wanted him to acknowledge his onscreen counterpart, and he did not disappoint.

Prompted by my question, Moore self-effacingly explained his version of how he was cast in the role that earned him international stardom. "Harry Saltzman and Cubby Broccoli, the producers, and I used to gamble. They owed me a lot of money. They thought it would be cheaper to put me in a movie."

Moore talked about taking over the role of Bond from Connery. He said, "People would ask, 'Aren't you nervous about taking over for Sean Connery?' And I'd respond, 'No, not really. There have been four thousand actors who have played Hamlet, and this certainly ain't Hamlet.' There's not much to say in the role apart from, 'My name is Bond.'" It could be argued that Connery was so successful and beloved as Bond that only an actor of great confidence could assume the mantle. Moore's bravado and fearlessness were not unlike Bond's. Furthermore, Roger Moore was suave, erudite, and witty—words that have been used to describe James Bond himself.

Later on, Moore admitted to having a few trepidations in taking over the part that Connery seemed to define indelibly. "I did get nervous when I was on my way to London for the first screening of *Live and Let Die*. I felt like I was in a delivery room waiting to have a baby. The baby's going to come out and that's it! There's nothing you could do about it."

Moore's fear about following Connery, at least the one that he'd admit to, manifested itself in a most unlikely way—in Bond's drink of choice. Fearing that he could not order a "martini, shaken not stirred" without a Scottish burr, Moore's

Bond never orders his preferred beverage. "I never ever said that in any of my Bond movies. But every waiter, every barman in the world knew that I wanted a martini shaken, not stirred."

When discussing how he prepared for the role, Moore singled out a concern that initially troubled him. "I asked myself, 'What sort of spy is he? Everybody knows him!'" Moore's point was the absurdity of Bond being a world-famous "secret" agent. If an operative is to be effective, his identity must remain concealed. Moore finally decided that Bond's audience had long ago suspended its disbelief about matters of this kind.

After some initial apprehension, the public embraced Roger Moore's interpretation of the role. His Bond was so popular that he played the part in seven consecutive movies.

Although Moore was modest about his popularity as Bond, he enjoyed the association. In an article for the *London Times*, Moore wrote, "I am an aficionado of James Bond—both the books and the films—and of course have a vested interest in the franchise. But more than that, I have a vested interest in the character. I feel protective towards him."[1]

Moore's Bond is strikingly different from Connery's. Connery was lethal, often unkind or cruel, and he introduced the world to Bond's sadistic tendencies. During the 1960s, Connery seemed to be the only possible Bond, and for many of his successors, including Timothy Dalton, Pierce Brosnan, and Daniel Craig, he will always be the gold standard.

Moore radically redefined the part in the 1970s and 1980s. Moore told me that he believed Bond did not like killing and he added that his interpretation of Bond as a reluctant assassin was the insight that proved to be the linchpin of his approach to the part. On the surface, suggesting that the world's most lethal spy could actually loathe killing is a little like proposing that the world's best race car driver hates making left turns. In Bond's world, killing is an essential part of the job description. Secretaries type, chefs cook, and Double-O agents kill—they even have a government-issued license to do so.

Although the Double-O prefix is thought of as an exotic indicator of an extraordinary spy's arsenal of skills and knowledge of spycraft, the actual meaning is decidedly less glamorous. In Fleming's first novel, *Casino Royale*, the literary Bond confessed, "It's not difficult to get a Double O number if you're prepared to kill people. . . . That's all the meaning it has."[2] These days, two kills hardly seem impressive. Matt Damon's Jason Bourne can kill two thugs with a rolled up magazine before breakfast.

Fleming added to the reader's knowledge of the Double-O section in subsequent stories. In *Live and Let Die*, *Casino*'s follow-up, Fleming added that a 00 agent is empowered to "use assassination as a weapon"[3] and in the fifth novel, *From Russia, with Love*, he wrote that the "numerals signify an agent who has killed and who is privileged to kill on active service."[4]

Whereas Moore's Bond killed a foe while holding one hand on his Walther PPK and the other over his nose, it sometimes appeared as though Connery enjoyed killing. Moore, in his article for the *London Times*, expounded on their differences: "Being a coward, I hated guns and would far rather have tried to disarm an opponent with a flippant remark, whereas Sean would knock them out cold. That was the difference in our characters."[5]

For Moore, Bond's killing was what he had to do so that he could travel to remote, romantic locales and meet and bed beautiful women. Moore's Bond carried out his assignments for the audience's vicarious enjoyment. Moore remarked, "I basically said [to the audience], 'I'm having a good time doing this, and I hope you're having a good time watching me have a good time.'" Moore's Bond is having the best time when he's seducing his nubile costars. Rather than fetishize the violence, Moore's Bond plays to the audience's sexual fantasies.

I bristle when Moore detractors suggest that he transformed Bond into an amiable rogue. After all, if Moore didn't make audiences believe that he was the world's most able spy and not merely a wisecracking ladies' man, the films wouldn't be as effective as they are. The spy-as-playboy paradigm only works if it's played for laughs—as it is in the Austin Powers movies. It's not a concept that could have been sustained over Moore's enduring seven-film reign as Bond. Moore's Bond was every bit as formidable as Connery's, but Moore chose to emphasize Bond's more dashing, less dangerous qualities.

Neither Connery's nor Moore's interpretations seemed to invite scrutiny of Bond's motivation. Surprisingly, even after the first twenty films, audiences didn't know much about James Bond's personal life. We knew what he likes to drink and how he likes it prepared (shaken and not—you know—the other way). We knew the order in which he likes to say his name (last name, first name, last name again). More avid fans could recall that he was briefly married to Tracy di Vicenzo but became a widower when Ernst Stavro Blofeld arranged her execution. It wasn't until Daniel Craig's conflicted Bond that the general public wondered about the man behind the number. Fleming's novels provide plenty of answers.

We know from the books that Bond became an orphan at eleven when his parents (Andrew Bond and Monique Delacroix) died in a mountain climbing accident. An aunt (Charmian Bond) became his guardian and he studied at Eton (the prestigious boarding school) before he was expelled due to an incident involving a maid (even then Bond was a lothario). After college, Bond joined the navy, rose to the rank of commander, and was recruited by Her Majesty's Secret Service, where he became its best agent.

In each book, Fleming gives us tantalizing morsels about 007's private life. In *On Her Majesty's Secret Service (OHMSS)*, Bond fondly recalls the "spade-and-bucket days" of his childhood when he would swim in the "dancing waves" and collect seashells, which, over the gentle objections of a parent, he intended to display on his bedroom windowsill.[6] In the short story "Octopussy," Bond says that the Austrian climber Hannes Oberhauser "was something of a father to me at a time when I happened to need one."[7] In the short story "From a View to a Kill," we learn that Bond lost his virginity in Paris at the age of sixteen during "one of the most memorable evenings of his life."[8] We discover that seeing his friend Quarrel survive the shark attack in *Live and Let Die* triggers Bond's "first tears since his childhood."[9] In *Casino Royale*, we find out that "Bond's car was his only personal hobby"[10] and that he considers boredom to be "the worst torture of all."[11] Elsewhere in *OHMSS*, Fleming confirms what readers have long suspected—that women and "gun-play" were the only things "that set James Bond really moving in life."[12] In *Moonraker*, Fleming reveals that Bond suffers from depression and that his goal is to "have as little possible in his banking account when he was killed," as "he knew he would be."[13]

Although the cinematic Bond is usually depicted as a carefree bachelor, the literary Bond is frequently heartbroken. In *Moonraker*, Bond develops feelings for policewoman Gala Brand. When Brand rejects him, a forlorn Bond tries to inure himself from "the pain of failure that is so much greater than the pleasure of success," and he resolves that from now on there "must be no regrets" or "false sentiment."[14] For Bond to successfully disguise his pain, he "must play the role which she expected of him. The tough man of the world. . . . The man who was only a silhouette."[15] In *OHMSS*, Fleming humanizes 007 again by revealing that Bond takes yearly trips to France so that he can visit his slain wife's grave. Yet in *The Man with the Golden Gun* (1965), we learn that Bond "knew, deep down, that love . . . from any woman was not enough for him. It would be taking 'a room with a view.' For James Bond, the same view would always pall."[16] In *Diamonds Are Forever*, Bond explains his aversion to matrimony: "Most marriages don't add two people together. They subtract one from the other."[17] But six novels later, in *OHMSS*, Bond has a change of heart. He comes to realize that he's looking for a woman who "above all . . . needs" him and, moreover, that he "wouldn't mind having children."[18] In *Diamonds*, Bond reflects on the kind of advice he might give to a son, should he ever have one: "Spend your money how you like, but don't buy yourself anything that eats."[19] In *You Only Live Twice*, the last novel that was published before Fleming's death, Bond might have finally gotten his wish. In it, Japanese diver Kissy Suzuki becomes pregnant with Bond's child.[20]

Fleming informs us that the professional life of a secret agent isn't always exciting. In fact, it's sometimes dull. We learn in *Moonraker* that Bond considers Mondays "hell" because it means "two days of dockets and files to plough through."[21] The literary Bond has two secretaries: first Loelia Ponsonby, then Mary Goodnight. He goes out on assignments only two or three times a year and during the remaining months he "had the duties of any easy-going civil servant."[22] Bond doesn't take vacations; he works from about 10 a.m. to 6 p.m., has lunch in the "canteen," and lives in a "small but comfortable flat," which is looked after by May, an "elderly Scottish housekeeper."[23] The mandatory retirement age for Double-O agents is forty-five. Although the films seem to suggest that there are numerous Double-O agents, we are told that at this point in the literary Bond's time line, there are only "two other members" of the 00 section.[24]

In *The Man with the Golden Gun*, we learn more about Bond's working methods: "The first law for a secret agent is to get his geography right, his means of access and exits, and assure his communications with the outside world."[25] And in *Thunderball*, while deliberating on how much unsubstantiated information to share with M, his superior, 007 reminds himself, "Wishful intelligence, the desire to pleasure or reassure the recipient, was the most dangerous commodity in the whole realm of secret information."[26]

Elsewhere, Bond speaks about his need for self-reliance. "What's the good of other people's opinions? Animals don't consult each other about other animals. They look and sniff and feel. In love and hate, and everything in between, those are the only tests that matter. But people are unsure of their own instincts. They want reassurance."[27] In *From Russia, with Love*, Bond philosophizes: "Never job backwards. What might have been was a waste of time. Follow your fate, and be satisfied with it."[28] In *OHMSS*, Bond soothes his troubled mind with the comforting notion that "worry is a dividend paid to disaster before it's due."[29] Taken together these details form a somewhat revealing portrait (or dossier, if you will).

But movie audiences didn't seem to have much interest in the private life of a character they so loved. It seems that, to his fans, what Bond did before his first onscreen adventure was irrelevant and, comparatively speaking, mundane. Through the first twenty films Eon (*Dr. No* through *Die Another Day*) and the first five actors (Connery through Brosnan), revelations about Bond's psychological makeup and particulars about his past were usually limited to information about previous missions or his preferences in relatively inconsequential matters, such as food (Beluga caviar), drink (Bollinger Champagne), and music ("That's just as bad as listening to the Beatles without ear muffs.").[30] But these scant details were meant to establish Bond's sophistication, build his legend, and add to the mystique of the already enthralling spy.

However, notable moments in the pre-Craig era hint at the depths of Bond's character. In *The Spy Who Loved Me*, we see Moore's Bond shed his unflappable exterior at the mention of his late wife's memory, and in *For Your Eyes Only*, he touchingly leaves flowers on her grave. In *The Living Daylights*, we learn that Dalton's Bond has become disenchanted with the spy game. When threatened with censure for not following orders, Dalton's Bond fires back, "Tell M what you want. If he fires me, I'll thank him for it." Bond's friend-turned-enemy Alec Trevelyan seems to have 007's number when, in *GoldenEye*, he wonders, "If all the vodka martinis ever silence the screams of the men you've killed. Or if you find forgiveness in the arms of all those willing women. For all the dead ones you failed to protect." Elsewhere in *Golden-Eye*, we are told that Bond's inability to form long-term relationships with women is a self-defense mechanism. Brosnan's Bond confesses that he must remain "cold" because, "It's what keeps me so alive." In *Tomorrow Never Dies*, Bond reveals that he left Paris Carver, a woman that he cared for, because she got "too close."

An assortment of throwaway remarks hint at Bond's self-image. Before skeet shooting with the austere Emile Largo in *Thunderball*, Bond confesses, "I'm not what you'd call a passionate man." In a deleted scene from *Diamonds Are Forever*, Bond tells Plenty O'Toole that, notwithstanding his polished appearance, he considers himself to be a "mere commoner." After Bond has been released by the enemy agents who had imprisoned and tortured him for fourteen months in *Die Another Day*, M rebukes 007 for not swallowing his cyanide capsule and thereby risking breaking under duress and revealing top-secret information. In response to M's reprimand, Bond sneers that he "threw [the cyanide] away years ago." The agent's confidence that he could endure sustained torture indefinitely and not be broken suggests a darkly hopeful outlook. Here Bond's well-earned world-weary veneer belies an underlying optimism.

These exceptions aside, insights into Bond's character and past were replaced with allusions to previous Bond films. In *OHMSS*, George Lazenby's Bond opens his desk drawer to find memorabilia from Sean Connery's Bond's previous adventures, including the knife that Honey Ryder wore in *Dr. No* and the garrote that Red Grant used in *From Russia with Love*.[31] In turn, when Connery returned to the role in *Diamonds Are Forever*, his Bond seeks revenge on the man who killed Lazenby's Bond's wife. Her memory survives through three other Bond actors—Roger Moore, Timothy Dalton, and Pierce Brosnan—in the previously mentioned Roger Moore movies, as well as in *Licence to Kill*, *GoldenEye*, and *The World Is Not Enough*. In *Die Another Day*, Brosnan's Bond visits Q's disused equipment supply room, which is filled with gadgets from previous Bond films, including the jetpack from *Thunderball* and the fake alligator from *Octopussy*.[32]

These allusions link the Bonds of the different eras and reinforce the notion that Connery, Lazenby, Moore, Dalton, and Brosnan were all playing the same character at different periods during his lengthy career.

Daniel Craig's Bond films make numerous references to prior adventures, but it can be argued that Craig's Bond is not the same character that the previous actors played, that he isn't the same man. But this radical departure from the series' formula wasn't immediately apparent at the dawn of Craig's era. His first movie, *Casino*

Royale, can be viewed as an origin story and as a prequel to *Dr. No*, the first Bond movie. *Quantum of Solace* and *Skyfall* seemed to fit into the same narrative. However, the perception of Craig's Bond changed when, in *Spectre*, archvillain Ernst Stavro Blofeld revealed that his father, Hannes Oberhauser, looked after the orphaned Bond for two years and had asked a young Blofeld to treat Bond as a brother. If Craig's Bond had a personal relationship with Blofeld, then Blofeld's previous encounters with Connery, Lazenby, and Moore's Bonds wouldn't make sense. The plot point, while controversial among Bond fans, suggests that Craig's Bond films need to be reassessed and viewed as part of a separate narrative, which is related to but independent of the previous movies' continuity.

For nearly sixty years, Bond movies have been escapist entertainment of the highest order. They are meant to transport us from the drudgery of our ordinary lives and to distract us from our more commonplace concerns about, say, our finances or our family's well-being. Sean Connery remarked, "Along comes this character who cuts right through all that like a very hot knife through butter, with his clothing and his cars and his wine and his women. Bond, you see, is a kind of present-day survival kit."[33]

Noted Bond expert John Cork argues in *Some Kind of Hero* that "Bond was a man who saw the big picture, whose arrogance and disregard for the rules and conventions was because he was on a larger mission, a mission that went beyond any single assignment."[34] James Bond seems to agree with Cork's assessment. When M questions 007 about his motives in *Quantum of Solace*, Daniel Craig's Bond defensively snaps, "I'm motivated by my duty."

For many years, audiences thought that there was one true Bond. In the 1960s, movie posters promised and audiences believed that "SEAN CONNERY IS JAMES BOND." But several actors have played the spy since then, and each actor has become the definitive Bond for his generation. There were subtle differences among their characterizations. Bondologist Mark O'Connell writes about the "masculinity of Connery, the vulnerability of Lazenby, the diplomacy of Moore, the instinct of Dalton," "the professionalism of Brosnan," and now about "the *conscience* of Craig."[35]

Bond's appeal is undeniable. And men, perhaps especially young men, live vicariously through the novels and the movies about this dashing, fearless, super-capable figure who is also irresistible to women. Raymond Chandler put it simply: "Bond is what every man would like to be."[36]

Even Ian Fleming wished he could be like Bond. Before Fleming was a novelist, he worked in naval intelligence during World War II. When the war ended, he returned to civilian life and wrote twelve novels and nine short stories about the spy he never was. Fleming said that the plot of *Casino Royale* was based on an incident from his own life. When on leave in Portugal, he tried to bankrupt a few German agents (and eventually, he hoped, the entire German government) at a casino. As

Fleming told *Playboy* magazine in 1964, "I thought it would be a brilliant coup to play with them, break them, take their money. Instead, of course, they took mine. Most embarrassing. This incident appears in *Casino Royale*, my first book, but, of course, Bond does not lose. In fact, he totally and coldly vanquishes his opponent."[37]

Like Fleming, Moore obviously knew that he was not Bond, yet there might have been a part of him that wished otherwise. Let's revisit Moore's statement that every time that James Bond enters a bar, a bartender offers him a martini unsolicited. It should be noted that in none of the *movies* do bartenders give Bond a martini unless he orders one. Perhaps, Moore's Freudian slip suggests that he confused his own offscreen adventures with Bond's on-screen ones. I imagine that Moore rarely walked into a restaurant without having a well-intentioned fan or bartender offering him Bond's drink of choice.

Notwithstanding Roger Moore's modesty, to audiences, Moore transformed himself into James Bond. And as noted, many men dream that they too could reinvent themselves in Bond's image. These men might have imagined that if Moore could become Bond, then perhaps they could too.

Moore was the Bond that we "realistically" could hope to be. Moore's Bond was the embodiment of our wish fulfillment. Most of us knew that Connery's cool was far from reach, but Moore humanized Bond just enough so that audiences had at least an outside shot at being like him.

Connery's Bond was perhaps a little too virile for an adolescent's nascent fantasies; he was too hard-edged and hairy for teenage boys to relate to as readily as they could to Moore's Bond. Don't doubt for a moment that the teenage boy inside us is an important factor in appreciating Bond. It takes a fourteen-year-old's mentality to laugh without embarrassment at such common Bond movie touches as the title of Moore's sixth outing, *Octopussy* or the names of several of Bond's women, among them, Pussy Galore, Chew Mee, Plenty O'Toole, Penelope Smallbone, Xenia Onatopp, and Doctors Holly Goodhead and Molly Warmflash.[38]

Viewers get the sense that Connery's Bond wouldn't want to spend time with them. Moore's, on the other hand, was Bond as your pal. Bond as your protector. Bond as your wingman. Bond as your father figure. With his disarming approach to the part, Moore welcomed you into his world of glamour and intrigue. He welcomed you on his adventures and he invited you to be just as Bond-like as he. Of course, most of us could never come close. Even in his eighties, Moore looked better and more like Bond than most of us ever will.

Moore retired his license to kill in 1984, after battling an ax-wielding Christopher Walken on top of the Golden Gate Bridge and after hearing Tanya Roberts utter her last "Oh, James!" while showering with him in *A View to a Kill*. Since then, other actors have "become" Bond. Though Bond is no longer Roger Moore, Roger Moore will always be James Bond.

Nobody did it better than Roger Moore.

ILLUSTRATION BY PAT CARBAJAL

What was the key to understanding Bond's character?

When I first took on the part, I read Fleming's books. There was little offered in them about the character. However, I remember reading one line that said Bond had just completed a mission—meaning a kill. He didn't particularly enjoy killing but took pride in doing his job well. That was the key to the role as far as I was concerned. [*Note:* Moore is referring to the passage in the novel *Goldfinger*, in which Fleming writes: "It was part of his profession to kill people. He had never liked doing it and when he had to kill he did it as well as he knew how and forgot about it. As a secret agent who held the rare Double-O prefix—the license to kill in the Secret Service—it was his duty to be as cool about death as a surgeon. If it happened, it happened. Regret was unprofessional—worse, it was a death-watch beetle in the soul."[39]]

Although there is deservedly much discussion about how suave and funny you were as Bond, you were also good at making him cold-blooded and lethal. How did you approach those scenes?

Well, if you read the internet blogs, they agree I was funny, but they're not so sure I was suave and certainly don't regard me as having been cold-blooded. There was one scene in *For Your Eyes Only* where I had to be rather cold-blooded in killing a villain. They say that scene changed the series tone for my films, but I wasn't comfortable with it, if truth be known. I was rather cold-blooded and mercenary on Fridays, though. That's the day I received my paychecks.

What was your approach to saying "My name is Bond, James Bond," 007's signature line? Audiences eagerly anticipate the line. It seems like an actor could go a bit mad thinking about it.

Oh goodness, I spent many, many hours committing that line to memory! Guy Hamilton, the director on my first Bond, said, "Don't say the line with a Scottish accent and we'll be fine." Words I heeded.

From the movies, we learn so little about Bond personally. What do you imagine his private life is like?

It's probably one bar to another bed. I'd imagine his private life to be rather limited as he's seemingly always on the job.

When people meet you, on some level—perhaps an unconscious one—they believe that they're meeting James Bond. What's that like for you? Do you feel any pressure to meet those expectations?

Oh, I don't think they think I'm Bond. Well, okay, maybe. I sometimes get comments like "Hello, Mr. Bond" and such like. I smile and keep walking, but if someone comes up to me and says, "Hey, you're James Bond," I'll say, "No, I am Roger Moore; I used to play James Bond." I don't pretend I am the character. Therefore, I have no expectations to meet other than those of meeting Roger Moore. I am, of course, charming, polite, and courteous.

Where do your and Bond's personalities converge and diverge?
Well, when I played the part, he looked and sounded like me. That's where the similarities and differences begin and end!

Men the world over have dreamed of being as suave, capable, masculine, and as appealing to women as Bond. Most of us come up a bit short. When you were in character did you ever allow yourself to feel like Bond?
How does Bond feel? I don't know. I never really absorbed myself in a role like some actors do. Many take the roles home with them and live the part. I'm quite happy to leave mine at the studio and return home as I left, simple old Roger Moore. I guess it would be easy to think I'm invincible and live as charmed a life as 007, but that would be foolish, wouldn't it?

You've played a wide variety of characters in scores of movies. You've also starred in memorable television shows including *The Saint* and *The Persuaders*, but the character you're most associated with is James Bond.
Without a doubt, you are recognized for the last role you played. When I was Bond, I was recognized as Bond. Before that, I was recognized as Lord Brett Sinclair, the Saint, Beau Maverick, Silky Harris, Ivanhoe. . . . Bond was later than those other parts, and perhaps bigger, too.

What are the positive and negative aspects of the association?
The positive aspects of Bond? A bigger paycheck. The negative aspects? A coward having to pretend he is brave and trying not to blink when explosions go off.

Can you please give us some advice on how to be as cool as Bond in our daily lives?
Stay in bed . . . with a pretty lady.

Roger Moore in *The Saint*. The show debuted in 1962, the same year as the first Bond movie.

ITV/PHOTOFEST

How has playing James Bond affected you personally? Not profession-ally but personally.

Personally, it has given me financial security. It has also provided me with a certain celebrity, if that is the right word, which has enabled me to work as a goodwill ambassador for UNICEF.

Speaking of UNICEF, how has playing Bond been an asset to meeting children in your travels for UNICEF?

It is a great asset. After all, who would want to meet a jobbing actor? But meeting an actor who once played James Bond, that opens doors. I find I'm able to meet with presidents, prime ministers, and people who make decisions. Bond has afforded me a great personal passport, which I use for UNICEF.

Why do you think the films have remained popular for fifty years and counting?

The films are hugely popular because they are entertaining. The producers never cheat audiences; the money goes on the screen.

To what do you attribute the character's popularity?

Every man wants to be James Bond; every woman wants to be bedded by him!

What drives James Bond?

He obviously feels a sense of duty and thrives on it.

Is Bond essentially a hedonist of sorts, who's primarily in pursuit of pleasure?

He takes pleasure along the way and uses it to great advantage at times in extracting information from certain ladies, but hedonist? No, I don't think so.

What do you think are the most significant ways the *character* of Bond has changed?

He has had six different faces! Each Bond is right for that generation. I'm sure my Bond wouldn't work today; just as Daniel Craig's 007 probably wouldn't have worked for 1970s audiences. The producers move and adapt with the times. They are very clever.

Until recently, the Bond movies have avoided exploring Bond's psyche. Would you have enjoyed exploring those elements?

Me? Act and think deeply? No thanks! I wouldn't say they avoided exploring his psyche, but I guess after twenty-odd films, you reach a stage where we know so much about the character without knowing that much about the man and it's interesting to take a look.

Can you talk a little bit about how you found the right note to play Bond?

Guy Hamilton told me to play it my way. We avoided some of the lines closely associated with Sean, such as ordering a vodka martini, but otherwise, I just played myself, as always.

Bond's movement appears effortless. Can you talk about how you approached the physicality of the part?

I never thought about it. I had doubles to make me look good!

There are some great moments in the films where you show Bond's vulnerable side. How do you approach those scenes?

I honestly don't read into it. I look at the script, speak to the director, and just say the lines.

Over the course of your seven Bond films, you experimented with different approaches to the part, from the tongue-in-cheek to the more realistic. What is your favorite approach?

I never really enjoyed the hard, gritty side of Bond. I much preferred being a lover and being a giggler.

Were there any moments in the Bond films that made you uncomfortable?

As I say, my Bond was a lover and giggler. I didn't think he should hit a woman [as he does in *The Man with the Golden Gun*] nor kill a man in cold blood. The storyline called for it, I know, but I personally don't feel comfortable with those types of scenes.

What do you see as the main difference between Sean Connery's Bond and yours?

Sean's Bond was a tough character who could fight his way out of a corner; my Bond would charm his way out of a corner.

What made Connery's interpretation distinctive?

Sean was the first Bond. He created and defined the part. He was distinctive in that there was no one else to compare him with.

What about George Lazenby?

George's film is a damn good movie. He could have been a great Bond and could have made quite a few movies, but it wasn't to be. We are friends.

Timothy Dalton?

Not long ago, I sat down to watch *The Living Daylights* for the first time and thought it a terrific movie, and Timothy, whom I've known years, is a bloody good 007 and a great actor. I was genuinely surprised by how much I enjoyed the film.

Pierce Brosnan?

Pierce played it much like me, though I did feel his films got a little too far-fetched—*invisible cars*?

Daniel Craig?

Daniel is certainly the best actor to ever play 007, and I think he will go on to become the best ever Bond.

What about that actor who played Bond seven times, Roger Moore? He's must have done something right. What did you admire about his approach?

Oh, he was very handsome, charming, talented, and modest.

Who is the best Bond?

Sean, because he was the first.

I have a silly final question. Who would win in a fight, your James Bond versus Sean Connery's?

Just after I had been announced as Bond, I took my eldest son, Geoffrey, to lunch at the White Elephant in London. He looked around the room and said, "Dad, could you beat up everyone in here?" I looked around. They looked a pretty frail bunch of folks, so I said, "Yes, sure." He then asked, "What about James Bond?" I explained that I was going to be James Bond. "No!" he protested, "I mean the real James Bond, Sean Connery." It's a wonder my son grew so tall.

HOAGY CARMICHAEL IS JAMES BOND

As told by his son Hoagy Bix Carmichael

Ian Fleming said that he imagined James Bond as having an angular face like that of Hoagy Carmichael, the singer, actor, bandleader, and composer who wrote the music for such timeless songs as *Georgia on My Mind, Heart and Soul*, and *Stardust*, and who was mentioned three times in two of Fleming's novels.

In *Casino Royale*, Vesper Lynd describes 007 as "very good-looking. He reminds me rather of Hoagy Carmichael."[40] For his part, Bond rejects the comparison. Later in the book, while sizing up his reflection in the mirror, Bond comes to the conclusion that the scar on his face makes him look like a pirate and that there is "not much of Hoagy Carmichael there."[41]

Apparently, Bond holds the minority opinion. In the third novel *Moonraker*, agent Gala Brand thinks that Bond "was certainly good-looking. . . . Rather like Hoagy Carmichael in a way. That black hair falling down over the right eyebrow. Much the same bones."[42]

Author John Gardner puts his own playful spin on the reference in his twelfth Bond continuation novel, *Death Is Forever* (1992). In it, Bond informs CIA agent Easy St. John that "Someone once said I looked like Hoagy Carmichael with a cruel mouth."[43] However, St. John tells 007 that she's not familiar with Carmichael. Bond, disappointed with her unforgivable naivete, dismissively replies, "Oh, Easy, if you don't know, I'm not going to explain."[44]

In this brief interview, Carmichael's son Hoagy Bix Carmichael shares his thoughts on his father's link to Bond.

Fleming modeled the look of Bond after your father.
Ian Fleming wrote that Bond had the angular look of Hoagy Carmichael.

What did your father think about this association?
Dad certainly dined out on the fact that he was possibly part of what Ian Fleming had in mind when he molded the character. He loved that fact. And he twisted it a little bit more, like, "After all, I am the model for James Bond."

How important was that to your dad?
He would get a big grin about it. But it's not like he had a picture of James Bond above his desk. He had enough accolades on his own.

Did your father ever meet Fleming?
I'm almost sure that Dad never met Ian Fleming.

Hoagy Carmichael.

What do you think of the drawing of Bond that Fleming commissioned?
I have seen the drawing of Bond before and have never thought it looked much like my father. It is a much stronger, he-man face and not much in the Carmichael vein. Until his death at eighty-one, dad had a full hairline. None of which takes away from how amused, almost proud, my father was that Ian Fleming felt that James Bond looked much like the guy from a small town in Indiana who could write a song or two.

BEING BOND

BOB HOLNESS IS JAMES BOND

As told by his daughter Ros Holness

Bob Holness was the first actor to play James Bond on the radio and the second 007 actor overall. Following Barry Nelson's 1954 performance as Bond in a TV adaptation of *Casino Royale*, Holness earned his place in Bond lore by playing the agent in the late 1950s in a South African Broadcasting Corporation's dramatization of *Moonraker*.

Unfortunately, except for the broad details, little is known about the production. Moreover, there are no known recordings of *Moonraker*. As a result, the radio drama has remained a long-standing mystery to fans.

However, Brian McKaig, who writes The Bondologist Blog, wrote Holness and asked him a series of questions about the broadcast.[45] Holness, in a letter dated February 24, 2003, wrote back to McKaig and answered many of his questions. Holness passed away in 2012 and his nearly two-page letter to McKaig is, to my knowledge, the actor's most detailed account about the production. McKaig, who hasn't previously disclosed the full contents of the letter publicly, has given me permission to quote from it.

In the letter, Holness, an Englishman, reveals: "I was actually *born* in South Africa, as was my mother. When I was six months old my parents decided to move back to my father's hometown of Herne Bay, Kent [England] and from there on to Ashford, when I was 11 years old. It was in 1953 when I was 25, that the whole family decided to return to South Africa—to Durban to be precise."[46] In Durban, Holness found work in a series of jobs in the theater, as a "stage manager progressing to juvenile lead."[47]

The actor recalled that in 1955 he "started a career in radio working with both Springbok Radio [a radio station] and the South African Broadcasting Corporation [SABC] and it was with the SABC that I was offered the chance to play Agent 007."[48] Holness explained that the cast of *Moonraker* was made up of "fellow members of the Durban SABC Radio Repertory Company."[49]

Because Bond hadn't yet become part of popular culture, Bond's radio debut was not considered to be particularly noteworthy. Instead, *Moonraker* was just one of many shows that the repertory company performed for the SABC. Holness remembered that "together we did a multitude of different productions from daily soaps to the classics."[50]

Holness confirmed to McKaig something that Bond fans have long feared—the production has been lost to time. "As far as I'm aware it was never actually recorded but done as a live theater radio piece."[51] There have been reports that the radio drama was rebroadcast on the BBC. However, as Holness points out, if the show was never recorded, then "it couldn't possibly have been transmitted later by the BBC."[52]

Bob Holness, circa the 1950s.

In the correspondence, Holness explains why he didn't play Bond on the radio after *Moonraker*. Holness writes that the broadcast was "a great success but when enquiries were made about the possibility of doing another adaptation we were told that there were plans to turn a novel into a film and they wanted to see how that went. The rest, as they say, is history."[53]

Although Holness hadn't heard of James Bond before *Moonraker*, the actor developed some affection for the character. Holness told McKaig that he has subsequently "read one or two of the earlier novels though and enjoyed them a great deal."[54] As far as the cinematic Bond, Holness explained, "When my children were younger I would take them to the cinema to see the latest Bond release but we all agree that after Sean Connery it was never the same."[55]

Holness, the first radio Bond, didn't seem envious of Connery, the first movie Bond. He recounted, "As far as playing Bond on the big screen, it never occurred to me to try. My strength lay, not really in acting, but in presenting and I was very happy to stay in that field."[56] Later, Holness found success hosting the game show *Blockbusters* in England from 1983 to 1994, an eleven-year run.

The letter to McKaig provides valuable context to the adaptation and to Holness's role in it. However, it does not provide us with all the answers. Holness lamented, "I'm afraid that I have no idea who adapted the novel for radio, how the rights were obtained or who else was in the cast."[57] Holness also indicated that he did not know exactly when *Moonraker* was performed: "I think that the recording was made in 1958 although I can't be sure."[58] Holness, underestimating the importance of his letter, sweetly added, "I fear I've been little help with regard to giving you specific information."[59]

It's problematic to write about Holness as Bond because, as previously indicated, his performance was not believed to have been preserved. Moreover, aside from the previously unpublished letter to Brian McKaig, there is little reliable information about SABC's radio adaptation of *Moonraker*. However, because I wanted to acknowledge Holness's contribution to the franchise and discover more information, I contacted his daughter Ros Holness, a member the pop group Toto Coelo, whose song "I Eat Cannibals" was a hit in the 1980s.

Ros confided to me that she made a discovery that provides new information about Holness's stint as Bond. Ros explained: "A while ago, whilst sorting papers in my late father's study, I stumbled upon a book of contracts that I'd never seen before. One of these contracts was particularly interesting as it was the one issued when Bob agreed to play James Bond in *Moonraker*."

Ros had originally planned to present this document herself but she has allowed me to include it in this book. Ros's discovery is noteworthy because it gives us critical new information about the adaptation. Before she found the document, even the most basic facts about the broadcast could not be corroborated—even the year was unknown.

The contract was prepared by the South African Broadcasting Corporation and it was made out to "Mr. R. [Robert] Holness." The contract reads: "We offer you an engagement to play the part of James Bond in "Moonraker" by Ian Fleming."

The contract also tells us that the novel was "adapted by Hugh Rouse." Hugh Rouse would later go on to become a popular broadcaster on South African radio. Rouse also narrated *The Avengers* radio program from 1965 to 1969 and acted in and narrated many other radio shows.[60] [*Note:* Given Rouse's experience, it's possible that, in addition to adapting *Moonraker*, he also served as its narrator, just as Martin Jarvis was the director and narrator of BBC Radio 4's eight Bond dramatizations.]

Thanks to Ros, we now know that the performance took place from 7:30 pm to 9:00 pm on January 30, 1958. From the date of the performance listed on the contract, we can also determine that Holness was twenty-nine years old when he played James Bond. Holness was also required to participate in three rehearsals, which were held on January 26 from 2:00 pm to 6:00 pm and on January 28 and 29 from 5:10 pm to 10:00 pm. The date of the agreement is January 23, just seven days before Holness was set to play 007, and three days before rehearsals were to commence. For his work as the first Bond on the radio, Holness was paid a fee of £11, which, adjusted for inflation, is about £252, or $326.

Although neither the letter nor the contract gives us all the details about the 1958 *Moonraker* radio play, taken together they help solidify Bob Holness's legacy as Bond. It should be noted that the contract also has sentimental value to Ros. She touchingly explained, "The contract is all I have as proof that Bob Holness was the first ever James Bond."

In the following interview, Ros gives her perspective on her father's contribution to the Bond legacy.

What do you know about how your father cast as James Bond?

Bob was part of a group of actors who were employed to perform in a radio repertory company for the South African Broadcasting Corporation. They offered him an "engagement" to play the part of James Bond in *Moonraker*, which was adapted by a South African man called Hugh Rouse. The company did weekly live performances for the "English service." My mother was also part of the company. Her stage name was Mary Rose Clifford. She married my father in 1955. [They remained together until Holness died at the age of eighty-three. It appears that Clifford did not perform in *Moonraker*.]

What do you know about the production?

South African Broadcasting Corporation

(ESTABLISHED UNDER ACT 22 OF 1936 AS AMENDED)

ARTIST'S CONTRACT FORM

Telephone 2-3576 (3 Lines)

P.O. Box 1588

Telegrams "Broadcast," Durban

REGIONAL DIRECTOR,
BROADCAST HOUSE,
120, ALIWAL STREET,
DURBAN.

23rd January, 1958.

SMOKING IS STRICTLY FORBIDDEN IN STUDIOS

Mr. R. Holness,
c/o The Foyer.

DEAR Mr. Holness,

We offer you an engagement to play the part of James Bond in "Moonraker" by Ian Fleming adapted by Hugh Rouse

in the English service on 30.1.58

from 7.30 p.m. to 9.00 p.m.

at a fee of £11. -. -.

PRODUCER JOHN JACKSON

A balance test

at _____ at which time you are expected to attend.

You will be required to attend the following rehearsals:—

Date: 26.1.58   Time: 2 - 6 p.m.

Date: 28.1.58   Time: 5.15 - 10 p.m.

Date: 29.1.58   Time: ditto

If no rehearsals are listed above you will kindly get in touch with the producer immediately to discuss full particulars of the programme and to arrange rehearsals. In the case of recitals, if no accompanist is hereon

specified, will you please contact our official accompanist _____
and make independent arrangements for rehearsals.

Kindly complete the attached form and return it to us before immediately

If we do not receive your confirmation by this date we shall take it to mean that you are unable to accept the engagement.

For SOUTH AFRICAN BROADCASTING CORPORATION.

Bob Holness's *Moonraker* contract.

PERSONAL COLLECTION OF ROS HOLNESS

The producer was a man named John Jackson. When John asked Bob if he would play James Bond, Bob was thrilled to do so. Incidentally, John Jackson and his wife Jean became good friends of the family and, in 1961, we all returned to England on the same ship, the *Stirling Castle*. Towards the end of his life, I questioned John about the recording but he didn't remember it specifically.

It's my understanding that there is no known recording of the radio drama. Sadly, in those days the rep performances were done live and, as far as we know, it was not recorded. It was one of many radio dramas that my parents acted in that were rehearsed for about four to five hours a day over three half-days and then performed live on air.

What would he have brought to the role?
Bob was always a charming man with a great sense of style. He had humor and a good brain, but he wasn't overly keen on violence. He was also a great dresser but, of course, that was irrelevant when working in radio.

Did he ever express the desire for another opportunity to play Bond?
The production of *Moonraker* was well received and so the producer asked the Fleming estate if they could try another one of his works. They told him they'd been approached by someone who wanted to make a film and that if it wasn't a success they'd get back to him and talk more. Well, we all know what happened next.

What did your father think about being James Bond?
Although we all think it was incredibly cool, my mother says that Bob just took it in stride. He loved acting and put his all into every character he played.

Did Bond fans seek him out?
I don't think they really did back then [when *Moonraker* first aired], but they certainly did in later days when word got around that he was the first actor ever to play James Bond. Then we had numerous requests for photos and autographs.

You said your dad was the "first" actor to play James Bond, not the second. Can you elaborate on that?
At some point in the UK, it was announced that Bob had been the first ever James Bond. Some people have contested this by saying he was the second. But Bond experts have noted that although Barry Nelson had played a character called Jimmy Bond in 1954, he wasn't a true Bond since he was portrayed as an American agent working for "Combined Intelligence Agency" or the CIA. Therefore, Bob Holness can officially be recognized as the first performer to play James Bond!

DAVID NIVEN IS JAMES BOND

As told by his son David Niven Jr.

Although David Niven isn't closely associated with James Bond, the charismatic actor's influence on Bond's legacy can be felt in myriad ways. Niven, of course, played Sir James Bond in 1967's *Casino Royale*, a movie that has little in common with Fleming's 1953 novel, the 1954 TV adaptation, or the 2006 Eon-produced movie. In the comedy, and in order to confuse the enemy, SMERSH, a number of operatives are assigned the name James Bond, including agents (Terence Cooper, Daliah Lavi, and Ursula Andress), Bond's daughter (Joanna Pettet), Miss Money-penny's daughter (Barbara Bouchet), and a baccarat expert (Peter Sellers) recruited to separate the villain Le Chiffre (Orson Welles) from his wealth. Along the way, the spies encounter 007's nebbishy nephew Jimmy Bond (Woody Allen).

The film features Burt Bacharach's Academy Award–nominated music and was directed by John Huston, Val Guest, Robert Parrish, Joseph McGrath, Ken Hughes, and Richard Talmadge, who performed uncredited work on the over-the-top finale. Niven captured the spirit of the spoof when he told *Life* magazine that it was "impossible to find out what we are doing."[61]

As the second cinematic Bond, Niven's restrained performance was an effective and welcome counterbalance to the absurd, madcap, and occasionally incomprehensible mayhem. At the premiere, Niven cheekily described *Casino Royale* as "a hodgepodge of nonsense, hardly a critic's film" while simultaneously predicting that it would be a hit.[62] Niven was correct: reportedly made for $12 million, *Casino Royale* earned more than $41 million worldwide.[63]

Niven's influence on the Bond legacy predates his sole appearance as Bond and extends beyond it. Niven, a former member of the British army, and Ian Fleming, a former member of Britain's Naval Intelligence Division, were friends. As an affectionate acknowledgment of their relationship, Fleming refers to Niven in 1964's *You Only Live Twice*. In the novel, Kissy Suzuki, a former actress who eventually becomes pregnant with Bond's child, names her pet bird "after the only man I liked in Hollywood. . . . He was called David Niven. He is a famous actor and producer."[64] Later, Suzuki elaborates on her feelings about the English gentleman. "They were all disgusting to me in Hollywood. They thought that because I am a Japanese I am some sort of animal and that my body is for everyone. Nobody treated me honourably except this Niven."[65]

The Niven references do not end here. Fleming depicts Bond as a fan of Niven. Fleming writes that Bond feeds the bird "in exchange for the pleasure he has given me in his other incarnation."[66] [It seems that Niven returned the favor in the television series *The Rogue* (1964–1965), in which he played a con man whose surname is Fleming.]

David Niven, one of Ian Fleming's choices to play Bond.
PHOTOFEST

The joke, meant as a tribute to Niven, also provides another glimpse into Bond's character. Moreover, it's amusing to imagine Bond, alone in a darkened movie theater, watching Niven in *Separate Tables* (1958), *The Guns of Navarone* (1961), or *55 Days in Peking* (1963), which I can only assume are Bond's preferred Niven movies. I have a harder time envisioning the sometimes-snobbish Bond buying a ticket to see Niven playing a cat burglar opposite Peter Sellers's bungling Inspector Jacques Clouseau in the comedy *The Pink Panther* (1963), which was released a year before *You Only Live Twice* was published.

We should not read too much into the Niven reference, but Fleming's inclination for name-checking real people and brands is a vital part of his writing. In an unrelated letter to Harry Saltzman, Fleming explained his thinking: "I have personally found that the use of branded names in my stories helps the verisimilitude, so long as the producers are quality products."[67] The same reasoning would seemingly hold true for Fleming's decision to make Bond admire Niven's work.

Bond is a fan of Niven, and the feeling was apparently mutual. According to Fergus Fleming in *The Man with the Golden Typewriter: Ian Fleming's James Bond Letters*, a collection of Ian Fleming's correspondence with his friends, colleagues, and fans, Niven hoped to play Bond in a television series. In prefacing an exchange between Niven and Fleming, Fergus Fleming wrote: "The actor David Niven, whose TV company had recently failed in its bid to acquire rights to James Bond."[68]

Although Niven missed this opportunity to play Bond, he did try to work with Fleming on another project. Fergus Fleming writes that on "23 October 1962 [Niven wrote] to ask if Fleming could think of a suitable character—a high-class crook, a la 'Raffles' or a super-modern 'Sherlock Holmes'—for him to play in forthcoming four-part series."[69] Fleming responded, "I have just this minute come back from New York working on just such a project as you suggest. . . . I think I should gracefully decline."[70]

When the proposed James Bond television series fizzled out, Fleming turned his focus to bringing Bond to the big screen, and Niven was one of the actors he thought might make an effective Bond. According to Robert Sellers in *The Battle for Bond*, Richard Burton in 1959 might have been Fleming's first choice for the role,[71] but by as early as January 1960[72] or as late as March 1960,[73] Fleming was lobbying for his friend Niven, who won the Best Actor Oscar for *Separate Tables* (1958).

Fleming wanted Niven to play Bond, but Albert Broccoli and Harry Saltzman, who in 1961 secured the rights to adapt the character into a film series, had other ideas. In his autobiography *When the Snow Melts*, Broccoli wrote, "It is important to understand that we never intended to play Sean Connery exactly as Fleming's Bond: the university graduate, the gentleman. . . . If we had wanted that kind of character, then we might have considered . . . someone in the David Niven mold."[74]

However, after Connery's first farewell as Bond in *Diamonds Are Forever*, Broccoli and Saltzman had a change of heart and sought to "create a new James Bond" in the 1970s.[75] The producers were attracted to Roger Moore, in part, because of his "Niven-like touch in his humor."[76]

Moore, in turn, has cited Niven as one of his favorite actors and as someone who influenced his persona. The duo, who became close friends, made four films together: *The King's Thief* (1955), *Escape to Athena* (1979), *The Sea Wolves* (1980), and *Curse of the Pink Panther* (1983), Niven's last onscreen performance. When discussing Niven, who died in 1983, Roger Moore said, "The saddest thing about aging is that most of my friends are now in the other room. I miss David Niven the most. I still can't watch his films without shedding a tear. There's a bust of him in my study, given to me by his son."[77] Arguably, Niven's effortless charm and onscreen persona had a greater impact on Moore's approach to Bond than Connery's depiction of the character.

I contacted Niven's son David Niven Jr., a film producer and actor, who produced *The Eagle Has Landed* (1976), whose cast included Michael Caine and Robert Duvall, and Niven and Moore's *Escape to Athena*, to get his perspective on his father's impact on the Bond legacy.

What did your father think of playing James Bond in *Casino Royale*?

He enjoyed playing Sir James Bond—the only senior citizen Bond—in the original *Casino Royale*, as it was fun, a total spoof and a lark. [*Note*: Niven was fifty-seven when he played Bond, who is brought out of retirement for one last mission in *Casino Royale*, and Sean Connery was fifty-seven when he played a semiretired Bond in *Never Say Never Again*. In their first appearances as Bond, Connery, Moore, Brosnan, Dalton, and Craig were thirty-two, forty-six, forty-two, forty-one, and thirty-eight. In his final performance as Bond, Moore was also fifty-seven but Bond's age wasn't brought up.[78]] Daddy once said that no actor had any idea how the movie could be cut together as there were five [credited] directors, with each doing "their own thing." He loved working with Joanna Pettet, Barbara Bouchet, Elaine Taylor, Jacqueline Bisset, and Alexandra Bastedo. All were young and gorgeous.

Your father and Ian Fleming were friends. How would you describe their relationship?

Daddy and Ian became friends during World War II. They both attended the Royal Military Academy Sandhurst—Ian only briefly and my father graduated later to become a lieutenant colonel—and were two years apart. Both chased a lot of women successfully. Their friendship, I think, started in World War II when daddy's father-in-law-to-be was high ranking in Royal Naval Intelligence.

I was surprised to learn that Niven was interested in purchasing the rights. Fergus Fleming wrote that Niven's company "failed in its bid to acquire rights to James Bond."[79] Do you know anything about his interest in playing Bond in a series?

Fergus Fleming's statement the company "failed in its bid to acquire the rights" is not accurate. My father and Dick Powell owned the then–most successful independent TV production company called Four Star. My father told me he had lunch with an old friend called Ian Fleming who offered him the rights to his James Bond books. Daddy was very excited so he discussed this with his partner Dick Powell, whose reaction was "Who in the USA do you think would ever give a fuck about watching a movie or TV series about an English secret agent?" My father didn't have a strong response, so he sadly advised Ian, "no." My father always wished they had made the deal, but that's life.

In the novel *You Only Live Twice*, Kissy Suzuki speaks fondly of David Niven and names her pet bird after him. What did your father think about the tribute?

In order to truly understand what the real joke is about the bird, one has to realize that in those days and up until the 1990s, well-bred upper-class Englishmen used the word *bird* as a code name referring to a penis.

How did your father describe his friendship with Moore?

Roger Moore and Robert Wagner were the two younger brothers that my father never had. He adored and loved them both, which was mutual, and their extremely close friendship lasted until daddy died. Roger drove with his daughter, Deborah, throughout the night from Nice in the South of France to daddy's house in Switzerland because he had told my youngest sister, Fiona, over the phone, "Don't worry, I will be there by mid-morning." Daddy had just died and the airport in Nice was closed—hence the seven-hour drive. Roger was leaving the next day to film in South Africa so couldn't stay for the funeral, which he organized (in a Catholic church later changed by my brother to a Protestant one). The church was full of sunflowers that Roger had flown in from God only knows where.

GEORGE LAZENBY IS JAMES BOND

James Bond aficionados often cite George Lazenby's solo outing as the secret agent in *On Her Majesty's Secret Service* as one of the best films in the long-running series. In his seminal book, *The James Bond Bedside Companion*, Raymond Benson, Bond scholar turned nine-time Bond novelist,[80] wrote that the film is an "artistic triumph" and that Lazenby's "performance is the most honest and sincere of any of the actors who have played Bond."[81] Steven Soderbergh, the Oscar-winning director, argued that "Lazenby has a vulnerability that Connery never had."[82]

On Her Majesty's Secret Service [*OHMSS*] is the film in which Bond, an inveterate womanizer, defies audience expectations by falling in love with and marrying Tracy di Vicenzo, the daughter of the head of a crime cartel. Because Bond must remain a perpetual bachelor, their relationship is doomed. In the end, Bond sees his new bride gunned down by an old enemy. In his book *The Man with the Golden Touch*, Sinclair McKay observes that the "emotional stakes are raised very much higher than they are in any other Bond movie save 2006's *Casino Royale*."[83]

OHMSS concludes with a deeply shaken and stirred Bond cradling his wife's lifeless body, holding back tears, and trying to convince himself that "It's all right. It's quite all right, really. She's having a rest. We'll be going on soon. There's no hurry, you see. We have all the time in the world."

Lazenby effectively strips down Bond's macho exterior, revealing a caring, sensitive soul inside, and he reminds viewers that 007 is not only a ruthless spy. McKay argues, "What everyone tends to forget now is that the literary Bond was not some form of callous automaton; very far from it. In the opening chapter of *OHMSS*, Bond even has a flashback to childhood seaside holidays. This is the Bond that we see in the nascent form in George Lazenby—a man who can outfight anyone, but whose heart is bigger and more open than anyone might think."[84] Lazenby's understated performance is all the more remarkable when you consider that prior to being cast as Bond, Lazenby was a model who had no formal training or acting experience.

Besides anchoring one of the best Bond films and despite the film's disappointing box office performance, Lazenby contributed something far more important to the Bond franchise in particular and by extension to franchise films generally: Lazenby's performance proved that an actor could take over a lead role that has become closely associated with another actor. Even though many enthusiasts of the Bond movies enjoyed identifying Connery with Bond, Lazenby's performance demonstrated that if a character is complex enough, the part doesn't belong to any individual actor.

In other words, despite Connery's blistering screen presence, the star of the 007 films was really Bond, not Connery. The character is bigger than any individual performer. As Albert Broccoli explained in his autobiography, "There was some brief media hysteria predicting that Connery's abdication would force the 007 empire into oblivion. It didn't happen, because of one fundamental truth: James Bond 007 is the real star. It is always one notch bigger than the actor who plays him. It is like a space station—it stays in orbit whichever hero is up there at any given time."[85]

Lazenby's performance paved the way not only for Roger Moore, Timothy Dalton, Pierce Brosnan, and Daniel Craig, it also provided the precedent for Val Kilmer, George Clooney, Christian Bale, and Ben Affleck to follow Michael Keaton as the Dark Knight and for Dean Cain, Brandon Routh, and Henry Cavill to succeed Christopher Reeve as the Man of Steel.

To celebrate the release of Roger Moore's autobiography, *My Word Is My Bond* (2008), *The New York Times* organized an event at which the paper's film critic A. O. Scott interviewed the seven-time Bond. During the interview, Moore stopped the proceedings and informed the audience that fellow Bond actor George Lazenby was seated among us. Lazenby stood up, and the packed crowd greeted him with warm applause. We were all delighted by the rare opportunity to be in the presence of two different Bonds. The following day, Lazenby agreed to do this interview with me.

What do you think motivates James Bond?
Bond is the personification of male desire. His drive to be the best. To be the winner. To accomplish whatever he sets out to do. He represents the male ego.

What is your view of his character?
James Bond is a villain and a murderous one. He deals with villains and he has to outsmart them. He has the villain's essence in his makeup. He'd be a pretty good villain himself. He knows how to out-connive, out-spy, out-charm, out-kill. The guy basically gets away with murder.

Did you take anything from Ian Fleming's novels to inform your performance?
I did—the end scene, in particular. When I read the novel originally, it made me cry. I had the book on my lap and I read it right before I did the scene. I wasn't an actor before the film started but [during the making of *OHMSS*] I had nine months of on-camera training. [Laughs.] By the time we shot that scene, I was really starting to get into it.

George Lazenby established that the character of Bond is more significant than any individual actor.

ILLUSTRATION BY PAT CARBAJAL

But whatever insecurities you had as an actor didn't appear in the film. Your Bond is, above all, confident.

I did the best I could. I felt that I had to copy Sean Connery in a sense. Connery could just be himself and let his personality emerge. Because I was following in his footsteps, I felt that I had to copy Connery's energy. I was at a bit of a disadvantage because it's much stronger when you're being yourself. Whoever first plays the character has the advantage of establishing the energy of the character.

Can you think of a specific example of that?

Normally, I swagger when I walk. I'm not as precise in my speech. Of course, I'm Australian and I don't normally speak with an English accent. But to evoke Connery, I had to change my walk, my speech, and my attitude. I'm certainly not always this charming.

Your performance doesn't come across as a Connery clone. Did you remember a time when you said, "I'm going to break away from Connery's interpretation and be my own Bond"?

Yes, when I cried at the end. The director said, "James Bond doesn't cry." I had full-on tears on the first take. During the second take, I didn't cry but I kept the emotion.

I don't think Connery's Bond would have cried in that circumstance.

No, he wouldn't.

What made that scene especially effective is how Bond, for the first time in the series, opens up.

Ian Fleming did it for me. He gave me that emotion out of the book.

What do you like about Bond?

It depends on the situation. If I'm in a casino, I love to win. If I'm in a fight, I love to win. If I don't like somebody, I'd love to shoot him. [Laughing.] You know what I mean? He can do all these things that I can't. Then I have the other side of myself, which is the peaceful side, and I don't like anything about Bond. I just want to be quiet. Look into my own feelings and thoughts. Bond is not into that. Bond isn't into mediation, for example. I am.

Bond is not an introspective character.

No, he's not. Bond's just a charmer and he's efficient at what he does. He gets away with a lot of bad behavior because he's the best at what he does. You wouldn't fire him no matter what trouble he gets himself into. In that way, he's like a used car salesman, which I was.

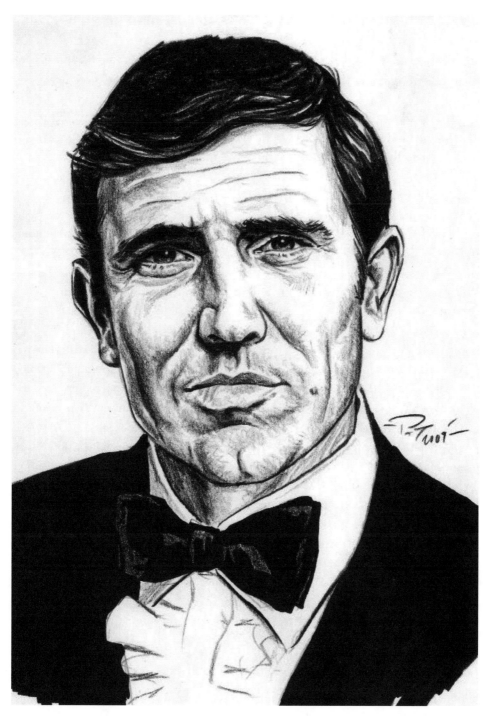

George Lazenby's emotionally vulnerable Bond.
ILLUSTRATION BY PAT CARBAJAL

What do you think motivates your Bond more, his job or his self-gratification?

I think for Bond, they go together. You can't make him do something that he doesn't want to do. He enjoys what he does. Otherwise, he wouldn't feel so confident.

Where do your personalities most closely intersect?

That goes back to the male ego. That's what's attractive. He lives the life most of us would love to live.

Did you ever allow yourself to feel the power of playing Bond?

That comes naturally. Everyone started to call me "sir," whereas before I was Bond they called me "asshole." [Laughs.] It changes your persona. It's a big image to uphold, and I didn't handle it very well.

What is the biggest perk and downside of having been Bond?

To me, the downside was being recognized when you don't want to be. The biggest perk was getting tables in restaurants. When you go into restaurants, they change tables around for you and you get the table you want. It's a different life altogether. But when I stopped playing Bond that changed a bit. I remember when it was announced that I was not going to be playing Bond anymore they took my photo down from a nightclub I used to go to. There was a restaurant that I used to go to and in the restaurant, there was a sign that read "George Lazenby is a premium Bond," but then that was taken out, too. I thought, "Oh, being James Bond does mean something."

How did women respond to your Bond persona? Did they respond to you as James Bond?

Yes. After playing the part, I met a different class of women. Many of them were—what should I say?—"society climbers." Prior to doing the part, I spent more time with the average girl on the street. I found the average girl on the street to be much funnier, more real, sexier, and I missed them. That's why you'd see me going out with a girl on the street rather than an actress I was working with. I still find that.

How has playing this part affected you personally?

I lost myself. At first, it took me away from the self that I thought I knew—but didn't. It made me into a new self, which I didn't know either. I was just playing another character in life. Now I'm beginning to understand life and I'm studying my own personality. I know that I am not who I think I am.

Who have you become?
I think I am a very fortunate human being who is a lot happier than I used to be. Now I'm happier knowing that there is something greater than me inside me.

One last question. Who would win in a fight, your Bond or Sean Connery's?
Sean's too old to fight me today. [Smiles.] If we were both eighteen years old, you'd have to toss a coin.

MICHAEL JAYSTON IS JAMES BOND

The first radio adaptation of a James Bond novel was the 1958 production of *Moonraker* with Bob Holness as 007. It would take another thirty-two years before the spy would return to the airwaves in the BBC production of *You Only Live Twice* (1990) with Michael Jayston as Bond and Ronald Herdman as Ernst Stavro Blofeld.

Though action sequences are the staple of the cinematic Bond, they don't always translate to the aural experience of radio. Instead, the different medium allowed writer Michael Bakewell to dramatize passages from Fleming's novel that are unlikely to appear in film. In one such scene, Bond plays the children's game rock, paper, scissors against the head of the Japanese secret service, Tiger Tanaka. As the two men face off, listeners are privy to Bond's inner monologue as he contemplates the best strategy for playing his opponent while ensuring that neither man "loses face": "If I beat him, he will lose face in front of all these women. If I lose, I shall lose face in front of him. So do I play to win or lose? But it's as difficult to play to lose as to play to win. And does it really matter?"[86] The short but compelling soliloquy provides a rare and unfiltered glimpse into Bond's thought process.

Jayston played a Bond who, because he is still in mourning for his murdered wife, has found that "all the zip has gone out of life."[87] Yet while on a mission in Japan, Bond "looks death in the face," exacts revenge on Blofeld, and emerges from his crucible reborn and reinvigorated.[88]

But his new sense of purpose is short-lived. In the process of destroying Blofeld's compound, an explosion knocks Bond unconscious. When he comes to, he doesn't remember his former life. The radio drama, like the like 1964 novel, ends with a cliffhanger, as Bond decides to go to Russia in an attempt to "awaken memories of his life."[89]

Jayston is also known to *Doctor Who* fans for his multiple appearances as the villainous Valeyard.

Did you have to audition to play James Bond?
Oh, no. It was just an offer that came through with my agent. They asked if I wanted to do Bond on the radio and I accepted it straightaway.

What was your reaction to being offered the part of Bond on radio?
At the time, I thought that James Bond on radio was a bit silly. Bond is not about cerebral activity. He's about action. And, of course, the girls. At the time, I thought it was rather odd that they'd do it on radio. Mind you, I didn't treat it as something that was silly; I did it to the best of my ability. We had a fine cast. Clive Merrison played Tanaka. We also had Burt Kwouk. [Kwouk played superintendent Ando and appeared in the films *Goldfinger*, *You Only Live Twice*, and the 1966 version of *Casino Royale*.]

Did you reread the book to prepare for the part?
No, not at all. You play it out of your own personality. If you think of all the Bonds, Roger Moore played it based on his personality, and Sean Connery played it based on his. In the end, they were totally different performances. Daniel Craig is very good indeed. They're all totally different. It's like playing Hamlet. [Roger Moore also made the Hamlet analogy.]

As you say, there are many different ways to play Bond. How would you characterize your performance?
I hope he was a bit gritty. But you never know if you can't see it. I tried to play it as slightly relaxed in some ways, because he knows he's in charge most of the time, although he does get into situations where he isn't in charge. But I didn't base it on any of the Bonds. I just based it on how I thought Bond would go over on radio.

In what ways are you like Bond?
Not much at all. How could you know Bond? Bond is nothing like the real people in the secret service. I've met John le Carré because I do all of his books on audio. John le Carré was in the secret service, and he said it wasn't like that at all. He said the people who were spies never stood out in the crowd at all. Whereas Bond goes into the roulette tables and you'd notice him because he's tall and he's personable. He stands out in the crowd. Whereas le Carré says you'd never look at George Smiley twice if you saw him in the restaurant or a pub. He looks like an avuncular gentleman who's there and not like someone who's there grabbing all the information.

How did you change your voice to play Bond?
I made it ordinary pronunciation English because, in the original novels, he was highly educated, and he would've had a posh voice. It was a more posh voice than Sean Connery's or Pierce Brosnan's. I generally tended not to shout.

Did you play the cinematic or literary Bond?
I just played the literary Bond, as it was written. The script was very good. We didn't change much of it at all. If you accept the fact that it's a radio production of Bond it holds up. But to me, it's not a radio drama.

What were the challenges of playing Bond using only your voice?
If the voice fits, if it's right, then all the people who are listening to it use their own imaginations to understand and visualize the character. If the voice fits, you can say, "I'm Alexander the Great" or "I'm Othello." Whereas on-screen, you've got to accept the fact that he looks in a particular way.

Michael Jayston in Carol Reeds's *The Public Eye* (1972). Jayston was thirty-seven years old when the film was released, the same age as James Bond in Ian Fleming's third novel, *Moonraker*.
UNIVERSAL PICTURES/PHOTOFEST

Can you talk about the internal life of the character?
Well, there really wasn't any internal life. You just accepted the fact that you were playing this character called James Bond, and you played it scene by scene. You can't do too much internal stuff on radio because it doesn't register. On radio Bond is not cerebral at all. He doesn't think to himself much.

When the radio play ends, Bond has amnesia. Was the plan to continue the story in another production?

Yes. I was supposed to be doing another two, but then they dropped it. Mind you, I didn't have a contract to do more than one, but I think they realized that Bond wasn't really a vehicle for radio.

But now they've recently reinvigorated it. [Toby Stephens, who was cast as a villain in *Die Another Day*, played Bond on radio in *Dr. No*, (2008), *Goldfinger* (2010), *From Russia with Love* (2012), *On Her Majesty's Secret Service* (2014), *Diamonds Are Forever* (2015), *Thunderball* (2016), *Moonraker* (2018), and *Live and Let Die* (2019).] But until they revived it on radio, I was the only one who had played Bond on the radio for [nearly twenty] years. I don't mean to deprecate it, but I still don't think Bond is the proper vehicle for radio. Do you think it's the proper vehicle for radio?

I enjoyed listening to it. I also think it's a fascinating exercise and an interesting way to try to reinterpret something that's familiar to us. What were the recording logistics like?

We did it in sequence, which is much better. But [Sayo Inaba] who played [Kissy Suzuki] was very polite and she used to put her hands together and bow when we were saying our lines. I told her, "You don't need to do that." But she continued to bow even when we were doing our lines to her. It was strange. But she was very good.

How long did it take to record the entire production?

I think it took two days altogether. Generally, we did a scene twice or sometimes three times, especially when you've got sound effects. We did a few scenes where we didn't have to retake them.

The sound effects were done live, in studio, while you're giving your lines?

Usually they were, although they'd say, "Can you pause for four seconds, because we're going to get the sounds of the sea" or something. But generally, we had the sound effects then.

Has playing Bond meant anything to you personally, has it affected your life?

No, not really. It was only two days of a radio show. I was doing a hell of a lot of work at the time, and it was just something that came along. And it didn't affect me at all, really. I liked doing it. But I wish nobody else had done it, because then they'd say, "He was the only guy who played Bond on the radio."

The peculiar thing was, along with two other actors, I was up for James Bond years ago, when Roger Moore was still doing it [but he'd hinted that he might be retiring from the role]. I went up for it and met Cubby Broccoli and all those people.

You met with Cubby? How did that happen?
They just wanted to see me. So I met Cubby Broccoli, the director [John Glen], and I think a light and cameraman was there for some reason. We had a great chat, and they said, "We'll let you know."

Did you do a screen test?
No. I was going to, but then Roger Moore decided he wanted to do some more, so that was it.

What do you remember from that meeting?
Cubby Broccoli was absolutely charming. His daughter [Barbara Broccoli] was there as well. His daughter was very young at the time. I only met him for about five or six minutes. Then I met the director.

What did you and the director talk about?
We just talked about how I would tackle it. But as I said at the time, as I'm saying to you, you play it out of your own personality. If somebody's played it well, that doesn't mean you can't play it in your own way and just as well.

But then Roger Moore wanted to do some more, so it was all dropped. Whether I'd have gotten it or not, I don't know. And when Moore stopped playing Bond for good, I think I was too old. It was about two or three years after I was first considered.

Do you recall the two other actors who were up to play Bond?
Patrick Mower, who's in *Emmerdale* [a long-running British soap opera]. He's about the same age as me, about seventy-five, and I forget who the other one was. I know there were two other people up for it with me.

What does Bond mean to England?
It really is flying the flag, whether or not most British people would think that's their idea of the British hero, but in some ways it is.

Do Bond fans seek you out?
A lot of the Bond fans know I did this on radio, but I'm not really an actor in the league of the other people who played Bond. It's only the absolute aficionados who would know me as Bond. But it was so long ago that few people would know about it, unless they looked it up.

Were you disappointed you didn't play Bond in a film?
It was one of those possibilities that lasted for only about two or three weeks, and then my agent said it's all fallen through. Other work came along, and I didn't think any more about it. I don't know whether I would have liked to have been Bond in the movies, because you're everybody's property once you become Bond. You become a figure of iconography.

JOSEPH MALONE IS (A DANCING) JAMES BOND

In the line of duty, it's occasionally necessary for James Bond to disregard his Walther PPK and to put on his boogie shoes. Such was the case in *Thunderball*, when 007 evades capture by taking to the dance floor and employing a perfectly timed turn that allows him simultaneously to avoid an assassin's bullet and to kill the enemy agent with whom he's dancing. In its remake, *Never Say Never Again*, Bond turns the villain's girlfriend against him during an elaborate tango routine. In the *A View to a Kill* theme song, Bond, who is presumably the protagonist, beckons a woman to "dance into the fire" with him.

But the most unexpected instance of Bond tripping the light fantastic occurred at the Oscars. On March 29, 1982, during the fifty-fourth Academy Awards ceremony, Joseph Malone was the dancing, spinning, high-kicking 007 during Sheena Easton's performance of her nominated song "For Your Eyes Only."[90] In the presentation, Malone, as Bond, drives a laser-firing sports car onto the stage, fights a cavalcade of bad guys, shoots a laser gun, tosses grenades, dispatches a villain with a sword, bests Bond baddies Harold Sakata's Oddjob and Richard Kiel's Jaws, who reprised their roles from the Eon films, scares away Dr. No and Blofeld, destroys a villain's stronghold, saves singer Sheena Easton, and escapes in a rocket ship.[91] No doubt about it, Malone's Bond is a weapon of dance destruction.

How were you cast as James Bond for the Academy Awards tribute to the series?

Originally, I was not cast in this role. A dancer named Blair Farrington was cast to play James Bond and I was one of the dancer henchmen who got killed during the number. As I recall, it was on the Friday or Saturday before the live performance on Monday night that Blair twisted his knee during a rehearsal. He was determined that he'd be all right and that he just needed to rest it. As many dancers have done similar things, we were sure he'd be fine by the next day. As it turned out, Blair's knee was not improving and it was still bothering him during the next day's rehearsal. But he absolutely soldiered on, doing his best to dance whatever portions he could while holding off on the more demanding parts of the choreography. After the second day of his injury, when it appeared he was not getting better fast enough, Walter Painter, the great choreographer who came up with that number, came to me on the q.t. and asked me to keep an eye on the staging for that part. He obviously did not want to discourage Blair in any way, hoping that Blair would be able to dance the role. I tried my best to learn the staging from my position on the stage after my demise.

By Monday afternoon, Blair's knee seemed to have gotten progressively worse, but Blair, like any of us with that great part, did not want to give in. He continued to rehearse. Eventually, the moment of truth came, and since the stage was now being used to complete all of the camera blocking for the awards proper, the entire cast went out into the lobby of the Dorothy Chandler Pavilion, and Blair tried to do the number one more time. It became obvious to all, sadly, that he was not going to be able to dance. So Mr. Painter called me over for a quick powwow with [the show's producers] Howard Koch Jr. and Michael Seligman, both of whom were there watching. Mr. Painter explained to them that he had asked me to watch and familiarize myself with the staging after my character's early demise and from my subsequent position on the set. They asked me if I knew the role and I said something like, "Well, I've never rehearsed it on my feet but I'm pretty sure I know the general staging." This was critical to this piece because this was one of the first times a production tried to integrate computer-generated effects as well as special effects in real time during a live performance. Obviously, with the graphics and explosions onstage, the timing was extremely important and particularly specific for the success of the number. And as you will notice, due to my lack of rehearsal time, much of it was a bit late.

Well, I did my best dancing on the carpet of the lobby while my fellow cast members approximated the levels and placement on the set. None of the principal villains or Sheena Easton were involved in this rehearsal. Truth be told, my fellow dancers basically talked me through the choreography and staging as I danced—and during the performance as well—shouting out to me where I was supposed to go next and the action that I was supposed to be doing. When I finished, I remember Mr. Koch saying something to the effect that he felt more of a Robin Hood energy from me than a James Bond energy when I did the number. He then asked if I thought I could do it. It was now sometime around 2 or 3 pm before a 6 pm live telecast. I promised that I'd do my best to change my energy, assuring him that James Bond was certainly one of my favorite action heroes and I would do everything I could to channel that energy on stage. I'm not sure he really had much of a choice at this point unless they were going to cut the number. You'll need to judge how you think I did. I think I got in one more rehearsal in the lobby before all of the dancers had to be released for makeup, hair, and dinner.

So, now I'm James Bond—at least the dance version.

As you can probably guess, I was a bit panicked that I didn't really know the number and that I was about to perform it onstage live for both a star-studded audience as well as about a gazillion people watching on television. I briefly met with all the villains that I had action with, as well as Ms. Easton, and we walked through the staging that I was supposed to do with them. Nothing in real time or on the set, though. Fortunately, it was the first of several dance numbers that I was involved in that night, so I spent every spare minute trying to remember what I was supposed to be doing, where and when. So, if you can picture me wandering around backstage with a cassette of the number playing on my Walkman, desperately trying to learn the number that had been rehearsed for the better part of a week without me doing this part—well, you get the picture.

There was also the added problem of having to drive 007's car onstage and hit an exact mark so that all of the graphic effects would line up. Unfortunately for me, since the set was already in the position for the beginning of the show, I never got to rehearse that nor even drive the car. The first time and only time I ever did that was when I drove it onstage live.

What do you remember about the costumes? First, you're dressed in a jumpsuit, then three dancers strip it off, and we see you're wearing a tuxedo underneath.

Obviously, I hadn't been fitted for the costume so there was now a mad dash to get Blair's jumpsuit fitted to me. Luckily, the brilliant Bob Mackie, our costume designer, was, as always, on it. Since the jumpsuit was very specifically designed and built to reveal the tux underneath, they had to alter the original to fit me. That led to a lot of wonderful folks doing last-minute pinning and sewing. I guess Walter and Bob had spoken at some point because it seems to me that they had a tux standing by in my size.

The boots I wore were another matter. Blair's feet were a bit bigger than mine and there was no way to get another pair of boots like that in time. It was a problem because I had to dance in them and they needed to fit as well as possible [but since there was no time for a better remedy], I think I wound up just putting on a couple of pairs of socks.

Richard Kiel plays Jaws in the performance. What do you remember about him?

Due to the circumstances, I did not really have too much interaction with the Bond villains or Ms. Easton. At one point, I decided I better try to eat something, as it had already been a long day. I went to catering and there was Richard Kiel, who invited me to eat with him and his wife. As we shook hands, I was impressed that he didn't squeeze my hand but rather let me squeeze his. Given the difference in our sizes, I felt a bit like a little boy shaking hands with an adult. As I didn't have much time, after we sat for a minute and exchanged pleasantries, I took him up on his offer to rehearse our part again, since we had some of the more specific staging. He helped talk me through that section at the end of the dance as we performed. He was such a wonderfully sweet, charming, and gentle man.

Did you ever feel like Bond?

The time I felt most like James Bond was when I drove onstage in the car. Next, when the girls unzipped my jumpsuit revealing me in the tux. And in the end with Richard Kiel, when I invited him into the shuttle first and then threw the grenade in after him. Finally, when I swept Sheena Easton up and took her into that rocket for the kiss.

What do you think of the nearly four-minute and twenty-second performance?

I'm sure that as you watch it again, you will see how much of it was a bit out of sync. What you probably won't know is that at the end of the number, as the ship is taking off—done with a forklift and as I kissed Sheena Easton—I was pulling desperately on a trip wire that was supposed to release a British flag. No matter how hard I pulled, I could not get it to release. It stayed rolled up until we abruptly stopped at the end of the number and then it released.

Mr. Koch called me at home the next morning thanking me for stepping in and saying that I saved the show or something like that. Hardly the truth, but I appreciated him saying so.

On my way offstage, the first person I saw standing in the wings watching was Roger Moore. He shook my hand, gave me a nod, and, in typical British fashion, said, "Well done."

COREY BURTON IS JAMES BOND JR.

Pairing James Bond and a children's cartoon might seem like an uneasy fit. But Bond producer and screenwriter Michael G. Wilson, along with Andy Heyward and Robby London, defied conventional wisdom and surprised Bond fans when they created *James Bond Jr.* (1991–1992), a half-hour animated series. *James Bond Jr.* was supported by a robust merchandising effort, which included comic books, novels, a video game, and action figures.

The show depicted the exploits of 007's daring nephew James Bond Jr., who, while still attending prep school, frequently saves the world from familiar Bond baddies—among them, Goldfinger, Dr. No, Jaws, Nick Nack, and Oddjob. With the aid of classmates Tracy Milbanks, Gordon "Gordo" Leiter, and gadget inventor Horace "IQ" Boothroyd III, Bond also faces off against outrageously named new villains like Dr. Derange, Barbella, Walker D. Plank, the Worm, Goldfinger's daughter Goldie Finger, and Scumlord, the enigmatic head of the SPECTRE-like organization SCUM (Saboteurs and Criminals United in Mayhem).

The animated series is not the first appearance of a character called James Bond Jr. In R. D. Mascott's *The Adventures of James Bond Junior 003½* (1967), Junior is identified as the son of Bond's brother Captain David Bond.[92] However, many viewers of the cartoon consider Burton's character to be the son of 007 and not his nephew. There is evidence to support their theory. As previously noted, Kissy Suzuki is pregnant with Bond's child at the end of the novel *You Only Live Twice*. In the 1973 novel *James Bond: The Authorized Biography*, John Pearson reveals that Suzuki gave birth to a son whom she names James. John Gardner, in his twelfth original Bond novel, *Never Send Flowers* (1993), specifies that Bond doesn't have any siblings.[93] Raymond Benson incorporates James Suzuki into the plot of his 1997 short story "Blast from the Past." Based on the continuity established by Fleming and expanded on by Pearson, Gardner, and Benson, it stands to reason that James Bond Jr. is, in fact, Bond's son. [Pearson also gave 007 a brother named Henry but it's unlikely both Bonds would have a son named James. In 1967's *Casino Royale*, Bond has a daughter named Mata Bond (Joanna Pettet).]

Lineage aside, *James Bond Jr.* is a curious part of the character's history. The creators of *James Bond Jr.* faced the unenviable task of translating the adult nature of Bond into an animated children's show. Corey Burton, the ubiquitous voice-over actor whose credits include work for the Walt Disney Company (feature films, animated television shows, and theme parks), LucasFilm Animation, and Warner Bros., played James Bond Jr. in sixty-five episodes.

In the following interview, which was conducted in writing, Burton looks back at the curious spin-off.

How were you cast as James Bond Jr.?

I don't exactly recall. It was most likely a standard audition and callback process. Probably influenced by my previous young teen hero role of Spike in the original Transformers series [*The Transfomers* (1984-1987)], where I worked with Sue Blu, voice casting and session director for the *James Bond Jr.* shows. Though my teen days were over by then, I was called back in after what must have been a rough couple of sessions with a more age-appropriate but still green voice talent, and Sue had to rework the pilot episode soundtrack with an experienced voice actor in the lead role, dependable enough to take on upcoming session demands smoothly and efficiently. We'd always gotten on well anyway, and I could still consistently sound youthful enough for the gig, so I was suddenly onboard for the whole series.

It was a lot of fun for us all, throughout, with a harmonious, agreeable air of camaraderie, though I'd always contended that teens mostly have lower pitched voices than typically cast, and I was a bit disappointed by the consistent reminders to keep my pitch up in the highest part of my range when I felt he should sound somewhat more mature than his goofy compatriots. I still contend that a young Bond should be disarmingly cool and collected and with a sly sense of mischief, but those decisions aren't ours.

Even though you weren't playing James Bond, you had to at least evoke his spirit. How did you create the character and determine what his voice should sound like?

Well, I am a traditionally schooled radio actor, so I instinctively take character cues from the dialogue itself and how the voices interact within the scenes as written, and I try to match the directors' vision of how it plays as a finished piece. While the character is based in the UK, and there were real Brits among the cast, we were told to keep accents light enough to be clearly [discernible] to American kids, and considering that James was supposed to have been raised internationally, I settled on something I'd call transcontinental BBC—with my native California teen guy musical structure underneath a basic Londoner accent, and figuring he'd spent time with family living down under, and as a nod to the underappreciated George Lazenby, I added a hint of Australian lilt and swagger to the delivery. To indicate that his was an "acquired accent," I made his annunciation of certain vowel sounds, especially the letters *I* and *O*, carefully formed as if he'd been trained in a BBC standard English study course as a child and as if he'd be reprimanded for not shaping a proper *O* with his lips or fully sounding out every long *I*, as in Welsh dialect. I'd be able to call his voice my own concoction, if not for the frequent reminders to keep his pitch as high as possible within my range at all times.

What did you use from the Ian Fleming novels and movies?

What established the whole feel of the dashing 007 world of espionage adventure fare for me boiled down to Connery's cheeky delivery of dark pun, "She's just dead." Wickedly cool, dangerous, and funny in what you might call an intensely subtle way. I have to confess to never having finished any of the Fleming novels, but those early films, along with 1960s TV series like *The Man from U.N.C.L.E.* (1964–1968), *Danger Man* (1960–1962 and 1964–1968), which was also known as *Secret Agent*, and even the comedy satire *Get Smart* (1965–1970) really made a huge impact on my childhood. I even fashioned Double-O credentials for a buddy and myself when I was maybe nine or ten. While certainly suave for his age, of course we had to avoid any real indication of randiness in his manner with the flock of fawning young groupies in his domain. I had to be merely playful—never horny as hell, as anyone would surely imagine a super-cool young stud like him to have been. And again, though I'd have preferred otherwise, the voice had to remain unmistakably teenage, avoiding all traces of maturity in tone and texture in every sound and syllable uttered.

Age aside, how is James Bond Jr. like James Bond? How is he different?

Completely the same outlook, though inexperienced in the ways of the world, without scars of battle or tragedy affecting his demeanor. Or expression of chest hair in his stance. He would also reflect a touch of fame-by-association syndrome, as if to intone that unfortunately familiar subtext with a constant yet unspoken refrain of: "My uncle (more likely his true scandalously absent father) is the positively legendary hero of Her Majesty's Secret Service, and I am his one true royal heir—so treat me accordingly, or else!"

Despite the show's title, James Bond Jr. is neither the son of Bond nor a younger version. He's a nephew. Why not just make him a young James Bond, which is an approach they eventually employed in the Young Bond novels?

Precisely. I figure the producers didn't want to set the show back in time to depict an earlier era, so the mature Mr. Bond we knew from the movies was tagged as the bachelor uncle, still off on assignment somewhere in the world of intrigue and unimaginable danger, while we could all be in on the kid-friendly hijinks that might transpire within the more wholesome and whimsical environment of Warfield's "young spies in training" program. Strictly Saturday morning fare. No smoking, vodka martinis, or conscious references about activities related to any character's naughty bits, even though the surfer-stoner persona of Gordo surely had a voracious appetite for all manner of forbidden fruit, presumably being furtively satiated just beyond the virtual camera lens.

There are many references to the Bond films. But there are many more instances in which the iconic heroes and villains have little to do with their on-screen counterparts.

My guess is that they wanted to steer clear of sociopathic and misogynistic inferences, making it all about having a jolly good time saving the universe from impending doom and disaster, in simplistic Good Always Prevails against innately, unjustifiably Cruel Forces of Evil—without muddying up plots and personalities with all those bothersome motivational complexities inherent in the full spectrum of emotional subtext behind either heroic or villainous human behavior.

There weren't any justifiably troubled or tormented souls in cartoon series back then. We found only noble warriors, goofy sidekicks, and reckless madmen on the cluttered game boards and battlefields of life in the syndicated realm of cartoon storytelling before cable made nuance and subtle human frailties possible to depict on the blurry low-res NTSC [the video standard used in the United States] canvas and monophonic "squawk box" low-fi three-inch speaker cones of the small screen.

What are your memories of Albert Broccoli?

He was so kind and gracious to all of us in the cast; he said sitting in on the session was like being in the studio audience for a radio show. With a warm handshake, it felt like a visit from our kindly old Uncle Cubby. And brushing off the compliments, I expressed polite regret that it wasn't one of our most engaging episodes that week, saying something like "I wish we'd had a better script for you to hear us perform today." To which he responded with a heartfelt gesture of complimentary protest, insisting that he'd tremendously enjoyed watching us perform the show and only regretted that he had to get back to "business" and couldn't stay longer. He was so dear and genuine.

Then there was a mysterious session scheduling gap for a few weeks, after which I was shocked to receive a conference call from the production office, somewhat tentatively addressed at first by the normally congenial Sue Blu, saying that she was there with the show's line producer, whom I'd barely ever spoken with previously, who abruptly began confronting me in a strangely brusque "I'm in charge here" tone. "Do you have any idea what you put us through these past couple of weeks? Since our last recording session?" I had no idea what he was going on about. [He repeated,] "What did you say to Mr. Broccoli!?" [I replied,] "Whaaaat? I remembered Cubby expressing how much he enjoyed sitting in, that it was like listening to a radio play and reminded him of shows like *The Lone Ranger* and Jack Benny when he was a kid. I really liked him and talked about old radio sho . . ." "I heard you," I was interrupted in a prosecutorial manner, never before known in my decades as a cartoon voice performer. "I wish we had a better script. Sound familiar?" "Oh yeah, probably something like that. It was all very friendly." "Well, we've been going back and forth about *firing* you. I don't know if you meant to trash our writers and make us look bad in front of Mr. Broccoli? Because that's what it sounded like you were doing."

I was aghast at the accusation of intentional assault toward the integrity of our show based on an awkward remark during a warmly personable moment of interaction with an iconic legend of the movie industry. Who would even imagine such a thing? And how dare this syndicated TV cartoon production clock-watcher accuse silly little me of trying to sabotage any animated series, especially one that had me in a leading role? I never much cared for teen boy or hero roles as it was, so didn't care about losing the gig—but over a paranoiac reaction to a casual expression of professional modesty?

For the record, it was one of our weaker episodes, and I honestly did wish he'd been there to hear us delivering snappier, cleverer dialogue. "Well, some of us fought to keep you on, but it was a close vote. I guess I can believe you probably didn't mean it that way, but it sure pissed everyone off." Now my temper was roiling. But I always remember the wisdom of my professional mentor, Daws Butler, who upon being told auditions were going around to replace him as the voice of Cap'n Crunch, simply accepted the career slap in the face with a knowing shrug, "Well, they're gonna do what they're gonna do." And I thought back on the good times with Sue and the fun-loving cast and held my tongue. "I had no idea. . . . Just trying to be humble about it, in my own awkward way," I apologetically fibbed. "Well, luckily for you, recasting at this point would be a lot of work, and nobody has time to go through all that in the middle of everything, so we decided to give you a second chance. But if you ever open your big mouth again, you're out for good. Do you think we can trust you to keep your mouth shut from now on, or do we have to call it quits?" Oh, what I'd have like to have said—but for the sake of all the positive aspects of working in an otherwise joyful environment, I intoned in my most reassuring broadcaster delivery, "Absolutely." There was a bit more hot air and negotiation wrapping up the call, but I've gone on too long already with this backstage tale and probably said too much.

This should be all about Cubby Broccoli anyway. But it was a rather sour note to tag onto the wonderful brief moment I lucked into, sincerely relating affectionate regards to the legendary cinematic showman who clearly welcomed the spontaneous candor of my remarks. I believe he'd have been horrified to have learned that our lighthearted exchange about a shared love of classic *Theater of the Mind* radio entertainment from that great bygone era was being jealously eavesdropped and scrutinized from behind our backs to be cynically interpreted as some inexplicably insulting act of arrogance and insubordination toward the production staff deserving harsh disciplinary measures and the ultimate punishment.

THE MANY LIVES OF JAMES BOND

Needless to say, if you've checked into my IMDb credits [four hundred and counting], I've since gone on to heights of career accomplishment, longevity, and respectability few off-camera performers have ever come close to achieving, more in demand now than I would prefer to be at this "mature" chapter of life. Sue Blu is as delightful, lovely, and successful as ever, and we've continued working together on fun projects to this day.

All I know is that Cubby Broccoli was one of the grandest gentlemen I've been privileged to encounter, and that James Bond would never have become the ever-lasting, monumental screen icon we've all come to revere in perpetuity without his inspirational passion and perseverance.

The show premiered two years after the release of *Licence to Kill*, which, at the time, was the most violent film in the series. The adult nature of the Bond character seems to be at odds with a cartoon aimed squarely at children.

I agree with your notion and feel that the cartoon production strayed too far from the essence of Fleming's cheeky atmosphere of dangerous intrigue and Bond's devil-may-care sense of masculine playfulness in the face of impending doom. But the market wasn't yet ripe enough to invest in animated series targeting the now-booming young adult demographic dominating the feature film box office and cable network offerings. In taming the tiger, they were left with more of a cute pussycat than the graphic novel superspy he might better have been.

It was closer to Johnny Quest meets Scooby-Doo, when the later animated Superman would have been a far better storytelling style to fit the Bond brand franchise, in my opinion. [Burton played supervillain Brainiac in *Superman: The Animated Series* (1996–2000).] Unfortunately, the industry was still focused on self-imposed limitations on violence and sexual innuendo, so essential to the universally compelling characterization of James Bond.

What is your assessment of the show?

It wasn't horrible, I suppose. Empowering for developing youngsters to emulate. The cast was decent, and a fair amount of dialogue and gags were amusing enough. But it wasn't really any discerning fan's notion of Bond: junior, nephew, or otherwise.

To what do you attribute its shortcomings?

Toy marketing profit goals over general audience entertainment values. They had the equation backward: great characters and their associated props sell products, but only extraordinarily successful toys can generate enough interest in a cartoon series to sustain a profitable following. And those toys have to prove themselves first, before a series can perpetuate those sales to stratospheric numbers. But if you've gone the extra mile to captivate a loyally passionate following, you can sell anything with that brand's official badge affixed. It probably would've done better to license classic props and RC model cars based on the film franchise than to strip the cool adult-themed soul out of the character and storyline to suit a Saturday morning cartoon demographic. But I can't complain—those were fun times.

The show isn't necessarily remembered well. In some ways it's like _The Star Wars Holiday Special_ (1978)—somewhat disavowed. Can you discuss its place in Bond lore?
From dialogue to animation workmanship—character design and execution, in particular—lackluster gadgetry and absence of novelty in storytelling, I was certainly disappointed with the quality of the series, in practically every aspect of production. Even down to its cheesy theme song and score, not to mention dreadfully off-sync facial animation and poorly posed physical expression that our recorded sessions seemed merely randomly tethered to.

On the upside, those sessions were a great deal of fun, with a warm and supportive roomful of kind and talented individuals on both sides of the glass. Okay, maybe a few not-so-stellar in regard to journeyman-level voice acting experience and prowess, but damn nice people at least. Just seemed to me like it missed the point on too many levels to accrue wide-ranging success as an entertainment venture, with sausage factory production standards setting the bar below any reasonable expectations of the vast 007 fan base.

Just look at what Saltzman and Broccoli did on relatively modest budgets with their inventively clever use of limited resources to expertly craft a series of blockbuster classics that swept audiences into a world of intrigue and excitement from that dazzling first blare of brass to their romantically satisfying conclusions, even thrilling the audience with the promise of another fabulous spin with Bond and company tagging out the end credits. Showmanship and transportive adventure don't need spectacular budgets to create memorably great spectacle, just passionate artistry and dedicated craftsmanship to combine great stories and talent into something transformative and distinctively rewarding, where your life is forever changed in the space of time between curtain opening to house lights up full again for that lost-in-rapture walk through the lobby and back into the ordinary world outside.

THE MANY LIVES OF JAMES BOND

SIMON VANCE IS JAMES BOND

Simon Vance has recorded the audiobook adaptions for all twelve of Ian Fleming's Bond novels and Fleming's two short story collections, as well as all of John Gardner and Raymond Benson's continuation novels. Vance, who has also recorded under the name Robert Whitfield, has narrated more than eight hundred books, including works by Fyodor Dostoyevsky, Charles Dickens, Mary Shelley, Bram Stoker, Oscar Wilde, Agatha Christie, Anne Rice, Michael Crichton, and Arthur Conan Doyle. Esteemed writers like Neil Gaiman have lavished praise on Vance's artistry.[94]

What were your initial thoughts about being asked to narrate a James Bond book?

I was excited because the books are so iconic. I remember being a child and seeing the paperbacks in my parents' bookcase. The covers were quite well done and stood out. I also love the movies. I grew up watching *Goldfinger* and *From Russia with Love* and so on. I think that when I was asked to do them, I didn't have quite the profile in the industry that I have now. It felt quite an honor to be given these books. While they're not literary productions, it was certainly something that I knew I had to get right. There was a mixture of excitement, honor, and some trepidation about doing the right thing by them.

Was it one at a time or did they just say to record all of them?

One at a time. Generally, when you've got a series like this, you're given the first one, but there was probably an understanding that I'd do the rest of them.

However, *The Spy Who Loved Me* was written with a female narrator and they sent me that book as well. I started reading and thought, "Ah, hold on." And I told the producers that I believed they should give this novel to Wanda McCaddon [who narrated the book under the pseudonym of Nadia May] or another British female. I said that it wouldn't be appropriate for me.

But, yes, I understood that I would get the rest of the series. However, in the last couple of years, another company got the rights to the Raymond Benson and John Gardner Bond books. In that instance, I was told, "Here are fourteen books, record them in the next few months." But that wasn't the case with the Fleming books. They'd give me one, and then a couple of months later, they'd give me another one, and a couple of months later, another one.

How do you prepare? I assume you read it in advance at least once?

Yes, it's particularly important with mysteries and thrillers because it's essential that one understands the dynamics and arc of the plot. But if I'm reading a nonfiction book—for example, a book on World War II, I know who won. That's not something I have to discover as I read. However, with a mystery or thriller, you want to be careful that certain characters don't turn out to be pretending to be someone else or the same character using a different name. And you can get caught out with accents and so on, where for instance a character can be called Smith and, at the end, you discover the author referring to this broad Scottish accent and you got that wrong. There's a lot of preparation.

As I said, I was familiar with the movies, but the movies aren't the books so it's important to read them ahead of time and to make notes. Getting the pronunciations correct is important. But that's not much of a problem with Fleming. He also didn't use a lot of convoluted words or sentences. I make a list of pronunciations and names and get authentic pronunciations. I didn't have to do much of that for Bond, but that's generally what I do before I launch into recording.

Do you audition voices for yourself before you start recording?
I tend not to. The important thing in an audiobook, I think, is to provide enough differentiation so that people know who's speaking. Only a bad writer puts "he said" or "she said" after every line of dialogue. You can have long stretches where people say things and, when you're reading it, you have a good idea of who's talking. But if you're just listening to it and it all sounds the same, then it gets confusing for the listener. You need *just enough* differentiation. I like to maintain some consistency throughout the book so that you have a clear idea that this is Blofeld and this is M. You have to make sure that they don't suddenly sound different from page one to page one hundred and fifty.

I did an Anthony Trollope book, and he had five sisters around the table. I had to give each of them a particular individual voice and it is not that easy. I tend to go by age and maturity to differentiate them. But if you took one of those sisters and put them in another scene later in the book, she may not sound exactly the same but, in the moment of the scene around the table, they sound different enough.

With Bond, I could hone in on the characters themselves and that helped a lot; in my mind, I'm seeing a movie in my head. When I'm reading any book it's like I'm playing a movie in my head. Now in the Bond books, there are often movies, so it helps me to visualize some of those characters. I may voice them thinking of the character I've seen in the movie, but I'm not a mimic. But thinking of an actor gives the character an anchor so that I can hear that voice throughout the book. Now, let's take M. In my mind, the classic M for these Bond books is Bernard Lee. In my head, I see Bernard Lee. My voice may or may not sound a bit like Bernard Lee, but that's my hook so that when I come back to it, it's Bernard Lee talking again and M's sound is consistent all the way through.

Simon Vance, the audiobook Bond.

When you do M from the first Bond novel, *Casino Royale*, and then return to the character eleven novels later in *The Man with the Golden Gun*, you go back to that anchor?

That's right, yes. It's especially important in a series like that, and one can make and carry over notes from book to book. These days it's much simpler. I can take voice samples and just put them to one side in a separate file so I can come back and say, "Oh yes, that's what it was."

How did you come up with your Bond anchor?

That's an interesting one. There's a style to Bond. He's cold. Hard. In my head, I see Sean Connery and Pierce Brosnan. I use Roger Moore for the humor and his wry comments. But because Bond is the central character, I don't necessarily need an anchor. I do have the picture of him in my head, but he's me as a spy. He's me as this tough, somewhat misogynistic male character. Very, very strongly male, no-nonsense. What he says goes. It just came out that way while recording the first book and I've kept that style all the way through. I just have to say "James Bond" and I can immediately see it in my mind.

Connery is Scottish and Brosnan is Irish. Are you playing with that? Are you doing some version of both of their accents?

No. I used a sort of standard British. When I visualize Bond's movie counterparts—Connery, Brosnan, and Moore—I take a sense of their persona from them. It's not all that precise. There are narrators who will make notes on everything and they will be precise and it's rigid. I'm a little more laissez-faire; I throw stuff at the wall and see what sticks and that becomes it. It's a looser approach but it works for me.

Thinking of Connery and Brosnan helped form your attitude toward the character?

Yes, certainly. I use their personas. It's the best parts of all of them. I'm not doing Pierce Brosnan. I'm not doing Sean Connery. I'm doing me influenced by some of their elements. What comes out is unique.

Do you have a recording booth in your house or do you go somewhere else?

Apart from a few occasions, I've always recorded at home. Let's quickly run through the history of audiobooks. At first, audiobooks were recorded primarily in New York and Los Angeles studios. Name actors would go in and be paid thousands and thousands of dollars to sit in a booth and be directed. There was also a sound engineer. When I came over from England to California [in the early '90s], I had been doing books for the blind for a charity in London. When I came over here, I was attempting to get into theater, and though I did a lot of theater in the Bay area, getting theater work was inconsistent. I was looking around for other work.

A friend of a friend was recording audiobooks in Ashland, Oregon, for Blackstone, the people who published the Ian Fleming Bond [audio] books. I auditioned for them and got the job. They allowed you to sit at home and record. We used tape cassettes and I recorded my first few books in the corner of the garage, surrounding myself with a few [padded] moving blankets to improve the acoustics. Slowly, I got better at soundproofing the room. I was good at self-direction. They used a few narrators around the country like that and slowly the business grew.

When the iPod took off around 2001, audiobooks also began to take off because people didn't have to change cassettes every forty-five minutes, turn them over or just swap them out—that was a cumbersome thing to do; iPods made it easier to listen to an entire audiobook in one go without having to change anything. The business started expanding and by that time I was recording digitally onto a computer. I think that's when I invested in my first small booth for my home. Around the time I started doing the Bond books, I had the booth in my house and I do all my work here. It's been working well for me.

Do you read from a manuscript or from a published edition?

At first, I read from the books themselves. I remember taking a razor blade to the pages of all the books so that I could take them all out. Then you could lay the loose pages flat and record from that. Sometimes they'd send photocopies of the books. Nowadays it's digital. I read off an iPad in the studio. It's more convenient. It gets quite hot in a studio if you have extra lighting. With an iPad, you can have dim lighting. Also, pages make a rustling noise, which has to be edited out. With an iPad, you just slide your finger to get to the next page.

How long does it take to record a Bond book?

About six or seven hours. Back in those days, I could do at least three hours a day. Sometimes I'd do four finished hours. A Bond book probably takes only two days in the studio. Three days at the most. That's apart from the prep and reading the book on my own. I've slowed down a little—getting older. Today, I do about two or two-and-a-half hours.

What do you think someone gets out of listening to a Bond book that they don't get from reading a Bond book?

It's an interesting question and it varies from person to person. I don't listen to a lot of audiobooks because I'm working on them all the time. It depends how detailed a reader you are. I know there are people who hate the idea of audiobooks and I'm sure those people probably read every single word on the page, or they analyze every sentence they're reading, and they can create in their heads an authentic picture that the author was intending. However, with authors from a different era like Trollope and Dickens, where a reader may not be familiar with the phrasing, I can bring out the sense of those sentences. For those books, it's often a lot easier for people to listen to an audiobook than to read it.

Fleming wrote in an easy style so I'm not necessarily bringing that extra aspect to the recording, but I am pulling it together. My sense of humor perhaps, my understanding of this style of writing may bring more out than somebody just reading the words and looking for the plot points. When some readers get to a long paragraph, they might say, "Oh, let me skip over this bit." But with an audiobook, you're forced to sit and listen to every word and that presents the greater picture. I'm not saying that's true for everybody. Some people are good at pulling everything from the text. I know some people say that audiobooks are for lazy people, but I don't think so. The listener still has to think.

What about the pacing as you are building to an exciting moment?
To be a good audiobook narrator, you don't necessarily have to be an actor. But you have to have an actor's sensibility and that feeling of the demands of the text. You need to know what the text needs in terms of emphasis, speed, pacing, and so on. It's not necessarily true as a narrator that when you get to the exciting parts you talk more quickly.

I don't want to do all the work for you. I hate it when American newsreaders put a lot of passion into what they're reading. "This is a serious story. This is terrible. Oh my god." Or "Here's a bright story." To me, that is doing the feeling for you.

With fiction, you have to go with the truth of the moment and at that moment you might be feeling passionate or sad or happy and so on, but I'm not going to suddenly change it up and emphasize, "Hey, here's a funny bit" or "This is serious." That's for the listener to decide. You want to avoid over-emotionalizing the part you're reading because not only does that do the work for the listener, but the listener can become less engaged. Listeners have to do the work and make those discoveries for themselves.

You don't want it to come across like a radio play.
Right, it's not a radio play. It can't be a radio play with one person doing all the voices. That is something different.

I've listened to the audiobook edition and radio adaption of *You Only Live Twice* **and they're two different experiences. When you're narrating, are you the voice of Ian Fleming?**

As you know, there are different styles of writing. There's the first-person narrator, the third-person narrator, and the voice of God. Now, is God Ian Fleming in this case? Yes, he's the creator. In a sense, yes, I am Fleming. But I'm the neutral voice of God. So, yes, it's Ian Fleming, but I'm not thinking Ian Fleming when I'm reading.

What is your impression of Fleming's writing style? Clean and crisp?

Yes, it's a very simple style. Ian Fleming was a very easy writer to read. That's not to say he was a bad writer. There's a facility to his work. He can write very complex things in a very simple way that makes perfect sense. The sentences are well constructed and they flow from one to the other. I get to read such a broad range of writing styles. When I encounter bad writers, I find that narrating them is like walking through mud; it's hard. It's so convoluted and it takes an awful lot of work, and I come out of a day in the studio absolutely drained. And then there are other writers whose work you fly through.

In your mind, when you narrated Raymond Benson's Bond novels, are you reading the same James Bond as Fleming's?

Yes, it's the same James Bond. That's the short answer. I don't think I went into it with an idea of rebuilding a character from scratch. When Glidrose Productions approaches a writer and says, "You're writing the next Bond novel," I don't think the writers go away thinking that they're supposed to create a new Bond. But there are subtle differences, obviously, as the years go by. In the movies, Daniel Craig is certainly very different from Roger Moore, so the writers are writing for a different Bond in that sense, and there will be appropriate changes. I did the Benson books before I did the John Gardner books, so they were recorded out of order [of the original publication]. As a side note, I loved the Raymond Benson books; I really enjoyed them, but I have to say I struggled with the John Gardner books.

Why is that?

Just didn't like the stories, it's as simple as that. I thought they were too outlandish. They were like the Roger Moore Bond movies; they were sort of silly. I don't want to knock John Gardner, but I liked Raymond Benson. The Benson ones seemed more truly Bond to me.

Raymond Benson also wrote *The James Bond Bedside Companion* and spent as much time writing about Ian Fleming's novels as he does the movies. He studied Fleming. You might be picking up on that.

That sounds like a book I would like to have discovered in the early days because I love it when people do analyses of whole series and the characters and so on because it does a lot of the work for me.

You've done so many books. Taken together, was Bond just one of many jobs—which is a completely fair answer—or does it hold a special place for you?

Oh, it does. It holds a special place. I'm a huge fan. Although I do love Daniel Craig, I've fallen in and out of love with the various movie Bonds. But I loved having the opportunity to do it. I'm very proud of what I did. I'm not sure I want to admit this, but it was during the early days of narrating and my American accents weren't very good. I would love to have a chance to do them all again. I'm not going to. I know famous actors [including Tom Hiddleston, Damian Lewis, and Sir Kenneth Branagh] have redone them. I remain proud of what I did, and I love being somebody who had the chance to record them all.

TIM BENTINCK, ANDREW BICKNELL, MAXWELL CAULFIELD, AND JASON CARTER ARE JAMES BOND

It might surprise those who don't regularly play video games, but three cinematic Bonds have lent their voice and likeness to 007-themed games. Two years after his last Bond film *Die Another Day*, Pierce Brosnan voiced the spy in *James Bond 007: Everything or Nothing* (2004), and Sean Connery played Bond in the game *James Bond 007: From Russia with Love* (2005). Daniel Craig provided Bond's voice in *007: Quantum of Solace* (2008), *GoldenEye 007* (2010) and *James Bond 007: Blood Stone* (2010).

However, it is the exception and not the rule to get the participation of a big-screen Bond. The movie star is usually unavailable or averse to submitting the time-consuming and often tedious task of recording lines and supplying the array of grunts, groans, and other vocal effects needed to simulate the sounds of intense physical exertion of running, jumping, and fighting, which is to say nothing of the exacting chore of producing and differentiating between the sound of a sock to the solar plexus versus a roundhouse kick to the head.

In most instances, voice-over artists are hired to play Bond even though the "official" Bond's likeness is often used. Tim Bentinck, Maxwell Caulfield, Andrew Bicknell, Jason Carter, and Timothy Watson were all recruited to provide James Bond's voice in different video games.

Tim Bentinck is the voice of Bond in *The World Is Not Enough* (2000) and *007 Racing* (2000), and he supplied additional lines for scenes in *Everything or Nothing* when Brosnan, who recorded the vast majority of the game, was not available for an additional recording session.[95]

Andrew Bicknell plays Bond in *Agent Under Fire* (2001).

Maxwell Caulfield provides the voice of Bond in *Nightfire* (2002), a sequel to *Agent Under Fire*, which used Brosnan's likeness in the game.

Jason Carter speaks Bond's lines for the agent's spy's brief appearance in *GoldenEye: Rogue Agent* (2004). The game also features the return of classic baddies Dr. Julius No, Auric Goldfinger, Oddjob, Pussy Galore, Xenia Onatopp, and Francisco Scaramanga, for whom his movie incarnation, the formidable Christopher Lee, provided the voice.[96]

Timothy Watson creates an effective imitation of Daniel Craig's no-nonsense Bond in *007 Legends* (2012).

It's worth mentioning that Kevin Bayliss and Adam Blackwood are often incorrectly credited with playing 007 in a number of video games. In separate written exchanges with me, both Bayliss and Blackwood set the record straight on their connection to the franchise. Bayliss, who is a voice artist for video games, told me that he had nominal involvement with the making of *GoldenEye 007* and that he didn't voice Bond's lines. Blackwood wrote: "Whilst I have played villains in a number of

James Bond games, I have never actually voiced James Bond himself. I hope this clears up a mystery and some misinformation out there on the internet." For good measure, Blackwood playfully added: "Shaken not stirred!"

My interview with Bond actors Tim Bentinck, Jason Carter and Andrew Bicknell were conducted separately and I have combined them. My interview with Maxwell Caulfield appears separately at the end.

How did you get the part of James Bond?

Bentinck: Well, I'm a professional actor who works in every medium—TV, film, theater, and voice—but the majority of my day-to-day work is voice related. I've been in the BBC radio series, *The Archers*. It's the longest running drama series of any kind in the world—the first episode was in 1951, and it's a kind of British institution. I have an agent for visual work, and another, Hobsons International, for voice stuff. One day a call came through, "Tim, how would you fancy playing Bond?" These were the words I'd been hoping to hear since I went to drama school, but when Timothy Dalton got the part, I knew it was never going to happen, Timothy Dalton, Timothy Bentinck—too similar. The joy was tempered slightly by the next question, "How's your Pierce Brosnan?" Curses, [I get to play] Bond, but no one would know it was me. Boo!

Carter: I believe I had a voice-over agent at the time who would have put me up for the part. I had also previously worked for that game company before.

Bicknell: As far as I am aware, I was put forward by my voice agent and selected [by the producers listening to my reel].

What did the game makers tell you about how they wanted you to play the part? What was their direction?

Bentinck: I've voiced a large number of video games, so I know what's required. The main thing they wanted was an exact voice match with Pierce, so it was not so much finding my Bond but finding his.

Bicknell: They gave me free rein to choose how I played each section and only commented if they needed more humor or drama.

Carter: The instruction was pretty much, "Play it like James Bond."

How did you arrive at the voice you used for Bond?

Carter: I was born with it!

Bicknell: I played the voice as laconic and interesting as I could and always with a hint of "Bond irony." Hopefully creating a character that was believable. There is a lot of my character in it.

Did you use the movies or Fleming's book to inform your interpretation of the character?
Bicknell: I didn't take anything from the films or books but was advised what the scene needed.

The Bond in your game looks like Pierce Brosnan. Did the producers want an exact soundalike or did they want you to simply evoke it?
Bentinck: Yes, they wanted it to sound like him. On each take, they would play me his voice through the headphones so I had a mental picture of his accent and delivery. Of course, he hadn't said the lines that I was performing, but it kept me on track. Brosnan has a unique accent, part Irish, and part mid-Atlantic, so he's hard to pin down.

Your video game came out during the Brosnan era. Did that influence your take on the character?
Carter: No, it did not. I grew up with Sean Connery and Roger Moore. However, I have just been made aware that I was voicing a likeness of Pierce Brosnan.

Bicknell: Not at all. I could not be as suave as he.

Andrew, can you talk about the look of your Bond in *Agent Under Fire*? Some believe he looks like you. Others say he is meant to resemble the cinematic Bond. Can you settle the debate?
Bicknell: As far as I am aware, the Bond game look is generic. I am not aware that it was modeled on me although there are similarities.

Talk about the process of recording dialogue for a video game.
Carter: I think I was there for three hours. There is a recording studio and you are watching video playback while you speak. There is an indicator line that moves along a path, which shows you the length of how long they want the audio.

Bicknell: The recording of the lines is directed by the team who made the graphics. They know what type of delivery is needed for the action on the screen when you often can't see it [during the recording session because] it's not finished. You keep doing takes slightly differently until one fits exactly.

What did you hope to bring to Bond?
Bentinck: Strength, charm, a raised eyebrow with hidden steel.

Do you have to find your inner James Bond to play him effectively?

Bentinck: Well, if I'd had the part for the movie, then, yes, I would have been in training for months and approached it differently. In this case, it was maybe two hours in a recording studio, so it was very technical with an emphasis on getting the accent right.

What motivates your Bond?

Bentinck: I recently went back and reread all the novels. The astonishing number of cigarettes he manages to get through. [In *Casino Royale*, Fleming writes that Bond] "lit his seventieth cigarette of the day," combined with slapdash preparation and a willingness to throw himself into ridiculously dangerous situations suggests a death wish above all else. He lives for the adrenaline rush and hang the consequences. This may be why he became such a hugely popular hero; he exemplifies a life that no normal person leads, and so he is the ultimate male fantasy character.

Carter: He is focused on completing the mission.

Who is your preferred James Bond?

Bicknell: Bond for me will always be Connery. [He played Bond as] a devil-may-care maverick who knows no rules.

How did you approach saying, "Bond, James Bond?"

Bentinck: Listening to Brosnan saying it, over and over! I'm a good mimic.

Bicknell: As an actor, you always play the script in the most believable way you can; it must sound authentic.

What parts of yourself did you bring to Bond?

Bicknell: I have a slightly maverick nature and, I hope, a good sense of humor.

Do you get a kick out of telling people that you're James Bond?

Bentinck: Oh, a huge kick. It's on the bucket list of every actor. I'm David Archer in *The Archers*, I was the voice of the [London Underground safety warning] "Mind the Gap" on the Piccadilly Line, and I've played James Bond. Three icons of England.

Carter: A gentleman came up to me at a convention recently and asked me to sign his game, telling me I was his first Bond. That was neat. Otherwise, I don't think most people who are my fans for sci-fi reasons are aware of my involvement with the Bond franchise. [Jason Carter played warrior Marcus Cole on the sci-fi show *Babylon 5* (1995–1998).]

What place do the video games have in the Bond franchise? How do you think they contribute to the Bond legacy?

Bentinck: That's really hard to answer. I've never played the games, although my sons have, and I've heard myself in context. I think the books and the films are the real deal; the games are less interesting really.

Carter: It's a cool way for Bond fans who also enjoy video games to be able to inhabit and/or play alongside their hero interactively.

Bicknell: I think the games are an integral part of the Bond [legacy] and keep the spirit of Bond alive.

What does it mean to you to have joined the group of official Bond actors?

Bicknell: Even when you are a small section of the Bond marque, it still sends a sense of pride through you to utter, "My name is Bond."

Carter: It's nice to sneak my way onto a list that includes Sean Connery, David Niven, George Lazenby, Roger Moore, Timothy Dalton, Pierce Brosnan, and Daniel Craig. I feel privileged that the video game voice-over I did has forever associated me with James Bond. That makes me smile. I didn't see that coming.

Bentinck: It's too late for me now to ever get the film gig, but no one can take away from me that somewhere in the world, someone is hearing me say, "The name's Bond, James Bond." I can die happy.

Maxwell Caulfield, who played Bond in Nightfire, set aside my questions and wrote the following illuminating response: I feel that to get my opinion of the experience of playing the fabled James Bond as a voice-over actor is a stretch. There's nothing really to it. You're reading lines off a tightly formatted script in tandem with the structure of an intricately constructed video game. Of course, you have to have the suitable tone and inflection and bring a certain nuance of character to the recording booth, but you are hardly living out a Bondian fantasy. Far better to be narrating an audiobook of one of the original Ian Fleming novels, all of which I read as a very early adolescent.

[Video game producer] Electronic Arts booked me to come into the hired studio in Burbank over the course of a long hot summer. I recall going in and picking up a standard fee on several occasions, with each recording session lasting no more than maybe six hours. I remember being pleased that fellow actor friends Samantha Eggar [who plays M] and Ian Abercrombie [who plays Alexander Mayhew, an employee of villain Raphael Drake, who helps Bond], were onboard for the project and it was nice to catch up with them whenever our sessions overlapped. The producers were quite sure of what they required from each line of dialogue, for what they felt would bring intensity and impact for the gaming experience. But this was not the same as being flown to multiple exotic locations around the world, bedding beautiful women, ripping off bullets, slugging heavies, tearing around in turbocharged supercars, and utilizing state-of-the-art gadgetry to foil villainous megalomaniacs hell-bent on global domination.

No, the closest I came to getting into the real mix was taking a meeting at Eon's front office on Piccadilly in London with their long-standing casting director Debbie McWilliams [who cast fourteen Bond films].[97] I didn't go on tape or even read any scripted lines as I recall. It was her mission to always be aware of potential candidates for the coveted "license to kill." Naturally, I was excited to have had respected agent Jeremy Conway submit me for consideration for a role that any red-blooded British male thespian with an inclination towards adrenaline-pumping, image-enhancing athleticism and displays of derring-do would naturally jump at. But we both knew I was almost certainly too young and frankly probably lacked the mettle at that point. It certainly never went any further and I never met a director or either Albert or Barbara Broccoli. I probably fit a certain profile during the time between Pierce Brosnan having been asked to do the role and Timothy Dalton being drafted in his place because of contractual issues [preventing the release of] their first choice from an existing television contract.

Double-O-Seven is a fantasy character and his staying power in the public's imagination and the seemingly ever-increasing success of the franchise at the box office is a tribute to the principal architects at Eon charged with sustaining their incredible run. It is their careful choice of directors, screenwriters, designers, composers, stunt coordinators, and myriad other departments that have been recruited from the ranks of Britain's finest film personnel that has made it what it is and hopefully what it will continue to be. But ultimately and crucially it is the selection of the man himself that truly determines if it works or not. I could elaborate on whom I feel has been most compelling and believable at being MI6's most lethal and suave superagent but that would be one actor's passing judgment on another—never a great idea, particularly as I've met almost all of them over the years, and terrific guys they are, too. You do require a combination of genuine cool, a wry sense of humor, and latent menace to make the character really click.

For my part, it was really brought home to me that I'd never get to chamber the Walther PPK, slip into the Aston or require a martini prepared in a specific way when I got a call from my Los Angeles voice-over agents, the same ones who'd booked me on the first one, to see if I'd be prepared to record an audition for Electronic Arts's very next installment of their best-selling Bond video game. Naturally, I declined.

DIETMAR WUNDER IS JAMES BOND

"Mein name ist Bond, James Bond." That's how Bond's classic introduction is uttered in German-speaking countries. The actor who has dubbed all of Daniel Craig's Bond's lines from English into German is Dietmar Wunder.[98]

But Dietmar's voice work isn't limited to the Eon films. Wunder has spoken Bond's lines in the German edition of the Craig-era video games, *James Bond 007: Blood Stone* and *007 Legends*. He is also the narrator for the German releases of the audiobooks of the Bond continuation novels, Jeffrey Deaver's *Carte Blanche* (2011) and William Boyd's *Solo* (2013).

When German fans curl up to a book on tape narrated by Wunder, they are listening to the voice of an official Bond reading to them.[99] Hearing a Bond actor narrate a book must be a pleasurable experience, even if it also results in a slight case of cognitive dissonance, as the Bond in question is reading a different version of the character from the one we know in the movies. It can be as delightfully disorienting as it would be to find Sean Connery reading Raymond Benson's *High Time to Kill* or Roger Moore narrating Anthony Horowitz's *Trigger Mortis*.[100]

As the voice of James Bond in movies, audiobooks, and video games in the German-speaking world, Dietmar Wunder is a full-service Bond.

How did you get cast as the German-speaking voice of James Bond?
There was a voice casting for the part of James Bond for almost half a year. They listened to actors whose vocal range was similar to Daniel Craig's. Then in September 2006, I received a call from the dubbing company Interopa Film GmbH and they said, "Sony Pictures decided; you are working for Her Majesty's secret service. The production company decided that your performance and your voice match the performance of Daniel Craig, aka James Bond."

How does the recording process work?
We watch the entire movie before the recording so we have an idea of the performance. Then we watch a short clip, known as takes, of each scene. Then we re-create the moment. We work intensely in the studio during the recordings.

How did you settle on the voice you used? Of course, it's your voice but you could have used a different timbre.
As an actor, I have my voice range from a high to deep. When I dub an actor, I use the timbre from my voice that best matches the original. It's important that it has to be believable. I used the deeper range of my voice with Daniel Craig. With Adam Sandler, I use the higher range. [Wunder has dubbed many of the comedian's movies.]

Dietmar Wunder, the German voice of Bond.

What are you trying to convey about Bond and his character through your voice?

To the best of my ability, I want to transmit the coolness, the calmness, and self-confidence of his character.

What aspects of Ian Fleming's Bond do you use in your performance?

Fleming created a man with a lot of baggage from his upbringing. Bond is also a [fiercely] loyal agent to MI6. But at the same time, he also follows his instincts with no mercy.

What do you think motivates Bond?

Daniel Craig's Bond is really close to Ian Fleming's books. He's a man who is driven by his job and by his duty. He's sometimes cold, with no mercy. Then he's fragile. He's always alone. But when the moment is right, he is the most charming man on Earth. After all, he is looking for love and the one woman in his life.

If you were voicing a different Bond actor, would you have used a different voice?

With my wide vocal range, I always try to match my voice to the original actor. That means that I probably would sound different under those circumstances. But those great actors before Daniel Craig already had brilliant German actors as their German voices.

You mentioned other German actors who have dubbed other Bond actors. It made me think about the other countries that are also listening to Bond in their own languages, as opposed to reading subtitles. For them, Bond's voice isn't necessarily exclusively English. Do you think that it's important for Bond fans to hear Bond in their native tongue?

Dubbing is always a wonderful way to transform a foreign-language film into a language that is your own. This way, you not only understand the words but you might also understand the culture a little bit better.

When you think of Sean Connery's Bond do you think of him with his Scottish accent or with the voice of a German voice actor?

For me, Connery's Bond with Gert Günther Hoffmann's voice is my Bond from my youth. Of course, later I heard Connery's original voice and I really like his Scottish accent, but when I think of Connery's Bond, he speaks German.

What was your approach to saying Bond's classic line, "The name's Bond, James Bond?"

First of all, it was a wonderful experience to say one of the most famous and coolest lines in film history. My approach was to listen to the original version and transport it with my feelings and soul into German. The most intense work is during the recording of that moment.

Has your approach to the part changed over the course of the films that you voiced?

Every movie is different, so my approach is always a little different. Also, my acting process has also changed over the years. Like Craig's voice, my voice has aged a little. But these [adjustments] happen unconsciously. At the same time, every time I go back to playing Bond, it is a little bit like meeting [an old] friend.

When viewers see a Daniel Craig Bond movie that is voiced by you, are they experience the same James Bond character as an English-speaking audience? Or are they experiencing a different Bond?

The original language of the film is English and our language is German. By their nature, the feeling is different. It has to do with how you experience the German language as compared to the English one. What I hear from the German audience is that the German version of the film conveys the charm, elegance, and coolness of James Bond very well. So I would say it is not a different Bond.

You've also played Bond in video games and narrated the Bond books *Solo* and *Carte Blanche*. When you narrate the Bond books, which are not based on Craig's interpretation, are you nevertheless playing the Craig Bond from the movies?

In all the books and video games, I always have Craig's interpretation of Bond in my head. Even if the books are set in a different time or Bond has a different hair color than Craig, I always think of Craig. So, for the audience, it may sound like the actual Wunder/Craig Bond.

How would you describe the Wunder/Craig Bond?

First of all, this is up to the audience, but I try to perform as believably as possible so that the performance that Daniel Craig [gives] is transported into German and everybody thinks, *wow, James Bond can speak German.*

When you play Bond, do you feel like Bond?
I am like a boy, so it is always so much fun to play one of the coolest agents in the world.

Are you recognized as Bond?
Yes, it happens often that people come up to me and say, "You sound so familiar." Sometimes they even say, "Aren't you the voice of Bond?" and "You know what? You sound like James Bond."

Do fans ever ask you to record their cell phone messages as Bond?
Yes, they do.

Have you met Daniel Craig?
No.

What is your favorite memory of playing Bond?
Actually, the whole experience, but to say the line, "My name is . . . ," is just awesome. In English, it's "The name is . . ." Also, the scene in *Casino Royale* on the train with Vesper. [In that memorable four-minute dialogue-driven scene, Bond and Vesper verbally flirt, joust, and jockey for dominance as they delve deeply into each other's psyches.]

What does it mean to you be Bond?
As a teenager, I wanted to become an actor after watching Sean Connery as James Bond. It means a lot to me. Who doesn't want to be James Bond and try to save the world?

Has playing Bond changed your life in any way? Not professionally, but personally?
One of my dreams came true. I am part of James Bond history in the German-speaking world.

KAI MARTIN IS JAMES BOND

The first time that audiences saw the movie version of James Bond was during the now-iconic gun barrel sequence that jump-starts *Dr. No*. In it, Bond confidently walks to the center of the frame, turns, and shoots at an unseen threat. The bright red blood that fills the screen indicates that Bond's aim is true. The entrance immediately and forcefully announced the arrival of a new hero. Two-time Bond director Sam Mendes referred to the sequence as a series highlight: "It's almost the best bit. Everything is possible in that moment."[101] But it wasn't Sean Connery who movie-goers first saw as Bond; it was Bob Simmons, Connery's stunt double.[102]

Stuntmen play a vital role in the success of the Bond movies. The series' audacious stunts function beyond mere spectacle; they also reveal aspects of 007's character. The dangerous maneuvers highlight Bond's ingenuity, his expertise, his athleticism, his penchant for risk-taking, his ability to improvise and adapt, and his unwavering need to do whatever it takes to accomplish his mission.

After all, only Bond could bungee jump off a dam and into enemy territory; ski off a cliff to his apparent doom only to narrowly escape death by employing a parachute decorated with the Union Jack; drive his car on railroad tracks to catch up with a moving train or on two wheels to fit through a narrow alley; or launch his car off a ramshackle bridge in order to perform a midair flip; run over the backs of snapping alligators; fly through the air while wearing a jetpack; speed down a mountain in a cello case; or drive his motorcycle off a mountain in order to board an plane in flight.

Due to the different skills required, it takes a coterie of stuntmen to double Bond.[103] One stuntman couldn't be expected to be proficient at fighting, running, jumping, skiing, snowboarding, parachuting, scuba diving, surfing, mountain climbing, bungee jumping, horseback riding, driving cars, motorcycles, rickshaws, and tankers, navigating speedboats and hovercrafts, and flying planes, helicopters, hang gliders, microjets, and gyrocopters, to name but a sampling of the requisite abilities on display throughout the series.

As the series' stunts help define the character, I wanted to interview one of the courageous professionals who performs them. To that end, I spoke with Kai Martin, who has doubled for Daniel Craig. Martin's dazzling work is on display during the parkour chase and in the tanker sequence at the airport in *Casino Royale*, during the foot chase and high-wire fight in the pre-title sequence of *Quantum of Solace*, during the opening credits of *Skyfall*, where an injured Bond sinks to his apparent death, and in its finale during Bond's underwater fight at his childhood home. In the thrilling pre-title sequence in *Spectre*, Martin played the helicopter pilot who Bond battles and then throws to his doom.

When I spoke with Martin, he was in the midst of training for Craig's fifth (and final) Bond movie.

How were you cast as a Bond double?

When Daniel Craig was cast as Bond, I remember thinking that I kind of looked like him. But it started when Adam Kirley and Lee Morrison, my friends and colleagues, were working as stuntmen on *Casino Royale*. Adam Kirley did the car turnover in *Casino*, which made a world record [for turning over seven times].[104] These are good friends of mine. Much of the film industry is based on trust and relationships, who you know. But you also need to offer the product. They started working on *Casino* in September 2005, and they said that they needed one more Daniel Craig double. In late December, I received a call from Gary Powell, the stunt coordinator. Receiving a call from him was like Christmas. It's something I've always wanted to do but never thought I would be given a chance. Then I got called on January 2nd for a fight audition. I got to meet Gary and the rest of the guys. I did the fight audition then met Martin Campbell, the director, by around 11:00. By about half-past twelve, I got the nod, ahead of another guy, to be one of Daniel's doubles. There is always a collection of doubles because of the array of skills needed. There are also different units that are running at different times. I got sent home in the afternoon, packed my bags, and the next day I went to Prague for six weeks. Then I came home for the weekend and went to the Bahamas for almost three months. It all happened in a bit of a flash.

After you're cast, they need to make you look more like Daniel Craig.

The aesthetics are important. Daniel's a certain height, a certain build, and a certain complexion, which, fortunately, I match. Then you go to different departments, like the hair department and the wardrobe department. Even though I have blond hair, they generally wig me. I have matched Daniel's hair before without a wig but it can be a bit hit-and-miss. Sometimes it comes down to how you look in the costume, in makeup, and in the wig. Those are big elements. They can make or break a career. A good wig can send you on your way up and a bad one can put you in the other direction.

Your job doesn't start on set or even with rehearsals. It begins with your training.

I am currently in that training stage. I want to be as fit as possible and ready for whatever they throw at me. My goal now is to get as close to Daniel Craig as possible. Generally, this is how my day goes. I get up at 5:00 in the morning, have coffee, take supplements, and meditate. I have about a half hour to myself. I leave the house at about a quarter to six. I get to the yoga studio at about 6:15. I practice yoga from 6:30 to 7:30. I go for breakfast. Then I will do my writing and reading. From 9:30 to 11:00, I do Thai boxing. Once I finish, I do cardio, which is about thirty minutes on the bike. I come home, rest, and eat. I will do any admin [administrative work] that life throws at me. Then I do weight training in the evening or go for a spa, a massage, or see the osteopath. I am training or investing in my body for a minimum of three to five hours a day.

How did the parkour chase at the beginning of *Casino Royale* come about?
Generally speaking, there is quite a lengthy rehearsal process before you shoot a stunt. If we're shooting on January 1st, then the stunt team will get together three months prior. The script will be broken down and we are aware of the potential stunts coming up. We break it down, plan, and rehearse. There are usually many rehearsals and, sometimes, they're painful. Stunts are a calculated business but sometimes there's a little trial and error. There's a lot of effort, too. Things creatively change on the day that you're shooting, and you have to adapt. It's an ongoing process.

Were other stuntmen playing Bond in the parkour chase?
Ben Cooke and I both doubled for Bond.

That sequence established that Craig's Bond is a different one than we've seen before. Bond is outmatched; he's not as skilled as the man he's pursuing.
That comes from the scriptwriters and the directors and their interpretation of the character. That's beyond my own scope as a stuntman. But I always have to slightly be aware of that. But let's take my brain completely out of this. I am told what to do. [Laughs.] Let's make no bones about that. I don't have any input in that. I'm told jump and roll, land and crash.

The essence of the stuntman is to mirror the actor's interpretation. I follow the direction of my stunt coordinator, who is adhering to the director, who is adhering to the script. It's a process where all the different departments work together to create the end product. It involves working with the actors, the stunt coordinator, and even the environment itself.

What do you remember about Casino's tanker sequence?
That was a great stunt. Bond is running on top of the tanker. He needs to catapult himself through the window so that he could fight with a driver, the baddie. At the start of the night, I was talking to my lovely stunt coordinator, Gary Powell. I have massive respect for him. I remember Gary's final words to me, "Don't fuck it up."

I'm like, "Okay, Gary, got that." [Laughs.] We all knew that it was a tricky shot. Martin Campbell, the director, said, "We need the shot tonight, Kai." I thought, "No pressure."

We're doing this to stunt and I'm running on top of the tanker with my safety wire on. We're going probably twenty-five or thirty miles an hour. But as I was catapulting in the cab, the wire was hindering me. I kept getting caught on the wire. It was preventing me from swinging around. I think we did it three times and I didn't get into the cab. But I was mindful of Gary's words and that Martin needed the shot.

Keep in mind that the engine of the tanker was exposed, although I don't remember why. You could see the engine turning over as we were driving. Ideally, you want the safety line on, just in case you get it wrong and you fall into the engine or off the side of the tanker. But I trust myself, and I know what I can and I can't do. I knew that I wouldn't mess it up. I asked to have the safety wire taken off. I wanted to get the performance right. Sometimes, to perform the stunt, you have to go to the next level. The safety line was taken off, and we got the shot. I did it three times. Then we were able to move on. It was a victory.

These are dangerous stunts. Have you gotten injured?
I was injured in rehearsals for that sequence. It was when the tanker goes up on its side. It was in the first or second day of rehearsal. There was a grill on top of the tanker and there was a thin bar, which you hold onto, that went across. Before we did it, I asked Gary if I should leave my helmet on and he said yes, so I put my helmet on. As the tanker went up on two wheels, it completely threw me and I smashed my head on the side.

Oh my gosh.
There you go, Mark! So I smashed my head on the side and, for a moment, I got disoriented. As I became disoriented, I lost my grip on the handle. I had the safety line on so I wasn't going anywhere. But I got my hand jammed under that bar. As it was coming down, my hand came down the other way, and that's when I broke a few bones in my hand. Looking at it now, I see that I still have a bump there. It swelled up immediately but we tested the stunt and got what we needed. Lee Morrison did a great job and Gary got the information that he wanted.

My hand swelled up massively. Fortunately, we had a little bit of a break after that when I was able to heal. But that's the nature of rehearsals. And that's where your determination is important. You could just say, "Oh, well," and then let the next person take over. But at that point in my life, to take that job away from me, you'd have to pull both arms off of me. You just grit your teeth, go through it, and get the job done.

After *Casino*, did you know they would call you back for the next one?
No, they don't tell you. But you hope they do. It can be a fairly competitive business.

But they did call you back.
I worked on *Quantum of Solace* next. I did the diagonal jump at the beginning.

That's when Bond and M are interrogating Mr. White and then Bond has to chase down the double agent.
Bond gets to the stairs and he doesn't run down them. Instead, he jumps across.

It's a character-defining moment.
Right. He says to himself that he can save a few seconds by jumping, even if it does rough himself up a bit. That's why audiences love him.

Then came *Skyfall*. You did the fight underwater at the end.
Bond shoots the ice and they go underwater.

In that case, it's harder to match Bond's movements. Are you just trying not to drown?
That was a difficult and demanding stunt. I hadn't fought underwater before. I also had to remember all of the fight choreography. We had safety divers just out of frame.

Was there an instance when you thought you'd double Bond and it didn't work out?
Because of the nature of James Bond, a specialist is often used. For the bike stunt on *Skyfall*, I rehearsed plenty. To prepare for that, I went to Spain and did some Enduro [mountain bike] riding for about a week. Then I came back to England; I probably would ride three times a week. But on the day, they brought a guy called Robbie Maddison, who is a phenomenal talent. I could be on the track 24/7 and I could still not compete with Robbie Maddison. He's a legend on a motorbike.

While I am investing in skills and cultivating myself, I have to be wise and understand what I can and what I can't do. Even if I could do it at a certain level, who else is out there? I have to think intelligently and focus on my strengths while recognizing in that competitive environment that it's not going to be adequate no matter how confident I become. There are specialists who are phenomenal talents, and, ultimately, you have to respect that.

In *Spectre*, you played the helicopter pilot who fights Bonds. What do you remember about the stunt?
I thought Daniel is very strong. It was a close-quarters fight and it was very physical. But by then Daniel and I had developed a lot of trust with each other.

Bond always has a goal, doesn't he? Bond's intention was to take control of the helicopter. And he doesn't always care how he goes about it. There is a moment where I got my head shoved against the dashboard. We did it so many times. That night, I went to the osteopath and he said, "Mate, do you know your nose is out?" Daniel is a very physical man and, like all fights, it was very physical and very brutal.

You doubled Bond, so when you're fighting Craig, it's Bond versus Bond.
[Laughs.] Exactly.

Usually Bond puts himself in danger, but that's one of the times where he endangers civilians. If Bond didn't take control of the helicopter, he could have injured hundreds of people below.
That's a good point. But that's not really part of what we do. That falls to the writers and directors. I just work on the stunts they ask.

Watching that scene for the first time in a movie theater, I had a strange, passing thought. I wondered if he was an evil helicopter pilot who worked for an evil helicopter agency or just a guy who happened to be piloting the helicopter that day.
He's probably a mercenary, isn't he? He knows what he signed up for. He's got a certain set of skills and he's getting paid for it. He's probably got the theory, "Tell me no lies and I'll say nothing." That was probably the character.

I don't have to feel bad for him?
[Laughs.] No, you don't.

I feel better now. It seems like the stunts most often used require running, jumping, rolling, and fighting skills.
That's a pretty good list. I'm a physical guy. So it helps.

You're training for *Bond 25*. Do they say you're definitely going to be doubling Craig? Or do they say keep your skills up and we'll figure out how to use you later?
I have spoken to the stunt coordinator Lee Morrison and Boris Martinez and I understand that there is a potential role for me to double Daniel. But nothing is guaranteed. I prepare myself for everything but expect nothing. That's all we can

do in life and in the stunt game. You don't really know what's going to come up. You might have trained, rehearsed, been through costume, but then there are last-minute script changes and they cut the scene. It's happened quite a few times now. But that's beyond your control. I get myself as fit as I can, as ready as I can, as focused as I can, and see where it takes me.

I prepare myself as well as I can in terms of mind, body, and conditioning. I can never go wrong having fight skills and making sure they are current at all times. Sometimes I dip in and out of gymnastics. These are all fundamental skills. It's a focus, a goal, and it's what gets me up at 5:00 in the morning.

The yoga, the training, the conditioning, the Thai boxing, the weight training is what is going to stand me in good stead coming into the next film. If the stunt coordinator calls me up and says, "Kai, we have a go-kart chase coming up," then I will say, "Okay, no problem." Then I find out where the local go-kart track is, and I throw myself into whatever discipline is required. At this stage of my life, I'm a good all-arounder. I'm a physical person. I am crashing and bashing for Daniel, maybe some fights. That's where I'm focusing my training.

Does eating like Craig play a part in that preparation?

A big portion of my career is looking like him. I'll speak to his trainer and find out what his body type is like. Is he bulky? Is he lean?

Do you need to study the way Craig's Bond runs or is it not that precise?

Copying how he runs and how he moves is crucial to your existence as a stunt double. You are always trying to match and mirror what he does. Whomever you double, you want to get a 100-percent accurate interpretation of what he's doing. The cut [between the actor and stuntman] needs to be seamless. You don't want the audience to think, *well that's the actor, and that's the stunt double.* I watched Daniel's films, trying to mimic and understand the way he moves. We all have a unique way we move. Matching it is critical to your success as a stunt double.

How does Daniel move?

Daniel's a very physical man, very capable. I'm talking about his Bond and the character and not Daniel himself, although he is a physical man, too. His Bond is very masculine, strong, and has a confident movement.

His fighting style is different from the previous Bonds. It's less polished.

It's been a great interpretation of Bond. He's quite rough. He will do what it takes to get the job done. It can be quite brutal. He knows what he wants and he always gets it. Pierce Brosnan's Bond was probably a little more precise and a little more suave. Daniel's Bond is more rough and tough.

Can you describe Bond's fighting style?

He really throws his entire body into it. He's been trained in different martial arts and he uses a combination of all of them. But it's not one style. I know on a Batman movie [*Batman Begins* (2005)] that they were basing his movements on Krav Maga. But I didn't hear any one style referred to on any of the Bond movies.

While performing a stunt, do you ever feel like Bond?

I was just listening to the Bond music and my friends will play it. But while I'm working, I have to put all that out of my head and focus on just the stunt. If I stopped and thought, *this is cool*, it might affect my work. Afterward, I might stop and enjoy it but not while I'm performing.

The stunts show how resourceful, brave, and prepared Bond is. In that way, Bond and stuntmen are similar. Do you relate to Bond at all?

Yes. Yes. Sometimes when I'm at a restaurant, I check out to see where people are sitting. I'll see what the easiest escape is and ask, *who can I eat beat in a fight*? I started checking out number plates. [Laughs.] So yes.

To double for Bond you have to be near the top of your game. You have to be sharp. You have to have awareness of your environment. Bond is an intelligent, aware, evolved person who is always picking up information. It's all-important to his survival. If he's not sharp, he'd be dead. For sure, there are crossovers.

What stunt are you most proud of?

It's from *Casino*. Bond is fighting a guy on a crane and he's holding on with just one arm. But before that, they're fighting. Bond goes to grab the man's backpack, and the other guy swings Bond around. At that moment, Bond is effectively off the crane. So while doing it, I grab the crane with my left hand and I'm swinging. Then I pulled myself up.

Before we did it, I was on the crane thinking, "I don't know how it's going to work." It was also super-hot, my wig is falling off, and I have to go to the toilet. I was stressed. I was 150 or 160 feet in the air. I felt like I was on my own. But that's the moment when you get the most out of me. We did the stunt and got it bang-on every take. For me, personally and professionally, that was the most important moment in my career so far.

Why is that?

I was still quite new to the Bond stunt team. A stunt like that can shape the future and it can curb the future. The fact that I pulled off the stunt, it projected and elevated me forward. Had it gone the other way, I could have gone to the back of the line.

In some ways, you were lucky that Craig was cast. If it was another actor, you might not have had these opportunities.
Absolutely. I never dreamed of working on a Bond because I don't look like the other Bond actors. Pierce Brosnan and Roger Moore look different than I do. I'm blond and fair-skinned. So there was luck involved.

What has being Bond meant to you?
It has been a huge turning point in my career. Prior to Bond, I had already been working in the industry for five or six years. I had done a lot of work, but I needed a bit more, and Bond certainly gave me more. Financially, it certainly changed my life. It has been a huge platform for me. To grow professionally, you have to constantly evolve. It has helped me grow as a human being. It's stretched me in a good way. I've had to learn more about myself so that I could evolve.

It's been an amazing life journey but it doesn't define me. Without Bond, I am still me. But Bond gives me a massive leg up in life. Knowing that I've been successful has also given me confidence. I am blessed with the opportunity that is coming along. It's been an amazing journey. It spills over into your personal life. I make sure that I'm grounded, humbled, and that I'm still me.

Stunt work requires calculated risks. But that's what you get paid for; that's why you train; that's why you stay sharp. It's so that you're ready for moments like the tanker stunt. Those ten months of preparation pay off in those ten seconds of work. That's what it all boils down to. You are judged in those moments. The rest of your life can be a reflection of those moments.

PART IV
DESIGNING
007

THE ILLUSTRATED BOND

ROBERT MCGINNIS

James Bond posters are designed not solely as marketing tools intended to attract filmgoers and sell movie tickets; they have also played a vital role in shaping the way we perceive 007. With the strokes of his brush, veteran artist Robert McGinnis has played a prominent role in crafting Bond's image.

McGinnis created the bold and suggestive poster artwork for *Diamonds Are Forever*, *Live and Let Die*, and *The Man with the Golden Gun*. With Frank McCarthy, McGinnis also illustrated the posters for *Thunderball*, *You Only Live Twice*, and *On Her Majesty's Secret Service*.[1] McGinnis painted the psychedelic image of a naked woman holding two guns for the poster of the spoof *Casino Royale*, and his depiction of Roger Moore for *The Man with the Golden Gun* was utilized for the *Moonraker* teaser poster[2] and the book cover for the novelization.[3]

In 1999, McGinnis created the cover art for a feature story on Bond for England's *Sunday Times Magazine*. It sumptuously combined depictions of sneering villains, contorted and nearly naked women, touchstone moments from many of the films, and the five Bond actors to date—his intricately detailed painting paid homage to the entire series.

McGinnis's pulp art helped forge the image of Bond holding a gun near his face into the public's consciousness. Though we do see Bond in that pose in the films, it's the movie posters that have played a significant role in creating and reinforcing that iconography. All six of the Eon-produced movies he worked on include Bond portrayed in this classic stance. In our interview, McGinnis proudly asserted, "I believe that for at least one of the poster images I created, that pose was shown eight stories high on a building in Times Square."[4] He is quick to point out that he did not create the stance. McGinnis observed that the "pose with him holding his gun up near his face had been used in James Bond images prior to the ones I created."

The seemingly inexhaustible artist is responsible for more than twelve hundred book covers and scores of movie posters, including *Breakfast at Tiffany's* (1961), *Barefoot in the Park* (1967), *The Odd Couple* (1968), *Barbarella* (1968), Sergio Leone's *Duck, You Sucker* (1971), *Gator* (1976), *Semi-Tough* (1977), and Pixar's *The Incredibles* (2004).[5]

In the rest of our brief interview, McGinnis shares his approach to his work.

How did you arrive at the concepts for your Bond posters?
The concepts were [devised] by the publicity department at United Artists. In part, because I had gained a reputation for, among other things, femme fatales on detective/mystery novel covers, I was requested through the marketing firm Smolen, Smith & Connolly to create poster art.

What direction did the studio give you for the posters?
My challenge was to compose all the desired elements and bring the most dramatic life and adventure that I could to each theme. For the most part, the producers knew what they wanted, but I was able to exercise creativity in making the image exciting. In the last stage of the process, I was left to sort everything out—including the various opinions, comments, and desires—and bring the image alive.

Once you've fleshed out your concept, how do you finalize the image you want to paint?
I translated those ideas to compositions done in pencil, which typically were referred to as "pencil studies" (or "pencils") or "rough drawings" (or "roughs") or "comps" (for "comprehensives"), and then the marketers would review the sketches and provide feedback as necessary. Usually, I would submit a variety of sketches and then the favored sketches and elements would be chosen.

What materials do you use?
In most cases I used Winsor & Newton designer's colors applied on plate-finish superior illustration board.

What are you given for reference material?
To record scenes for publicity, photographers took still pictures on the set of each film, and I was supplied with [and worked from] some of those reference pictures by the marketing firm Smolen, Smith & Connolly.

When creating a Bond poster, what is your main goal?
The main goal was to create the most exciting image possible—an image that conveyed Bond's handsomeness, sophistication, masculinity, cunning, and dangerousness. And, of course, the image also had to feature the other characters and allusions to scenes of danger, violence, sensuality, and romance.

How long does it take to create a poster?

From preliminary pencil studies to finished painting, creating a poster image could take anywhere from about three weeks to a month or maybe even as much as two months, depending on variables. Sometimes nearing a deadline and making revisions would impose pressure, but I enjoyed the challenge.

What did you want to convey about the character of Bond?

A main goal of mine was to depict his suave charm and masculinity.

What aspects of Bond's character did you want to convey through his expression?

I sought to impart a commanding attitude of strength, courage, worldliness, and cunning.

How did you use body language to convey his character?

Body language—alert and cat-like. [Harry Saltzman asserted that one of the reasons that he and Broccoli cast Sean Connery as Bond was because the actor moved "like a cat."[6]]

What's your favorite Bond poster and why?

Diamonds Are Forever gets a slight edge! I particularly enjoyed painting the diamond-encrusted satellite in space, the two ladies surrounding Bond, and the oil rig explosion in the sea below.

What has your Bond association meant to you personally?

To follow in the wake of Ian Fleming, even in a small way, has been a privilege and blessing that I enjoy.

RUDY OBRERO

The artists Robert McGinnis and Frank McCarthy were instrumental in creating the template for the Bond movie posters that began with *Thunderball* in 1965 and informed the style used through *The Living Daylights* in 1987. Many other artists, including Brian Bysouth, Bill Gold, Bob Peak, and Dan Goozee, have also made significant contributions to the look of the posters during this era.[7]

This twenty-two-year period is for many Bond fans the golden age of Bond posters, coming after the posters for the early Bond films, which are not representative of the cohesive style that would evolve, and before the post–*Living Daylights* artwork, which relied heavily on still photography and digital techniques that were in keeping with the industry standard and have also resulted in striking imagery like the moody *Casino Royale* teaser poster, which heralded a new, introspective Bond. It was also during this period that Roger Moore and Sean Connery appeared in two different Bond films (*Octopussy* and *Never Say Never Again*, respectively) that were released the same year. The Eon-produced *Octopussy* poster was in keeping with the design elements of the earlier posters, whereas the poster for the rogue Bond movie *Never Say Never Again* took a different approach.[8]

Dan Goozee, the artist behind the poster for *Moonraker* and, later, *A View to a Kill*, also created the poster for *Octopussy* in the grand tradition of the painters who preceded him. Illustrator Rudy Obrero—who painted the art for *The Postman Always Rings Twice* (1981) and who would later work on the advertising campaigns for *A Fish Called Wanda* (1988), *The Cat in the Hat* (2003), and *Master and Commander: The Far Side of the World* (2003)—was selected to create artwork for posters for the domestic release of *Never Say Never Again*, a film made without the budget or filmmaking expertise of Albert Broccoli's Eon Productions.[9]

The legal constraints under which *Never Say Never Again* was made extended to all aspects of the production, including the advertising campaign. Speaking to the Bond fan website MI6, Obrero lamented that his artwork could have used a splash of brighter colors: "If you'll notice there [are] no flames in there. No fire, no explosions. We had to keep the fire out, [and it] is kind of weird for an action movie not to have explosions [on its poster] . . . there was no big orange flame."[10] Against a blue background, Obrero's uncluttered but vivid painting for the film depicts a tuxedo-clad Sean Connery flanked by two much smaller renderings of Bond women Kim Basinger and Barbara Carrera.

When *Never Say Never Again* was first released on VHS (remember those?), my local video store set up a large standee of the poster. After a little pleading, the manager gave me the four-and-half-foot and nearly three-foot-wide display.[11] Though I admired the art, which contained elements that appear in most posters of the

Rudy Obrero, with three different versions of his *Never Say Never Again* poster.
PHOTO COURTESY OF RUDY OBRERO AND THOMAS NIXDORF

franchise—Bond in a tuxedo, beautiful women, and guns—little did I know that Obrero was dissatisfied with the finished work.

How were you chosen to work on the *Never Say Never Again* advertising campaign?

I believe I was selected to work on the *Never Say Never Again* poster because I had established myself as an artist who could depict action images and still paint celebrities with some accuracy. I was hired by New York West, an ad agency specializing in film advertising. David Fairrington was the art director for the project. His creative partner was Tami Masuda.

Can you walk me through the process of creating a poster?

I came in the creative process when David and Warner Bros., the client, agreed on a direction for the art. He gave me some rough thumbnail sketches to develop more comprehensive drawings from. Sean Connery had a "size clause," his head was to be the largest image, with Kim Basinger and Barbara Carrera being smaller. The original concept was to fall in line with all the other Bond movie posters. There were action elements included with the celebrities, scuba divers, Bond in a one-man hovercraft, a shark, a helicopter, and a yacht.

After that, I did three color comps. Comps are tight paintings to help the client visualize what the poster will look like. Titles and credits are put on clear acetate over the illustrations to simulate the final poster.

And here's where the nightmare began.

This poster art was directed by a bunch of lawyers. Because *Never Say Never* was a film that was not done by the Broccolis, the lawyers at Warners started to hack up the art, worried because of possible infringement lawsuits from the Broccoli folks. Warners was concerned that the poster looked too closely like all the previous Bond posters. So one by one I had to remove the action elements until none were left. What was left was only Sean and the two ladies. The blue background, which was supposed to be the ocean, no longer made any sense. As for me, of the four pieces I painted, the last one was the worst. I was embarrassed by the outcome. Remember the old adage: "A horse designed by committee is a camel." Sometimes I just have to shake my head and move on.

Let's talk about Connery's expression. There's a twinkle in his eye and a slight suggestion of a smile. You could have depicted him another way; he could have been a little more stern and determined. But your Connery is somewhat welcoming.

Sean's expression is less intense because that was my understanding of his character. Sort of the "wry spy." More cool than killer. He's a ladies' man after all. Was I wrong?

Many of the Bond posters created for Eon traditionally depict Bond holding a gun. Yours doesn't. But you incorporated guns into the art— two slanted guns suggest the outline of Connery's lapels.

As for Bond not holding a gun, the lawyers again butted in here as well. Because all the previous [Eon] posters have Bond holding the gun in his hands, we had to come up with a different solution for having a gun in the image.

What does your poster suggest about Bond and his character?

Not much. I ended up painting an image that didn't portray James Bond the way he should've been. The three unused comps say a lot more.

[*Note*: In comp 1, the portraits of Kim Basinger and Barbara Carrera are the same size as the portrait of Connery. Beneath the three figures is a montage of different action sequences, including Bond with a diver's knife facing off against a shark and Bond and Bernie Casey as Felix Leiter flying through the sky on human rocket platforms. The skull from SPECTRE's secret headquarters rests near the center of the painting. Directly beneath the images of Bond and the two women, Maximilian Largo's yacht, the *Disco Volente*, and his harpoon-wielding frogmen are also shown, all over an expanse of a blue sea.

Comp 2 consists of full-body illustrations of Basinger and Carrera, which are smaller than the head and chest image of Connery, and they are seductively leaning against two guns, which point upward and overlap the lapels of Connery's tux. The gold skull has been replaced by a relatively small but central image of Bond on his rocket platform. Other images depict Bond jumping through the air on his motorcycle, a helicopter, Bond fighting off a shark with his knife, three of Largo's frogmen in attack mode with spearguns, and other henchmen using underwater sleds. Felix Leiter has been dropped from the art.

Comp 3 is the approved art.

Comp 4 is similar to the accepted art but retains the action elements from comp 2. Connery's portrait, the two women, and the action components are all flopped—facing the opposite direction. As is the case with the finished poster, Basinger and Carrera are not supported by the guns.[12]]

Can you talk about the placement of the two women around Connery?
Sir James surrounded by beautiful sexy women usually clinging tight or close to him. That's what you should expect, right? Lawyers again. I had to put some distance between him and the two ladies for the same reasons stated above. You should see a pattern here. Sexy was okay, though.

Aesthetically, what should a Bond poster do?
A Bond movie poster should convey a suave spy action thriller of the highest order. I grew up reading all of Ian Fleming's Bond books. Those paperback covers are the reason I got into illustration in the first place. A chance to do a James Bond movie poster was a dream come true. And I took it as quite an honor. Too bad we had to do it with one hand tied behind our backs. It practically broke my heart to keep taking out the action elements. We can just execute the art to the best of our abilities. Personally, I would've opted for more explosions and wreckage.

What are your thoughts on the finished poster?
I wished that any one of the first three comps would have ended up as the final. They all contain the elements and attitudes that belong on a Bond poster. Don't get me wrong, despite some of the craziness that went on, I am extremely glad and proud to have had the opportunity to be on that project. I just wished the final outcome of the art was a bit more comprehensive and exciting than it was. I want all the Bond fans out there to know what we had to deal with at the time. And that we didn't have much control over what went into the illustration.

For me as an illustrator the *Never Say Never* poster was one of the major highlights of my career. Not to mention that the fee for that poster set up investments that continue to pay off today.

DAN GOOZEE

Many effective James Bond posters are jam-packed with montages of action, promises of breathtaking stunts, and eye-popping pyrotechnics. But Dan Goozee, who painted the artwork for *Moonraker*, *Octopussy*, and *A View to a Kill*, often takes a different approach. A few of his best Bond posters strip away the action in order to keep the attention focused squarely on James Bond. His *Moonraker* teaser poster is an unadorned but effective image of Bond wearing an astronaut suit as he is floating in space, and his posters for *Octopussy* and *A View to a Kill* feature a tuxedoed Bond standing beside a beautiful adversary set against a white background.[13] Even when Goozee amps up the action, as he did in his more elaborate *Moonraker* poster in which he places 007 in Hugo Drax's crowded space station, the viewer's eye is drawn to Bond, and all other details seem relatively insignificant.

For me, no artist has surpassed Dan Goozee's renderings of Roger Moore's Bond. As a teenager, my bedroom walls were covered with his posters. He depicts Moore's Bond just as I imagine him to be—debonair, unflappable, confident, fearless, and in command. In my formative years, Goozee's artwork helped to inform, reinforce, and even expand my already deeply held love of Bond.

In addition to his work for the Bond movies, Goozee is an award-winning fine artist whose work has been displayed in many galleries. As a commercial artist, he has also painted the posters for *Poseidon Adventure* (1972), *The Towering Inferno* (1974), *The Clash of the Titans* (1981), *The Black Stallion Returns* (1983), and *The Mission* (1986).[14]

You created the artwork for three Bond movies.

I painted three separate images for *Moonraker*. *Octopussy* was pretty much one image. However, some of the paintings have additional action elements. There were also a few different paintings for *A View to a Kill*.

Did the advertising agency you were working for have a clear idea of what it wanted?

It's different in each case. For the first piece I did for *Moonraker*, they already had the idea of Bond wearing a space suit and floating in space. Tony Seiniger, the head of the agency, had already been in London, talked to Roger, and, while standing on a ladder, had taken a photograph of Moore in his space suit. The steep angle of the reference photo required redrawing because Roger looked like a little person from that perspective. Of all the images I did for the Bond films that was the simplest one. For other posters, like *Octopussy*, they just said, "Come up with ideas and do some thumbnails." Of those ideas, the one they used was the image of Octopussy with eight arms. They were intrigued by that, so then they said, "Let's try a full figure drawing." It was a pretty smooth process.

I saw that reference photo on the Illustrated 007 website, and Moore is not wearing a tuxedo underneath the space suit.[15] Did you add that?
Yes, I did that because James Bond and a tuxedo go hand in hand. James Bond is a cosmopolitan guy, so why wouldn't he be wearing a tux underneath his space suit? A glimpse of the tux also helped with the identification factor.

What elements of Bond's character are you trying to capture?
Bond is bigger than life so that's always what you want to portray. It doesn't matter that on the poster he's going up into outer space without a helmet. No one thought twice about it; it wasn't going to raise any eyebrows.

You also painted a detailed poster with Bond in a space station.
I worked for about twelve years in the art department of 20th Century Fox before doing motion picture advertising. My job was to do storyboards and set illustrations. I had to create perspective drawings of the set and draw interiors and exteriors architecture. That background was helpful in painting Drax's space station. I had some reference photos of guys in space suits so I included those. I put Drax in the background and had Lois Chiles leaning on Bond. I don't think she liked her depiction; it showed a little too much leg.

I saw a version of the poster in a newspaper and someone retouched it and made it look like Roger Moore had [unflattering] jowls. It made him look older. I thought, no, Roger has to look chiseled. They also added more of those guys in space suits in the background. Once it leaves your hands, it's out of your control. It's just one of the pitfalls of illustration.

Let's talk about the depiction of Moore on the *Moonraker* posters. He looks serious and determined. He doesn't have a raised eyebrow, which would have undermined the character and the element of danger.
Right, he looks pretty intense. He's looking right at you with a wolflike stare. You know something bad is going to happen [if you cross him]. I only used a raised eyebrow once—in the *A View to a Kill* poster—where he is standing back-to-back with Grace Jones. I liked Grace Jones's head the most in that one. Sometimes the secondary figure is easier to paint because the pressure's not on.

But of all the portraits I did of Roger, my favorite piece is the one I painted of him for *Octopussy*. Maude Adams is standing behind him and her arms are wrapped around him. I came as close to nailing Roger on that one as I did on any of them. I may have romanticized him a bit for *Moonraker*, but I liked it. Most motion picture stars have likeness clauses in their contracts in which they have final approval of how they are portrayed in advertising. There's a little rock in the stream that I have to avoid. I want to paint something that they feel will be flattering.

The head is always the part I spent the most sweat over. It had to be as perfect as possible. I'd paint on a fairly large board and it was almost always located in a spot that was awkward to reach. I would paint the head on a separate piece, strip it, and hard glue it to the surface of another board. It's a little bit of a collage.

What about Bond's body language? In *Moonraker*, he's in an action stance.

He looks like he's ready to spring into action. I based the action stance on an image from the Bond films. Each begins with Bond looking down the barrel of a gun. Bond enters almost in silhouette, walks, and when he gets to the center of the frame, he turns, drops into a half-couch and points his gun directly at you. I painted a variation of that but because he's in space where there's no gravity, he's floating. But he's still holding that same stance. Other poster artists have used variations on the image. But whenever I hear the Bond theme that's the image that comes to mind.

Bond is always holding a gun in the movie posters. In *Moonraker*, you swapped his Walther PPK for a ray gun.

The gun is always pointed upward at a slightly erotic angle. If he were holding a tiny little Walther PPK, it wouldn't be too exciting, so I painted him with a laser gun.

One of the variations on your *Moonraker* poster has three action panels.

I only did the central figure. Once it got to the New York agency, someone else created those background panels. The panels make the poster confusing. But that happens when other art gets slipped in. I had Roger looking lean and mean, and sometimes they'll retouch it so that he looks weightier. Somebody else also retouched the interior of the space station in *Moonraker*.

For the *Octopussy* poster, I intentionally extended Roger and Maude Adams's legs a little longer than normal because I didn't want Roger and Maude to look too stubby and I was planning on bringing another element at their knee level. It was either going to be the titles or some action. I also painted the vignettes of the Haram girls fighting the Mujahideen and Bond flying the small beach craft plane, where Roger is knocking someone off the tail. They combined them together and another artist in Italy added some explosions and some other stuff. I'm probably not giving him enough credit; he might have just painted one similar to mine. I've seen other posters that look like my paintings that were painted by someone else in Europe or elsewhere; it's hard to say for sure.

What materials are you working with?

Acrylic is the medium of commercial art because you can just paint over it again and again without dragging up [the colors underneath] to the surface. I did most of those paintings fairly large, forty-by-sixty inches, which was quite larger than reproduction size. I thought that I could paint them looser so that when they were reduced to print size they would look a little tighter. Those works are all acrylic. The full-figure thumbnails were probably twelve by sixteen.

For *Moonraker* you painted three different but similarly themed designs. Each one has Bond in a space suit. Did you have to paint Bond from scratch on three separate occasions?

Right, they are separate pieces. I got paid for three separate pieces, which is the nice part. They agreed to buy the first reproduction rights so most of the original art was returned to me. I sold a lot of it at auction to a buyer in Germany named Thomas Nixdorf. He has a nice Bond collection.

Then came *Octopussy*. The central image is the one of Maude Adams standing behind Roger Moore. She has eight arms, all of which are doing something different.

It was hard thinking up enough things for her to do with her hands. Maude's holding the Fabergé egg and the martini glass in two of them. They wanted some things that were threatening, like the dagger, but she's also caressing him. In the original thumbnails, she was kind of giving Bond a little kiss behind his ear. But they decided that they wanted Maude to look a little more in charge, so instead of kissing Bond, she's giving a come-hither look.

Did you put her behind him so we don't get too lost in the anatomy of what an eight-armed woman might look like?

Yes, the feeling was that Maude would look too much like a spider if you could see the whole thing. It would be a distraction. Keeping her behind Bond simplified it so that you could concentrate on her arms. Plus the fact that she's kind of coming up behind him and enticing him with all these little gewgaws is more intriguing.

A View to a Kill **was next. You painted the image of Roger Moore and Grace Jones standing back-to-back.**

For reference photos, we hired a ripped female bodybuilder to portray Grace Jones. Then I put Grace Jones's head on the model's body. The person who posed for James Bond was just a nineteen- or twenty-year-old guy who worked at the agency. We grabbed him and put him in a suit and I then turned it into a tux. I also gave him a gun to hold.

What about the images of Bond on the Golden Gate Bridge wearing his tux?

The most interesting one was for *A View to a Kill*. It was the image of Bond on the Golden Gate Bridge. The high angle looking down was there so that I could see San Francisco in the background. The scale is probably off on the cables of the bridge that they're standing on, but I've never heard a word of complaint about it. Apparently, most people are just looking at the main figures of Roger Moore and Tanya Roberts.

You have another *A View to a Kill* poster that's with Moore on the Eiffel Tower. The concept is similar to the Golden Gate Bridge image. In both posters, Bond is positioned at a precipitously high level with a high-angle view of the city, and he's wearing his tux.

That one also has an exaggerated perspective. That's the poster where James is looking straight forward and Grace Jones is coming up behind him on the paraglider. That one was harder to do than the one with San Francisco Bay Bridge in the background. That was the first teaser poster, the one with Grace Jones and Roger back-to-back was the second teaser, and the one on the Golden Gate Bridge was the final piece and the release poster. It was a nice chunk of work. I learned a lot working with Tony Seiniger; he's one of the unsung heroes of motion picture art direction. He's trained a lot of people who ended up working for studios and sometimes in competing shops. Illustration is more collaborative than most people realize. I communicate with a lot of people while I'm working on a poster. I'm not one of those diva types who never listens to anybody. I'll listen to whoever is on the board about something I'm working on. But I've kind of retired; my eyes aren't good enough for close work anymore.

Bond posters aren't just art, they're also marketing tools.

They call it show*biz*, not show*art*. Even though you want to make it as heartfelt as possible, the basic premise behind a poster is to sell the movie and to get across that flavor of James Bond as best you can. Movie poster art has gone through a lot of transitions. As time went on, posters created on computers replaced illustrated movie posters. Also, movie posters are no longer a major draw for audiences to get them to see a film. Now, television and the internet are used to let audiences know about upcoming movies.

Also, painting is a slow process, and a lot of studios want to see many different versions, and computers are just faster. Today, they can take three of our basic compositions and quickly put them together with a computer. When I did *A View to a Kill*, they had Christopher Walken leaning out of a big dirigible. I got a call saying that they have good news and they just wanted a small change. They wanted to move

Christopher Walken and the dirigible two inches lower. I said, "Move it two inches or one foot; it's the same amount of work." Nowadays, you just put the whole image into a computer and you can use Photoshop to move the image.

You bring up an interesting point. Bond fans savor your art as a straight-forward expression of love for the character. But it's also a job.

It is a job. There's a difference between fine art and illustrations. Fine art is art. Fine art exists for itself. With fine art, the artist is giving his impression of something. If people appreciate or empathize with what the artist is trying to say or express, then it's a success. But it's not the same type of success as an illustration, which is a more quote-unquote "commercial" form of art. Illustrations are created to help entice you to spend time with a product, to watch a movie, or to read a story in a magazine. The *Saturday Evening Post* had great illustrations. For me, it's more of an accomplishment if you produce something that was also artful in the selling. It's helpful to have parameters—it's like a rope ladder you can walk on when you're going over a cascading waterfall. You hold on to it, watch your step, and make sure you don't stray too far.

Who is Bond to you?

James Bond is the ideal urbane, cosmopolitan stone-cold-killer type masculine fig-ure. My mental idea of Bond's character was set from what I had read in the books. When I first saw Sean Connery, I thought, *that's Bond*. Sean Connery and Daniel Craig look physically the closest to Ian Fleming's Bond. Fleming's James Bond is not a particularly nice guy. He's basically a hit man for the government. That's why they gave him a license to kill. The Bond of the books would not say, "shocking, positively shocking," after throwing an electric fan into a bathtub to kill someone. Everybody who's played the role has to keep the humor. Roger Moore's Bond is a different char-acter from the Bond in the books. Roger has a crooked smile and a raised eyebrow. Roger was a good James Bond, and he brought work my way. But I would have loved the chance to draw Sean Connery.

If you had drawn Connery's Bond, would you have taken the same approach?

No, no. I think I would have to make it a little darker. Back in those days, Sean Connery had a kind of saturnine face and the bone structure in his face was more prominent. Even when he smiles, he looks lean and mean.

How much time does it take to paint one of these?

I'd say a couple of weeks. Because of the size of the image, I had to paint standing up. The days were long. The kind of day that when I'm done, my back and my feet were sore. But the thumbnails, creative sketches, and color comps, which were smaller, could be made at the drafting table while I was sitting in a chair. That was always easier. In the early days, I did work out of a bedroom in a house. Because the paintings were so large, I had to literally take it out in the hall just to take a look at it.

Of all the work I've done, the most time-consuming part was drawing the illuminated space suit on the *Moonraker* poster, which had all these little reflections on them. To get the space suit right, I ended up mixing various colors and putting them in various screw-on lidded containers so that I could keep them wet all the time.

Once you have completed a painting, do you take your only original to the agency?

Right, you take it to the agency so that they could shoot the work and return it. I got back some of the originals because they were paying for the full reproduction rights, but if they wanted the painting itself, that was extra. However, I never got the *Octopussy* poster back. That was the one and only time that the agency didn't return my painting.

Do you have a favorite of your Bond posters?

I like the simple ones. I like the first one, where it is just Roger blasting up from the Earth and floating in space. Strong, simple images tend to attract the eye more than complex and busy ones. Once you have people's attention, they will stand and pore over a busy thing for a long time. But they may walk by it if it doesn't immediately grab them. A simple design grabs the eye faster. I also like the *A View to a Kill* poster with Roger and Grace Jones and *Octopussy* with Roger and Maude. I like them all and I was happy to do them.

Did you keep in mind how similar or dissimilar they were from the previous Bond posters?

It was probably youthful ignorance on my part, but I did not want to go back and look at them. Mitchell Hooks [*Dr. No*] and Bob Peak [*The Spy Who Loved Me*] have a strong design style. A movie poster has to make a more graphic statement than, say, a magazine illustration, where you're trying to portray depth and perspective. You can have a guy standing on a hill and a battle going on in the background. Most of the really successful artists are the ones who have a sense of graphic design, and my work was done with a sense of illustration. It took me a long time to realize that. It came from working in storyboards for twelve or fifteen years, where you are showing the movement of the camera. My Bond work reflects a [camera's] point of view.

Your posters have a strong sense of perspective.
Look at Drax's spaceship. I was dealing with the perspective of the environment. I made the shapes a little asymmetrical and used them to create a sense of depth. All parallel lines lead to the vanishing point; they all come together at the infinity point.

I love your *Moonraker* poster. There's a lot to look at but it's not busy. You tend to strip all that away and keep the focus primarily on Bond.
I figured he was the tent pole of the movies. It's all about Bond, so let's make Bond the most prominent figure or place him in the vanishing points to help make him prominent. To make a figure prominent you silhouette them by using a contrasting light or dark source. Or you can make all the parallel lines meet behind the figure or their head. This way your eye is irresistibly drawn toward that spot.

In the *Moonraker* poster, Bond is dead center. There are many lines from the space station that lead to the center, which converge right behind Roger Moore's face. And you have Drax pointing at Bond. You're using different techniques to lead the viewer's eye to Bond.
Right. Your eye follows Drax's hands, which are pointing at Bond. The more people you have pointing at the main character, the more the viewer will look at the main character as well. It's all a bunch of tricks that you learn in any art school.

Do you think that paintings capture something that photographs do not?
I think that more emotion carries through in a painting than a photograph. You can emphasize or exaggerate aspects of a character in a painting that don't necessarily come through with a photo or when a computer does it. But, of course, I'm biased.

Is the Bond of your posters literally the Bond of the films? Or are you creating another version of the cinematic Bond? Perhaps the ideal version?
It's the Bond of the films. It's the Bond you want him to be. But it's also the artist's interpretation of the first two. It was all of those things. The books set my mental idea of Bond's character. But you have to look at the appeal of Bond from a number of angles, including the social psychology of why he's become a cultural phenomenon to the idea of what people think is heroic.

The other thing about Bond is that he's doing things that are superheroic, although he wasn't wearing a cape. But then he would laugh it off. His humor takes the edge off. Look at his character. Bond is totally different from Gary Cooper's character in *High Noon* [1952], who is forced into a situation that he doesn't feel he can avoid. But Bond seems to have a love of or even an addiction to danger. Although he's a servant of government leaders, he is primarily his own man. That's why he'll circumvent his orders to get things done.

Do you think Bond's primary motivation is to serve queen and country? Or do you think that he is attracted to the lifestyle, violence, and excitement and that serving his country is a by-product?

You can make that point. It comes down to the question of how addicted is he to his job? Movies about hit men often leave you unsatisfied because they are one dimensional. And that's what separates Bond. Bond is definitely multidimensional. He can get down and dirty and fight in the mud or tear up a train in a physical altercation, but he's also cultured. He knows how to play Baccarat and how to dress well; he knows a proper martini should be shaken not stirred. He's a Renaissance man.

Can you sum up what it's meant to you to do the artwork for three Bond movies?

The other day I saw an article on a website about the top ten Bond posters of all time and they listed three of mine. That was nice. I'm amazed that I got to be part of something that has been around so long. When I was in art school in the '60s, I was reading the Bond paperbacks. I never dreamed that I'd end up doing the poster work on them. I didn't even wish for it. It was floating around in the back of my head and then it turned out that I'd work on them. I was pretty lucky.

THE LOOK OF BOND

JANY TEMIME

"Everyone who's ever put on a tuxedo thinks he's James Bond," mused 007 screen-writer Bruce Feirstein in his interview with me. Though Feirstein might have been half-joking, I tend to agree. The notion is similar to novelist Michael Chabon's observation that just as a towel tied around a neck turns a child into a superhero, a tux transforms an otherwise levelheaded adult into a handsome and suave secret agent.

But it's not just his tux. In fact, Bond's entire wardrobe is inextricably linked to our understanding of his character. His impeccably tailored and carefully curated clothes are his uniform. Bond dresses smartly not solely due to vanity: he is also selecting his garments based on the calculated effect they will have on those he encounters. In other words, there's a reason that Bond is always dressed to kill.

Through his clothes he's deliberately sending a message to the villains he intends to vanquish, the colleagues he hopes to bend to his will, and to the women he means to seduce. In these instances, his wardrobe is a weapon, a shield, or an invitation; it's his wordless opening salvo in the dangerous and high-stakes world of international espionage.

Although it's easy to imagine Bond shopping on Savile Row when he's not off globetrotting, in the decidedly less-glamorous world of movie making, the costume designer, supported by the wardrobe department, is responsible for designing, fitting, buying, pressing, and steaming the clothes that James wears. In the case of the two Sam Mendes–directed Bond films *Skyfall* and *Spectre*, costume designer Jany Temime dressed Daniel Craig in his dapper duds. The French-born Temime also worked on six Harry Potter movies and the nail-biting Sandra Bullock/George Clooney sci-fi thriller *Gravity* (2013), the Barbara Broccoli–produced *Film Stars Don't Die in Liverpool* (2017), and *Judy* (2019).

Can you describe your process? After you read the *Skyfall* script, what happened next?

First, I had a meeting with Sam Mendes. I found that we were both James Bond fans. It is necessary to be a James Bond fan if you want to work on a Bond film. We both think he is an amazing character. Then I go through the script. I take note of things

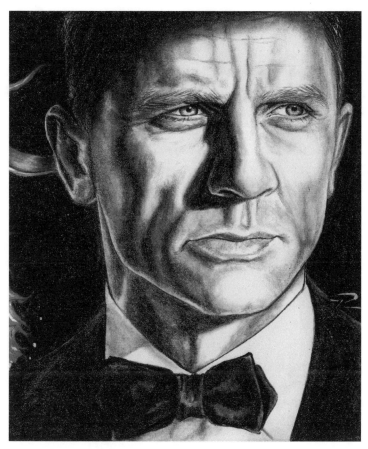
Daniel Craig's 007 is well-suited for any adventure.
ILLUSTRATION BY PAT CARBAJAL

that are constant in every James Bond film. Bond always meets one or two ladies, he has to save England two or three times, he will always have a car chase or boat chase. You have these things, which are a constant of James Bond. But usually, the films don't talk about where he was from or his parents. While we know a lot about his professional life and his sexual life, we know little about his private life. But *Skyfall* was the first time we learned about his personal life. It was the first time we learned about his childhood and that's what fascinated me.

That's what fascinates me, too. His clothes are his armor and he's using his wardrobe to send a message to everyone he meets.
It's good that you say that. It's exactly why I put the cufflinks with his coat of armor. I thought it was important in the twenty-first century to understand where he's coming from. Where Bond's coming from says a lot about his personality. The fact that he belongs to the Scottish aristocracy and to the United Kingdom says a lot about his attachment to the queen and his devotion to the country.

What did you and Daniel Craig talk about in your discussions about Bond's look?

We were in agreement about Bond's clothes. I like a suit that's a second skin. I like a suit that is molded to Daniel's body and shows his body. I don't like it when it's too heavy. Although I used that approach for Ralph Fiennes's M, who likes the stature of his office. For him, I'm emphasizing his power and not his sexuality. But when you are proud of your body like Bond, when you're using your body like Bond and when you're a playboy like Bond, then why not show that body? It's very sexy. So I use that and I dress him that way. Daniel completely agreed. Daniel is very aware of fashion; he has a good fashion sense. Even when he's dressing for himself, he always dresses extremely well. We talked about it a lot.

How would you describe Bond?

He is an English superhero. He is also an old hero; he's been around for decades. He has some quality that people love about him. His appeal is the mixture of him being a gentleman, being a superhero, and being capable of doing things that no one else can.

He's a charmer. He wins us over. Even when he's a bad boy we love him. We sympathize with him. There is nothing casual about him. He is extremely prepared for every situation. From seven years old he was in school and then he went into the military. So he is a guy who has always lived a code of discipline. He's calculated and organized in every aspect of his life.

Let's discuss some of the outfits that he wears throughout *Skyfall* and *Spectre*. In *Skyfall*, after he fails his mission and is presumed dead, he's living on a beach. He doesn't have to dress for work; he can dress for himself.

Bond's down and out. He's rundown. He's drinking all the time. He's dressed like someone who is living on a beach. He's shabby. He's not dressed up like the James Bond we know.

Psychologically, he's not himself. In his heart, M is his mom. He's been let down by M who ordered Moneypenny to shoot at him [in an attempt to kill an enemy agent]. Bond felt that his mom didn't care if someone killed him and that broke him completely. He comes back not only to save the country but also to prove to mom that he's worth much more than she thought he is.

He learns of the destruction of MI6's headquarters while he's drowning his sorrows at a bar on the beach in Turkey. When he confronts M at her flat in London a day or so later, he's wearing the same outfit. Bond went right to M. He didn't stop to change.

Sam wanted to show the urgency of the situation by having Bond go directly to M. In a previous draft of the script it indicated that Bond goes home, shaves, and then goes to her. But because he's presumed dead, that's not possible; all of his possessions have been given away. Bond has no home anymore, so he goes directly from the plane to M.

But once he's deep into his mission, he's dressed the way we've come to expect Bond to dress.
He's dressed for work and he's wearing his armor. Everybody's clothes are their armor. Even if someone is wearing a tracksuit, that is his armor. Everybody shows who they are by the clothes they're wearing. Bond's clothes are his armor and he's impeccable. But don't forget that he's an English gentleman.

Look at the education he had. He was in a public school [what Americans refer to as a private school] from seven years on. From seven years old on, he's worn a tie. You cannot dissociate the character of James Bond from being an English gentleman or from the aristocracy. He was sent away when he was seven and he had to wear the correct school uniform with a tie every day since he was a child. That is such a part of himself that when he goes to work every day he wears a uniform, which is a perfect suit. That's what he's accustomed to.

In *Skyfall*, once he goes to his parents' house, he's wearing his day-to-day clothes and not his professional wardrobe.
You're right. He leaves London in his suit. But then he changes right away into country clothes. So now he's dressed like a gentleman farmer. Not only working on a farm but wearing clothes that are adaptable to a country house environment. But he also knows that he's going to have to fight the villain and his men. He has to wear something that he can fight in. What he's wearing is completely adaptive to Scotland.

He's also wearing a scarf. I wanted a scarf that looked like the one worn [in World War II by British] General Montgomery. That was the reference I had. I also thought it suggested the high collars and the look of the military in the eighteenth century.

Let's move on to *Spectre*. When we first see Bond in the pre-title sequence, he's dressed like the dead. It's an unexpected look for our hero.
Right, it's the Day of the Dead in Mexico so he's dressed like a cadaver, like a skeleton. He's wearing a long coat, a top hat, and a mask. It's a reference to the folklore in Mexico about the bride and the bridegroom to the dead. That's how that costume originated. It's a little grander than the traditional outfit but that's where it came from. I designed fifteen hundred costumes for the extras and the one Bond wears is just one of many.

I dressed him in that particular coat for a few reasons. One, even in a long shot from far away the audience should know who he is, and the coat gives Bond an elegant silhouette. Two, the outfit had to be practical. Bond goes into the hotel room and takes off his coat and he has a suit under it. He takes off the hat and the mask, and then he has to go complete his mission. Finally, it also has to be sexy.

Later on, we get a rare glimpse at his personal life. When we see him in his flat, he's wearing a bathrobe.
Yes, it is a Turkish antique bathrobe. Bond travels a lot. I wanted to get something that he could have brought back from one of his exotic holidays. [*Note: Spectre* is not the first time that audiences saw Bond dressed for comfort in his home. In *Live and Let Die*, Roger Moore's Bond wears a dressing gown with the initials J.B. embroidered on it.]

The white jacket he wears on the train became the poster image.
Yes, it was very important. I said to Sam Mendes that I could not do another tuxedo suit better than the dark blue one we used in *Skyfall*. I had to go in another direction. I was thinking of Morocco, traveling in trains, the 1940s, and then I thought of Humphrey Bogart in *Casablanca*. So I put him in the same white suit as Bogart. The open lapels and double-breasted jacket would give it a 1940s look.

I know that I *should* have thought of Sean Connery's white tuxedo in *Goldfinger* but I promise you that I didn't. Everybody said to me that it was an homage to Connery. I am pleased that it became an homage to Sean Connery, whom I adore, but it's not that.

At the end of *Spectre*, after Bond resigns from the secret service, he returns to Q branch to retrieve his beloved Aston Martin. Theoretically Bond would be dressed for a life outside the purview of his profession. Yet he's dressed like James Bond, impeccable and ready for anything.
It's funny that you say that because we discussed that. I wondered, should he peel off that suit and wear something else? We all thought about it but then we decided against it. Logically, he should be in jeans but James Bond should never be wearing jeans. Never. So he's back in a suit. But it's a light-colored suit. It's not really a business suit. Because he's picking up the Aston Martin, he might also be meeting someone in the office. He's wearing a suit because he might also be there for business. Don't forget that he's stealing the car, so he better be dressed up for the job, even though he was not ordered to do it by somebody.

But there is another reason. We decided that if he's going to take the time to pick up the "James Bond car" he should be dressed like James Bond. After all, Madeleine is in love with James Bond. That's why we put him in the suit.

James Bond (Daniel Craig) is dressed to kill in *Spectre*.
ILLUSTRATION BY PAT CARBAJAL

I love that you said that Madeleine fell in love with James Bond, the professional, as opposed to the man.

Of course she's in love with Double-O-Seven. Double-O-Seven saved her. If it weren't for Double-Seven, she'd be dead. She falls in love with the man who jumps into an abyss with her to save her life. She doesn't think, *I love him because he* cooks *so well*. Of course not. It's the element of danger in his personality that she loves. The danger is why women love James Bond. Even if they resist the danger, they still come back to it.

As a costume designer, do you have to figure out how many suitcases he needs to pack before embarking on a mission?

It's not that many outfits. He'll pack a sportswear outfit, a classic suit, and a tux, because you never know what you're going to need. It's familiar to him. It's also a social class thing. He will wear a suit because it's the most elegant thing a man can wear. He dresses like that also because the people he meets will also be dressed like that. Three pairs of outfits and two pairs of shoes, it's not that much.

It must be a challenge to make Bond fashionable but not simply of the moment. You don't want to date the look of the film.
Completely. When you see the films later on, Bond should still look impeccably dressed. I want to make Bond look like an English gentleman and that has nothing to do with fashion. When you are dressed up classically, you can be dressed in that style for ten years and it still won't change. The suits are not "fashionable"; they are well made, and that is a big difference.

There are websites like Bond Lifestyle, The Suits of James Bond, and The Bond Experience that pore over every detail of all aspects of his lifestyle, including his wardrobe. The Bond Experience has created videos with titles like "The Belts of James Bond" and "The Gloves of *Spectre*." "The Jackets of *Skyfall*" video has around one hundred thousand views.
Oh, you have no idea! I was at the opening of an exhibition at the James Bond museum. There were so many boys dressed up as Bond.

They came dressed up in the exact outfits you selected for Daniel Craig?
Yes, yes, yes. When I come to a lecture, they come dressed up as Bond. With the trousers, with the sweaters. Exactly. They spend all this money on his wardrobe.

What do you think when you see that?
It reminds me of a story. When I was a student, I was working in Paris in a bathing suit shop. You know the scene in *Dr. No* with Ursula Andress coming out of the sea in her bikini? We were selling an imitation of that bikini, with a little knot on the side. You have no idea how many women came in to buy that bikini. I'm not talking about supermodels; I'm talking about every body type and every kind of woman. From young to old. They thought that when they were buying the bikini they were buying the body as well. I'm sure that when those guys dress up as James Bond, they think they are James Bond. It's pretty easy to get the clothes; all you have to do is buy them. Then you go out, hang out with your friends, and you're James Bond for a night.

GAMING BOND

GLEN A. SCHOFIELD

The last time Sean Connery played James Bond was not in the 1983 film *Never Say Never Again*, it was as a voice-over actor in Electronic Art's 2005 video game *James Bond 007: From Russia with Love*. The game, which also features his likeness, mostly adheres to the plot of the 1963 film, but it playfully diverges from the source material with appearances by the Aston Martin from *Goldfinger* and the jetpack from *Thunderball*. *From Russia with Love* also features a new ending in which Bond squares off with henchman Donald "Red" Grant and raids the headquarters of OCTOPUS, a SPECTRE-like organization.

For 007 fans who aren't necessarily interested in gaming, the most interesting aspects of *From Russia with Love* are the multiple nonplayable scenes that, if strung together, would form the basis for an animated Connery-era Bond film.

In addition to *From Russia with Love*, Electronic Arts also made the Bond video games *Tomorrow Never Dies* (1999), *The World Is Not Enough* (2000), *007 Racing* (2000), *Agent Under Fire* (2001), its sequel *Nightfire* (2002), and *Everything or Nothing* (2003).

Glen Schofield, the executive producer of *From Russia with Love*, who would later become vice president at Electronic Arts, directed Connery in his final portrayal of Bond.

How did you get Sean Connery to play Bond one last time?
Pierce Brosnan wasn't doing the Bond films anymore but EA [Electronic Arts] still had the license to make more video games. But the question was, what would that game be and what would Bond look like? I liked the idea of making a game based on a Bond film from the '60s. The people I worked with initially thought it was a pretty unconventional idea but I thought it would be fun. I really wanted to do it. So we built a bunch of elements for the game. We put together a good pitch, which included a potential scene from the game.

I first pitched the game to my boss at EA and he said, "There's not a big chance that we're going get this one through, but you guys have spent so much time working on the pitch, I'm going give you a shot." When we were done with our pitch, Don Mattrick, who was the president at the time, said, "Why wouldn't we make this

Dinner with Sean Connery in the Bahamas. Glen Schofield on the far left,
audio director Paul Gorman, and Sean Connery.

game? We have to get Sean Connery." I don't know all the details about how they got
Connery but I was thrilled that they were going ahead with the game.

Where did you record his lines?

He wasn't going to come to the States so I had to fly down to the Bahamas, where
he lived. I had the best time working with Sean Connery. But before we started
working together, I wanted to have dinner with him and I was nervous about what
he'd say. I'm sitting by a pool waiting, and I'm nervous. I don't normally get nervous
but it was Sean Connery. I get a call a few hours later and he says, "Yep, we'll go to
dinner, and we'll go to this place that I know." I went with a colleague to meet him.
When we arrive, this extra-long golf cart pulls up with a driver and Sean Connery
is sitting in it. He says, "Hop in." We hopped in the cart and drove to the restaurant.
It was just a wonderful evening where we listened to Sean talk.

What do you remember about that dinner?

I remember Sean's stories. I would tell a story about making a game or something
[relatively inconsequential]. But he'd tell a story about Desmond Tutu, Nelson Man-
dela, or the Scottish government. Sean would say, "I was having dinner with the
queen the other night." I'm like, "Man, I got nothing." He'd also tell us stories about
being a celebrity and that sometimes he just wanted to keep to himself. I remember
the music was a little loud for him, and he pulled the waiter over, and said, "We like
that we're talking over here." Immediately, the music was turned off.

THE MANY LIVES OF JAMES BOND

One more thing. He would call me [imitating Connery] "Schofield." But when he says "Schofield" it sounds like he's saying "Blofeld."

That's what I was thinking.
Yeah, yeah, it was great. I loved it.

Did you ask him Bond questions?
Sean told us stories about making the movie *From Russia with Love*. He talked about [Pedro Armendáriz who played Kerim Bay] and who was very sick while filming it. He died shortly after [his work on] the film was complete. Sean said he was a great guy; it was a big loss. He said that he had a really good time making that one. It was his second Bond film. It was a lot of fun because it was brand new, and it was just starting to get big. It was an exciting time for him. I remember him calling my house a few times and leaving messages like, "Glen Schofield, please. This is Sean Connery." Like he had to say his name. Like I wouldn't have recognized his voice. My wife used to save those messages.

What do you remember about the recording session?
There were a number of them and they were all done in a well-known studio in the Bahamas [Compass Point Studios]. A lot of important musicians recorded there including Bob Marley, AC/DC, and the Rolling Stones. There were gold records all over the walls. Sean has used that studio for twenty years to record lines for his movies.

We tried to get him to match his voice from the film. But he was [more than forty years] older, so trying to get him to be the same voice was tough. He would get a little gravely at times, but what a trouper.

What kind of direction did you give him?
His digital agent, which was a new thing at the time, kept telling me, "You have to bring a director down. You have to have a director." I said, "Well, I've directed these sessions many times." But he insisted, "You have to bring a director down, Glen. A professional director." So we fly a director down. This director was this sycophant. "Oh, Sean, that was wonderful." But I'm also in the booth and I know I need it to be a certain way. So, I'm changing things. I said, "Sean, we need you to do this." At the end of the day, Sean comes up to me and says, "Glen, you have to fire the director and do it yourself." So I did. I directed the rest of the sessions myself. It was a little daunting to tell Sean Connery, "You need another take." But he was really professional. He would just say, "Okay," and then he'd do another take. I knew when it was fine to ask for another one. But I didn't have to do a heck of a lot of them. I would say, "I need it a little bit this way." He was easy to direct.

Do you recall any specific direction you gave him?

There were times when I would say, "Oh, Sean, in this scene, there is supposed to be a helicopter in the background, so you'll need to yell it out a little bit more" or, "When you're saying a line, you just need to have an emphasis on a different word."

We would discuss the scene before recording it and he would say, "Oh, I should probably do it this way." He added a little flavor to it, too, and it was great. A couple of times he'd say, "Bond wouldn't say that."

Well, he knows the character.

He also said, "Well, here Bond would not be so forceful. He's more of a matter-of-fact kind of guy." He just knew Bond.

What do you remember about Sean doing the classic line, "Bond, James Bond?"

I don't think we had to do too many takes on that one. Most of the time he nailed it right away. The biggest issue was not performance but that his voice would give out because we were working for hours and hours. He hadn't done this sort of thing in a long time.

What's your strongest memory of Connery in the booth?

I remember sitting there and saying to myself, "Wow, I'm just an artist from New Jersey, and I'm sitting here directing Sean Connery as 007." I remember thinking that this is a time I will remember my whole life. Instead of having us stay at a hotel he said, "Stay in my friend's bed and breakfast."

In the recording booth, did he physicalize the role and embody Bond a little bit?

A little bit, but it was mostly his voice. He would sit and drink his tea. But it was his special tea. I said, "Sean, can I try it?" He replied, "Oh, sure." He made me some tea and said, "I got this tea from Michael Stipe of R.E.M. Are you familiar with them?" [Laughs.] The next day Sean comes in and he hands me a canister of that tea.

I wonder if his gesture was a small thank-you for helping him reprise his role.

As I mentioned, his agent at the time said he was a tough guy. Sean is a tough guy but I'm also a fairly big guy. I lift weights. We kinda hit it off on the tough guy thing. Mind you, I'm not really a tough guy.

I'm a little surprised that he was so easygoing. I would have thought that given his mixed feelings about playing Bond he might have been a little prickly.

Not at all. Let me tell you another story. We finished the recording session on Friday. The guy who ran the place checks the tapes and he goes, "Oh, my god. I don't have the recording session."

Something happened to Connery's recording?

He said, "For the first time in my career, something happened. I don't have it. Glen, I don't have it." My heart just fell. I didn't have any more money in the budget to re-record the entire session. I didn't know what to do. He said, "Let me call Sean. I've known him for twenty years."

He calls me back and says, "Sean said he'll come in tomorrow, no problem." It was just amazing, to have Sean say he'd do that. I called Sean and said, "We'll pick you up in a limo." He said, "Oh, I'll drive myself, Schofield." That day he drove up in this modest little truck. He didn't have the trappings of fame. Sean came back in that Saturday, and we recorded for four hours. Four more hours of him and we got everything we needed. Any other actor I know would've charged us for that day.

Here's a little anecdote. In the Bahamas, there's a ritzy billion-dollar casino. Of course, there's no parking immediately in front of the casino. Instead, a valet takes your car. There is one exception. When we got to the casino we saw that right up front is Sean Connery's little truck. It's just sitting there. You knew the respect that this man got.

Why do you think he agreed to do a video game?

He said he had grandkids. His grandkids were more excited about video games than they were about his movie career. So we gave him a bunch of free video games. We gave him a console so he could bring it back to them. For him, it was about them.

He normally tries to distance himself from Bond, so it's surprising he came back. He didn't need the money.

No, no. It was all about his grandkids.

Marlon Brando did voice work for the *Godfather* video game, which came out a year later. Does it pay well or is it a chance to try something new?

For the number of days they work, it is good money. But it is also a chance to do something they haven't done before.

In addition to capturing Connery's look, the Bond in your game also moves like him.

We spent a lot of time trying to get that right. We studied the way he moved. He moves in a unique way, right? Back then, we didn't have motion capture, so it was all hand animation. But the entire experience was fairly smooth. I remember my boss at the time saying, "This is the smoothest Bond game we've ever done, without a doubt."

Working with the Broccolis and all those people can be tricky, because they're particular about their brand, and they should be. But my main contact there—I can't remember his name—said, "This has been the best Bond game I've ever worked on." We all had a good time.

The Broccolis know Bond better than almost anyone but I can understand why you might want to put your own creative stamp on it. What discussion did you have about what's good for the game versus what's good for the Bond franchise?

I wanted it to be authentic. I wasn't worried about putting my stamp on it. I wanted to make it a true Bond game and bring back the feel of 1963. Those were my personal goals. I also wanted to make sure the Bond people were happy with the game, and they were.

What were some interesting creative differences on the other games?

We wanted Bond to carry two guns. But the licensor said, "Bond doesn't carry two guns." So there was no way to get around that.

That's true. Bond wouldn't normally carry two guns.[16]

But they did offer a compromise. They said, "If you want, Bond could pick up the gun of an enemy and use that gun. But then he'd throw it down in that scene. If you want to do that, we're okay with that." There were a few other creative disagreements here and there. I don't remember the circumstances, but I said I wanted to do something and they said no. I argued for it. But they were concerned with the integrity of the brand.

Do you remember what that disagreement was about?

I don't remember the particulars but they were saying, "Look, Bond doesn't do that. We're telling you, that's not what he does, and you're not going to do it." And we'd say, "Well, this is fun," but they'd respond, "You have to find something else because Bond wouldn't do that. We're not going to allow that." I was told that they would rather not do the game than do it in a way that goes against their idea of Bond.

Glen Schofield's memorabilia display showcases Sean Connery's digital likeness, a baseball signed by the actor, and the photo of Schofield's dinner with Connery. Cate Latchford, producer, far right.

PERSONAL COLLECTION OF GLEN SCHOFIELD

Why do you think the Broccolis allowed the Bond video games?
The games make a lot of money. They really do. But they also keep Bond relevant when they're between films. The video games also help introduce Bond to a younger demographic.

Why did you choose *From Russia with Love* and not another film from the Connery era?
We went through all the titles. *From Russia with Love* seemed to be one that would make a good video game. Especially from a game-play point of view.

You broke continuity from that film by including touchstones from other Bond films, such as the jetpack from *Thunderball*.
We had to talk to the license holder to get them approved. I don't know why, but that one seemed to go over pretty well.

In that particular case, they didn't have any objections?
I don't know why. They have their own set of rules, and I remember that one wasn't that hard to get through.

What about people's reaction to the game?
The game did okay but it wasn't a critical darling. It's funny because I talk to people later, and they're like, "Yeah, I loved that game." The critics at the time didn't necessarily love it, but they loved Sean.

Was there talk of doing another Bond game after that?
They did want me to make another Bond game right after that, but there wasn't enough time. It took a year to do this one, and they wanted the next one in about nine months. Nine months would've killed me. They wanted me to direct it. But with the amount of time they wanted to give me, it would have failed. So I turned it down.

I'm a huge Bond fan but I wasn't aware of the game when it was first released in 2005.
I was a little disappointed in EA for not doing more to promote the game. I'm not there anymore, but I love EA. I was disappointed that they didn't use Connery in in-store standees and other display items. I would've loved to have seen him on a late-night talk show. Of course, there might've been financial reasons why they couldn't do that. I remember they were also a little worried about what he might say. I thought that it doesn't matter what he says because he's still Sean Connery and he'd still be talking about your game. We should've done more at the time to promote

Baseball autographed by Sean Connery. Connery told Glen Schofield that it
"was the first baseball I ever signed. And probably my last."
PERSONAL COLLECTION OF GLEN SCHOFIELD

the game. We could've sold more. We had this great opportunity. But like you said,
we brought Sean Connery back. I was quite proud of that. I still am.

Do you have any keepsakes from your time with Connery?
I got him to sign all sorts of things, too, which was nice of him. We created a digital Sean, and he signed that for me. I'm also a big baseball fan and I have this weird
collection in which I get celebrities to sign baseballs for me. Anyway, I said, "Sean,
would you sign this for me?" He looks at it and he goes, "Is this a baseball?" I said,
"Yeah, would you sign it?" He said, "Sure, never signed one of these before." It's now
one of my prized possessions.

Working with Connery was just a wonderful, wonderful time. It's a time I'll
always cherish. The whole experience was something to behold.

PART V

BOND WOMEN

LANA WOOD

There's a memorable exchange between Sean Connery and Lana Wood in *Diamonds Are Forever* that seems to appear in every television special about James Bond. In it, Connery's Bond is about to play craps when Lana Wood, wearing a low cut dress that emphasizes her plentiful décolletage, introduces herself, "Hi, I'm Plenty." Bond dryly observes, "But of course you are." She continues, "Plenty O'Toole." Bond opines, "Named after your father perhaps." The brief interplay encapsulates some of the appeal of the series—an übercool ladies' man, a breathtaking woman, and the perfect risqué line.

How were you cast as Plenty O'Toole in *Diamonds Are Forever*?
I got a call from my agent who said that Cubby Broccoli and [director] Guy Hamilton wanted to meet with me for the new Bond film that they were casting and I said, "Wow." They also said, "Try to look tall." I said, "Tall? Great." I'm five-foot-two so for me to look tall or even pretend to be tall is going to be rather difficult. I bought an outfit specifically for my interview and wore pink hot pants, which were in style at the time. I wore a matching top and tall-heeled shoes that looked like gladiator boots. They went all the way up to my knee. I went out to the studio and had a long chat with them and [screenwriter] Tom Mankiewicz, who was also there. Tom was an old family friend. Tom said that he suggested me and that they were really interested. I said that I was thrilled. I hadn't seen all the films but I was an avid Ian Fleming fan and had read all the books, which I thought were fabulous.

I had a relaxed nice chat with them. We didn't talk about anything in particular; they wanted to get a feeling for my personality. They said they had seen a couple of the television shows that I'd done and they thanked me and I left. About a week or two later I got another call from my agent who said that they liked me and they wanted me to be in the film but that due to problems related to shooting in Las Vegas, they could not offer me the lead role, but they asked if I would consider playing the smaller role of Plenty O'Toole. I said I don't even need to think about it. I said absolutely—I just want to be a part of it. I'm just delighted and absolutely I would and that was it.

I traveled to Las Vegas with two cats, always have. They were on the plane with me and one of them was meowing and uncomfortable so I stuck my finger in one of the little round breathing holes and my finger got stuck. I got to the hotel and my finger was still stuck in the cage. I was standing at the desk and they said that my room was not ready. Here I am with suitcases and two cats, and Sean Connery, who was walking through the lobby, saw me. He said, "Lana, what's the problem?" I said that my room's not ready and so he told the desk, "Have her use my suite. I'm going to be at work all day long." They took me up to Sean's suite. They got butter from room service and put it around my finger and we finally worked my finger out of the cat cage. Then my room was ready I moved into my own place with my two kitties.

You didn't have to do a screen test?
No, nothing.

How did Guy Hamilton and Mankiewicz describe Plenty O'Toole to you?
They didn't describe the character at all. Tom did say that he came up with the name and that he thought it suited me perfectly and that was about it. I didn't care who the character was; I was happy to do it.

Tell me what you remember about the scene where you and Bond meet.
It was literally the first scene that I shot, so I was a little bit nervous and I didn't know what to expect. They were concerned about the size difference between Sean and me. They had me stand on an apple box to make the size difference a little bit less obvious. Even though I had heels on, it was not working. I think our size difference was part of was the problem we had with Sean and I walking to have dinner.

By then, I had cornered Guy Hamilton and said that I'd been thinking about the character, and I did not want to portray a hooker with a heart of gold. It's such a cliché. I wanted to make Plenty not stupid and without cunning. Her motives are clear-cut; she's doing a job the same as if she were working in a department store. That's her attitude about her work. She's very matter-of-fact, "Hi, how are you? What do you do for a living? I'm a shill." There isn't any embarrassment for her. I wanted her to be straightforward and without filters. I went on and on. Guy sat there and listened to me and then he said, "Lana, anything you want to do is just fine." I said, "Are you serious?" And he said, "Yes, we want you to do this part. So do whatever you want to do."

For the voice, I thought of Minnie Mouse, Leigh Taylor-Young [the high-pitched actress from the soap opera *Peyton Place*], and a Betty Boopish voice. Years later, people have said that someone else dubbed me, but it's my voice. Normally, I have a deep voice but I just thought she would come off too much of a sexpot. If I used a deep, melodious kind of a voice she might have seemed like a little sexpot shill who isn't likable. So that's what I chose to do. To this day I've wondered if I made the right decision.

The Academy of Motion Pictures made a short video on Bond that they planned to run during the show [to commemorate the fiftieth anniversary of the Bond franchise]. They grabbed me and asked, "What did it mean to you to be in a Bond film?" I said, "If I had realized it was going to follow me for the rest of my life, I would've tried harder."

[I laugh.]

Thank you for laughing. You got that it was a joke. It's funny that the other roles that meant so much to me at the time didn't go anywhere but Bond persists. Sometimes I think that I should've made Plenty more animated, but I wanted to keep her simple. She's not thinking about what she's doing or making any judgments; she's just working on the assembly line. I didn't want to make her too multifaceted.

It doesn't seem like she's putting on an act.

Oh, absolutely, without question. She doesn't know who he is other than he's a great good-looking guy she's attracted to and who's winning at the craps table. She's impressed by him.

I think that's a correct choice. Like us, she seems to be legitimately impressed by Bond. Your character feels the same way about Bond as the audience does.

I'm glad you said it, because I still question it. This one role has followed me forever. It's absolutely incredible. I had no idea that it would continue on like this. When it was first released, the studio sent me on a world tour for the film. I hadn't even seen the film and I left on tour—Europe, the Orient, everywhere. I returned home, went to the Grauman's Chinese Theater, and sat down to watch the film for the first time. That's when I discovered that they cut out an entire section of the movie with Plenty. I was absolutely shocked and I felt rather betrayed. I was upset and I called Guy Hamilton. He said the additional scenes with Plenty were sweet but they weren't moving the plot forward.

In terms of his craft, how did Connery approach the part?

Sean knew that he could do Bond in his sleep, and he is James Bond. Bond must be a killer and come across as someone who shouldn't be messed with. But, at the same time, he's so charming that he overrides it.

As moviegoers, we sit back and we watch Connery, but you had a unique perspective. You're in that world with him when you're doing a scene. What is that experience like?

You are very much taken there, that's where you are, and that's who you are. You're not aware of the fact that you're acting; you are completely sucked in by that entire experience at that point in time. Sean is very much that character and by the time we worked together, he had him down pat. I don't think there was a great deal of effort in trying to sustain a character. He was very comfortable with Bond.

What was his attitude about returning to the character?

You can't fault anything that Sean did because he was James Bond. But I think that he wasn't finding anything new or a great deal of joy in playing the character. He was always true to his craft but I got the feeling that he was waiting for them to say, "It's a wrap," so that he could play golf.

Are you in touch with other Bond women?

Maude Adams and I are dear friends. We travel a lot together to various Bond conventions. It's usually George Lazenby and me and Maude and me. Before one of the screenings, she asked if I wanted to leave and I said, "More than you know." We got up and snuck out of the theater. I told her, "I felt sort of dismissed by Guy Hamilton. Did he talk to you at all about your character or give you any direction in the scenes [for the Hamilton-helmed *The Man with the Golden Gun*]? She said, "No." I said, "I thought perhaps he didn't care for me or didn't find my character of that much importance because he didn't give me any direction at all." Maude explained that Guy allowed people to do their thing and took the Bond films as they were, which is a great action-adventure fantasy and escapist entertainment. After speaking with her I felt better because I had always thought that he just didn't care for me and that he was disappointed that I was hired.

I imagine there is kinship among the Bond women?

Absolutely, it's quite wonderful. The first time we all got together for the *Vanity Fair* shoot that Annie Leibowitz did [in 1999], it was quite amazing. Then, I guess because we kept being thrown together, we've become friends. I traveled extensively with Maude, with Gloria Hendry [Rosie Carver in *Live and Let Die*], and with Lynn-Holly Johnson [Bibi Dahl in *For Your Eyes Only*], who directed me in a short film that she was making a couple of years ago. Tanya Roberts [Stacey Sutton in *A View to a Kill*] is sweet. I was one of the producers on the Mike Hammer TV movie *Murder Me, Murder You* [1983] with Stacy Keach, and I had cast Tanya in it.

I have a particular affection for Maude Adams, Caroline Monro [the helicopter-flying villain Naomi in *The Spy Who Loved Me*], and Martine Beswick [Zora, one of the two fighting gypsies in *From Russia with Love* and MI6 operative Paula Caplan in *Thunderball*], whom I just absolutely adore. Yes, there's an interesting camaraderie, even though most of my friends worked with Roger Moore. I think he's wonderful; he's funny, relaxed, and works differently than Sean does. He's a lot of fun on the sets but I just didn't care for him as Bond. I tease Maude about that.

Is being a Bond girl a part-time job?

Certainly. It is something that remains with you. I had no idea that it would continue on like this. It was a part that I was doing that I was thrilled to do, but I did not think that it would have the continued impact that it has. After it was over, I went back home, back to my old-time boyfriend and back to my life and onto the next film. Bond went out of my mind and I just went back to doing TV. I then got married, had a child and more or less dropped off the face of the Earth for a couple of years. But then about ten years ago—and I don't know what began the parade again—Bond nostalgia and all the films seemed to come to the front of people's memories. I was suddenly caught up in going to shows and traveling and going from this photo shoot to that photo shoot and people would request, "Please film something for this show." So, I've been busy with Bond.

What's it like to be back in the Bond spotlight after it dimmed for a while?

It's surprised me when the Bond thing started catching up with me again, but I'm delighted because it meant a lot to me. Now I wish people would say, you were so wonderful in *QB VII* [a 1974 miniseries] in your scenes with Ben Gazzara. But I'm Plenty O'Toole. There are far worse things that one has to cope with.

Are there any drawbacks to being a Bond woman?

As with any actress, you are under a microscope and that can become uncomfortable. I do feel scrutinized. It's tough at times. I feel a great deal like Natalie [Wood, Lana's sister and a three-time Academy Award nominee] did. She used to tell me that when she steps foot outside the door she always has to be "Natalie Wood." At the time, I never understood it. But because of Bond, I finally do. I know that when I walk out of my hotel room door to go to the convention or to film an interview, people want to see me looking terrific and want me to be witty and well-spoken. Being examined like that can be tough sometimes, and I don't have the best self-image. But I do the best I can and that's all I can do. I'm content with that.

On the other hand, I was at my pharmacy last week standing in line and one of the pharmacists said, "I'll take care of you at the front register." Then he said, "I'm sorry that you had to wait." I couldn't figure out why I was suddenly getting this lovely treatment. But then he said, "I'd love to get an autographed photo." That sort of thing is a plus. I can't speak for other actors, but every little bit of kindness is nice. It keeps you going. I'm delighted with it.

I've made some absolutely wonderful friends, so it's all been good. When I was producing another TV film for ABC [*The Mystery of Natalie Wood* (2004), directed by Peter Bogdanovich], I called Sean to see if he would say a few words about Natalie. He was very sweet and he called me back immediately. He would've been happy to do it if we could have accommodated his schedule a little bit better but we just weren't able to. But he was very charming and very nice.

When you're flipping the channel and the movie comes on, what goes through your mind?

I pick on my choice for the character every time. As long as no one else walks in the room, I'll sit and analyze it. I try not to watch a lot of things that I've done because I don't want to spend that much time wishing I had made a different choice. But the more time that passes and the more people that I speak with and the fans who seem to identify with Plenty more so than the other Bond girls, I think that perhaps I did make the right choice in making her simpler and without guile. I get mail constantly and fans tell me that Plenty O'Toole is their favorite Bond girl. That's nice to hear. In terms of the performance, I'm tough on myself, but I guess you never get any better if you're not.

I hope someday you could look at your performance through other people's eyes; it seems like you're just beginning to.

I think I do. I don't know to what extent I do, but I think I do and it's really lovely. The fans are amazingly kind and so happy to say hello. It's been terrific.

THE MANY LIVES OF JAMES BOND

LISA FUNNELL

In order to understand Bond's character, it's necessary to understand the role that Bond women play in the franchise. That's the task Dr. Lisa Funnell undertook when she envisioned and edited *For His Eyes Only: The Women of James Bond* (2015), a collection of essays examining the different ways women are depicted in the films and novels. Funnell, who also contributed an essay, contends that "Bond has been historically defined by his relationships with women." Sabine Planka, one of the book's contributors, similarly argues that "James Bond, as a character, is virtually inconceivable without women. Women serve as his enemies, allies, and lovers, and their characters are defined almost exclusively by their relationships with him."

Dr. Funnell is an assistant professor in the Women's and Gender Studies program at the University of Oklahoma. She examines gender in the Bond series, as well as in Hong Kong martial arts movies and Hollywood blockbusters. She also wrote *The Geographies, Genders, and Geopolitics of James Bond* (2017) with Dr. Klaus Dodds. Dr. Funnell responded in writing to my questions about Bond women.

You explore the function and range of women in the Bond franchise in your book *For His Eyes Only: The Women of James Bond*. What are some of the types of women who appear throughout the series of films?

One common type is the damsel in distress who requires saving by Bond. She functions as a mediator of threat—that is, a threat to her is a threat to Bond—and her capture/targeting by the villain compels Bond into action. As a hero, Bond has his roots in the British lover literary tradition and is presented as a man of action who risks everything for a higher cause: to secure the physical safety and geopolitical interests of Britain and its allies and for the women he loves.[1] As a result, Bond's ability to safeguard and sexually satisfy beautiful women confirms his libido-based masculinity.[2] Solitaire in *Live and Let Die* and Stacey Sutton in *A View to a Kill* are good examples of Bond Girls who function as damsels in distress. Additionally, Madeleine Swann from *Spectre* qualifies, as she is kidnapped by Ernst Stavro Blofeld and imprisoned in the derelict MI6 building. The film ends with a "rescue the princess" scenario in which Bond is framed as her knight in shining armor.

Another common type is the kept woman who serves as a (sexual) companion to the wealthy villain often in return for money or a lavish lifestyle. Over time, some of these women feel imprisoned and look for an opportunity to break free. And so Bond steps in to seduce the kept woman and save her from the villain. A good example is Domino Derval in *Thunderball*, who initially agrees to be the kept woman of the much-older Emilio Largo, only to be imprisoned and tortured by him after she discovers that he killed her brother. In a similar way, Andrea Anders becomes imprisoned by Francisco Scaramanga in *The Man with the Golden Gun* and tries to have him killed by Bond. Finally, in *Tomorrow Never Dies*, Paris Carver marries Elliot but still pines for Bond and even sneaks away to warn him of her husband's plans. She returns home knowing that she will be punished for this betrayal.

A third figure is the sexy siren whose role in the film is to sexually distract, tempt, and/or seduce Bond, rendering him vulnerable for attack. Both primary and secondary characters have functioned as sexy sirens. For example, Miss Taro in *Dr. No* invites Bond over to her home for a rendezvous and he is attacked by a group of men on his drive over. In *The Spy Who Loved Me*, Bond is distracted by Karl Stromberg's assistant Naomi, who wears a brown bikini and flirts with him. She later attacks Bond while flying a helicopter, only to be shot down by Bond's Lotus Esprit. Finally, in *Die Another Day*, Bond sleeps with Miranda Frost, who [seems to have] literally disarmed him by taking the clip out of his gun as they have sex on a bed of ice.

What is a "Bond Girl?" And is that an accurate descriptor?

The term "Bond Girl" is problematic because it is frequently used to describe nearly all of the women who appear in the series (with the exception of M and Moneypenny). This works to collapse very different women into a single category regardless of their role, narrative agency, time onscreen, or allegiance to Bond. Since all of the men in the franchise—from villains like Goldfinger to henchmen like Jaws to allies like Felix Leiter—are not referred to as "Bond Boys," why is the term "Bond Girl" used to describe the vast majority of women in the series? There is a difference between a primary character and a secondary/supportive figure. In *Goldfinger*, for instance, Pussy Galore plays a pivotal role in the narrative and helps Bond thwart the evil plot of the villain. In comparison, Dink appears onscreen for only ten seconds, merely to say "hello," before Bond smacks her butt and shoos her away to have "man talk" with Leiter. The general descriptor "Bond Girl" does not allow for a distinction to be made between these women. Additionally, there is a difference between protagonists and antagonists in the Bond franchise, as heroic women are represented differently from villainous women. In *Thunderball*, there is a difference in the narrative treatment of Domino Derval, who is depicted as a kept woman and damsel in distress, and Fiona Volpe, who is presented as a sexy siren and black widow assassin. There are different gendered and sexual terms for "good" and "bad" women, and these distinctions also need to be drawn out.

In my essay "From English Partner to American Action Hero" (2008), I theorize that the term Bond Girl refers to a particular female character type of the Bond film. She is a nonrecurring character and lead female protagonist, central to the plot of the film, and instrumental to the mission of James Bond. However, the defining feature of the Bond Girl is the strong, intimate, and intense relationship she builds with Bond.[3]

One goal of *For His Eyes Only* is to untangle the "web of women" in the series and draw attention to the range and diversity in female characterization. Various scholars in the book define, differentiate, and theorize about the variety of women who appear in the films. These include "Bond Girls,"[4] "Bond Girl Villains" (or Bad Girls),[5] Secondary Women/Girls,[6] Miss Moneypenny,[7] and Judi Dench's M.[8]

Another issue is with the term "Bond Girl" itself. In his novels, Ian Fleming frequently refers to Bond's love interest as "the girl." His lexicon is carried forward into the films as well as into the subsequent discussion of female characters in academic, critical, and social discourses. Language reflects and relays cultural views and values. Women are often described through terms that objectify and diminish their capabilities, such as being discussed in relation to food (e.g., sugar, sweetie, and cupcake) and animals (e.g., chick, catty, and bitch). In addition, women are often depicted as being immature or juvenile through the use of terms like "girl," "babe," and "baby."[9] Just as the term "boy" can be used to put down a man, the term "girl" operates in the same way to put down a woman.

In the Bond franchise, James Bond interacts with *women*. The rare exception is Bibi Dahl, in *For Your Eyes Only*, whose infatuation with Bond is rejected by the hero, who finds her to be too young (i.e., not yet a woman) and thus deems sexual interaction with her to be inappropriate. But otherwise, Bond interacts with many women over the course of the novels and films. So the persistence of the term "girl" to describe these professional women is troubling as it reduces their social importance and arguably relays a condescending view of them. Given the cultural pervasiveness of the Bond franchise, it will be difficult to move away from using the term "Bond Girl" altogether. But it is important that if/when it is used, we remain mindful of the messages being relayed through it and strive to use other descriptors like "Bond Women" when discussing female characterization in a broader sense.

There is one additional problem with naming in the franchise. In the novels, Fleming refers to male characters by their full names upon the first mention and afterward by their last names. This is a common practice in literature as well as literary and film criticism. However, when Fleming refers to female characters, he introduces them with their full names and then afterward refers to them only by their first names. This has been carried over into academic, critical, and popular discourse. If you refer to James Bond as Bond then you have to refer to Vesper Lynd as Lynd. Otherwise, just as the descriptor "girl" infantilizes women, this gendered naming convention diminishes the importance and capacity of women. Though the first names Honeychile/Honey, Gala, and Domino certainly have a ring to them, these figures should be referred to as Rider/Ryder, Brand, and Derval respectively. [*Note:* Honeychile Rider and Honey Ryder are the names of the character in the novel and film, respectively.]

How have the "Bond Girls" changed over the years?

The "Bond Girls" have developed across four key phases of representation. Initially, the Bond Girl is positioned in the role of English Partner (1962–1969). Her relationship with Bond mirrors the male-female partnership made famous in the British television series *The Avengers* (1961–1969). In fact, two women who starred on the television show were cast as "Bond Girls" during this era: Honor Blackman as Pussy Galore in *Goldfinger* and Diana Rigg as Tracy di Vicenzo in *On Her Majesty's Secret Service*. The other Bond of this era (with the exception of Tatiana Romanova in *From Russia with Love*) have been cinematically Anglicized and speak with a British accent regardless of the nationality of the character or actor who plays them. The voices of Honey Ryder, Domino Derval, and Kissy Suzuki were dubbed in postproduction and replaced with that of Monica van der Zyl. [*Note*: Monica "Nikki" van der Zyl is a voice-actor of German decent who was trained at the Royal Academy of Dramatic Arts in England.[10]] Thus, the initial "Bond Girls" are aligned with British culture and positioned as British/Anglicized partners who work alongside Bond.[11]

Across the Moore and Dalton eras as well as in the final Connery film, the Bond Girl is positioned as an "American Sidekick" (1971–1989). In addition to being romantic interests, these Bond Girls are often depicted as American ally agents or professionals who effectively replace CIA agent Felix Leiter as Bond's American ally in the films. During this era, the Bond Girl and/or her corresponding actress tends to be American and represents American geopolitical interests in the film.[12] Much like the English partner, she plays a supportive role to Bond in the mission.

In the 1990s, the Bond Girl shifts into a third phase and is depicted as an Action-Hero Bond Girl (1995–2002). This shift coincides with the rise of women as action heroes in Hollywood blockbusters. These women are depicted as being intellectual, physical, and sexual matches to Bond, if not superior in these regards.[13] In *GoldenEye*, Bond relies entirely on Natalya Simonova's knowledge of computer programming; while she provides "the brains," he takes care of "the brawn." In *Tomorrow Never Dies*, Wai Lin is trained in martial arts, appears in her own action sequence, and arguably outfights and outshines Bond in every scene they share. Finally, in *Die Another Day*, Jinx Johnson challenges, if not dominates, Bond in bed during their initial sexual encounter.

Since the mid-2000s, the Bond Girl concept has been reworked. The qualities typically associated with the figure have been distributed across two different characters. In *Casino Royale*, they are divided between Vesper Lynd (who is depicted as a Bond Girl Villain) and James Bond (who is presented as a Bond–Bond Girl hybrid). A similar division occurs in *Quantum of Solace* between Camille Montes (who serves as a platonic partner) and the late Vesper Lynd (whose memory is frequently evoked through the Algerian knot necklace and the martini). In *Skyfall*, it is M who is framed through the conventions of the Bond Girl, and she is depicted as an M–Bond Girl hybrid. According to Christopher Holliday, her depiction recalls the English Partner Bond Girls of the 1960s.[14] The only woman who appears as a Bond Girl proper is Madeleine Swann in *Spectre*, and she drives away with Bond at the end of the film, presumably to continue their relationship. Although the Bond Girl concept has been reworked in the Craig era, it ultimately reverts back to a traditional model of femininity in the franchise.

In my essay in *For His Eyes Only*, I argue that Severine is one of the most tragic and disempowered women in the entire Bond franchise. She is depicted "as a disposable object of pleasure and struggle between two white men and the identity of Severine is defined solely in terms of her relationships with Bond and Silva. She has limited dialogue, little to no personal agency, and . . . her role could be entirely eliminated from the film without significantly altering the storyline."[15] Regressive in its depiction of women, *Skyfall* is a good example of why it is important not to make assumptions about gender progress and explore the actual depiction of women in the films.

Who is the quintessential Bond Girl in the films and why?

Honey Ryder from *Dr. No* is the quintessential Bond Girl, as she is the first and helped to establish the archetype. Although the 1960s Bond films are not as formulaic, Ryder set the standard for female representation, and subsequent Bond Girls are depicted with similar personality traits (such as independence and intelligence) and images (such as being costumed in bathing suits or lingerie). In fact, Ryder is memorable for her introduction into the film—emerging from the sea wearing a white bikini with a dagger attached at the hip. This arresting image of Ryder is iconic in the franchise. Moreover, her introduction has been referenced in two subsequent Bond films: to introduce Bond Girl Jinx Johnson in *Die Another Day* on the fortieth anniversary of the film series and to depict Daniel Craig's Bond in *Casino Royale*. These intertextual references draw attention to just how iconic Ryder is as a Bond Girl.

Who is the archetypal Bond Girl in Fleming's novels?

The Bond Girl concept was not defined in Fleming's novels in the same (formulaic) way that it has been in the Bond films. Bond typically works alongside a "girl" in each novel, with a few exceptions like *Goldfinger*, in which Bond engages with Tilly Masterson and Pussy Galore at the same time (as opposed to the film, in which Masterson is killed before Galore is introduced). However, the quintessential Bond Girl of the novels is Honeychile Rider in *Dr. No*. On numerous occasions, Bond expresses his deep attraction to Rider and especially for her independence. Although he is sympathetic to her backstory—from the death of her parents to her subsequent rape—he is also impressed by her local and self-taught knowledge, which he relies on throughout the mission. Unlike some of the previous novels with such memorable women as Vesper Lynd in *Casino Royale*, Gala Brand in *Moonraker*, and Tatiana Romanova in *From Russia, with Love*, *Dr. No* ends on a positive note with Bond in the loving arms of Rider.

What did the welcome addition of Judi Dench's M reveal about Bond's character?

The casting of Judi Dench as M helped to shift the gender dynamics of the franchise. *GoldenEye* was the first film to convey the notion that the world around Bond had changed (over the six-year hiatus in the series) in terms of its gender politics and geopolitics. The film questions if the world still needs Bond and his old-fashioned ideas and approaches. It is Dench's M who most clearly articulates this when she refers to Bond as a "sexist, misogynist dinosaur" and "a relic of the Cold War" during their first meeting in her office. In the Brosnan-era films, it is M who explicitly draws attention to Bond's shifting and somewhat uncertain relationships with women. For example, in *GoldenEye* alone, Bond is (jokingly) accused of sexual harassment by Miss Moneypenny, is frequently yelled at by Natalya Simonova (e.g., "Do something! Get us out of here!"), and is almost killed during a sexual encounter with Xenia Onatopp, who asphyxiates men with her legs while they have sex. It is Dench's M who informs both Bond and the audience that the gendered landscape has changed (in addition to geopolitics). This sets the stage for Bond to prove why Britain specifically and the world more generally still need him.

Did Brosnan's Bond and Craig's Bond have the same relationship with Dench's M?

The nature of their relationship changes with the maternal positioning of M in the Craig-era films. This is a topic that is addressed in detail in *For His Eyes Only* in "Section 6: Judi Dench's Tenure As M." In *Skyfall*, most explicitly, the relationship between M and Bond is framed in mother-son terms. As noted by Peter C. Kunze, *Skyfall* "perpetuates the 'M as mother' interpretation: her agents addressing her as 'Ma'am' can almost be heard as 'Mom,' and when Silva bombs MI6 headquarters—her symbolic home—M must take charge to protect her subordinates/children."[16] Lori Parks contends that "the dynamic that Silva sets up between himself and Bond is of competitive brothers vying for their mother's attention and affection. . . . Silva is presented to us as deranged, broken, effeminate, and ultimately second best (this is even referenced in his name Silva/Silver)"[17] in comparison to Bond, who is M's "golden child." According to Michael Boyce, "the representation of M as mother culminates in *Skyfall* when Bond takes her to his childhood home . . . [where] M allows Bond to settle the unresolved 'childhood trauma' Silva mentioned."[18] The maternal repositioning of M fundamentally changes her relationship with Bond, especially since she strongly rejects serving as a surrogate mother to her agents in the Brosnan era.[19]

THE MANY LIVES OF JAMES BOND

Daniel Craig's Bond, while as physically tough and masculine as any Bond, is also one of the most emotionally vulnerable and sensitive.

Casino Royale presents the origin story of James Bond from the moment he attains his license to kill. As a revisionist film, it deconstructs the Bond genre and reworks many of the characteristic elements in the process of rebranding the franchise. In my article "I Know Where You Keep Your Gun," I argue for a new heroic model in the Craig-era films—the Bond–Bond Girl hybrid—that is informed by Hollywood heroic masculinity and Bond Girl iconography.[20] On one hand, *Casino Royale* places consistent and explicit emphasis "on Daniel Craig's exposed muscular torso rather than his sexuality, libido, and conquest."[21] He is the most battered and bloodied Bond in history, and the film's predilection for body-focused (rather than sexually oriented) imagery aligns him more strongly with Hollywood models of muscular masculinity than the lover literary tradition from which he has his roots. On the other hand, *Casino Royale* presents Bond through iconic Bond Girl iconography when he emerges twice from the sea in a bathing suit, an image that recalls the introduction of quintessential Bond Girl Honey Ryder in *Dr. No*. As a result, there is no Bond Girl proper in the film, as characteristics of this figure have been divided between Vesper Lynd (who is presented as a Bond Girl Villain) and Bond (who is presented as a Bond–Bond Girl hybrid).[22] This results in a hero who "is simultaneously active and passive, masculine [i.e., tough] and feminine [i.e., emotional], British and American, and Bond and Bond Girl."[23]

There's a moment in *Casino Royale* where Craig's Bond, who is wearing a tuxedo for the first time, admires himself in the mirror. What's your take on that moment?

In *Casino Royale*, Bond is presented as the object of the (female) gaze occupied by Vesper Lynd. Lynd literally "sizes him up" to order Bond a custom tuxedo and then catches him looking at himself in the mirror seemingly impressed by the results. The scene relays a shift in gender roles and representations uncommon to the franchise. It also recalls the way in which Lynd figuratively "sizes him up" on the train:

> By the cut of your suit, you went to Oxford or wherever. Naturally, you think human beings dress like that. But you wear it with such disdain, my guess is you didn't come from money, and your school friends never let you forget it. Which means that you were at that school by the grace of someone else's charity, hence the chip on your shoulder. And since your first thought about me ran to "orphan," that's what I'd say you are.

Lynd offers insight into the personal history of Bond and informs him (as well as the audience) of how "green" he is on his first Double-O mission. However, this tuxedo scene depicts the transformation of Bond as he discovers that he not only looks good in a tailored suit but he looks the part. In a visual media like film, internal changes are often signaled externally through changes in costuming as well as behaviors and mannerisms. It is not simply the suit but the way in which Bond wears the suit that draws attention to his self-realization that he belongs at the card table and can be successful. This is the moment when Bond starts to get his mojo as a superspy.

There are a few instances in which the Bond Girl doesn't sleep with Bond. How does not sleeping with him impact our understanding of their character?

There are a number of "Bond Girls" who do not sleep with Bond onscreen, but their films still imply that sexual intimacy will be likely in the future. This has an impact on the way that their characters are depicted and interpreted. For example, in *Tomorrow Never Dies*, Wai Lin's rejection of Bond's advances strengthens her heroic competency by freeing her from the sexual/sexualized expectations of the Bond Girl. The same can be said about Melina Havelock in *For Your Eyes Only*, as a sexual encounter would detract from her mission to avenge the murder of her parents. However, in the case of Pam Bouvier in *Licence to Kill*, it appears to have the opposite effect, as she spends most of the film pining away for Bond only to have him choose her after sleeping with Lupe Lamora. The same is true of Anya Amasova, in *The Spy Who Loved Me*, whose effectiveness as an agent diminishes after she sleeps with Bond.

The only film in which Bond parts ways with a female partner without the suggestion of future sexual/romantic intimacy is *Quantum of Solace*. Bond is still clearly in love with Vesper Lynd and cannot commit emotionally to Camille Montes (even though he sleeps with Strawberry Fields). Unlike his romances with Lin and Havelock, which seem forced and contrived as afterthoughts, *Quantum of Solace* does not push the issue with Montes. Instead, she walks away from Bond, having avenged her family and taking out a threat to her people in Bolivia. This is reminiscent of Gala Brand in Ian Fleming's novel *Moonraker*, who does not end up with Bond, as she is engaged to another man. *Quantum of Solace* inverts this dynamic by having Bond be the one who is emotionally/romantically unavailable (so as not to show him being rejected).

Bond will sleep with almost anyone he can. However, Bond doesn't pursue Moneypenny (although it's possible that they consummated their relationship in *Skyfall*). Why doesn't Bond sleep with Moneypenny? Is that an odd form of respect for her?

The nature of Bond's professional yet flirtatious relationship with Moneypenny was first outlined by Ian Fleming in relation to Loelia Ponsonby, the personal secretary to Bond and other Double-O agents. Fleming describes her as a patriot who has committed her life to the service rather than to a family and should be held in high regard for this. Even though Bond describes Ponsonby as being very beautiful, he understands that she is not romantically available. This dynamic was subsequently shifted over to Moneypenny, who is the personal assistant to M.

The franchise presents a similar impression that marriage is not sustainable for James Bond and other secret agents. This is relayed in both the novels and the films. For example, in Fleming's *Diamonds Are Forever*, Bond explains why he has little interest in marriage: "Matter of fact I'm almost married already. To a man. Name begins with M. I'd have to divorce him before I tried marrying a woman. And I'm not sure I'd want that."[24] He then comments on fatherhood: "Like to have some [children]. . . . But only when I retire. Not fair on the children otherwise. My job's not all that secure."[25] Marriage becomes a central issue in the film *On Her Majesty's Secret Service*, which ends with Bond marrying Tracy di Vicenzo and resigning from the service. She is murdered shortly after by the henchwoman Irma Bunt, and Bond returns to work in *Diamonds Are Forever* without any mention of him being a widower. *Licence to Kill* offers a similar depiction of the dangers of marriage (particularly for a bride who weds a secret agent). The film opens with CIA agent Felix Leiter marrying Della Churchill, who is murdered on their wedding night by the crew of the villain that Leiter had just arrested. As Stephen Nepa explains, the Bond franchise presents the impression that marriage is unsustainable for a secret agent as it "put[s] at risk not only the Bond Girl but all of MI6; Bond simply cannot divide his attention between his responsibilities to the queen (his first and primary love/wife) and his potential domestic responsibilities to the Bond Girl."[26] As a result, these brides, as well as the women Bond deeply loves (like Paris Carver in *Tomorrow Never Dies*, Vesper Lynd in *Casino Royale*, and M in *Skyfall*), are destined to die as they distract/pull Bond away from the service.

Has there been a Bond Girl who is truly an "equal" to Bond? And what does it mean to be an "equal" within the context of these films?

Wai Lin in *Tomorrow Never Dies* offers the most equitable match to Bond and she is depicted in the film as his Chinese counterpart. She is a trained superspy and secret agent of equal rank. She is just as intelligent as Bond, following the same clues and arriving at the same conclusions and destinations as he. She is equally courageous, as she is willing to put herself in harm's way for the mission. And yet she also appears to be superior in physical and emotional terms. Lin is formally trained in martial arts, and she physically outshines Bond in all the action scenes that they share. During the motorcycle sequence, it is Lin who maneuvers from the back to the front of the bike to provide him with information; she does all of the physical labor while Bond remains stationary and steers. Unlike Bond, Lin does not get swept up by her emotions (as he does with Paris Carver). She remains focused on the task at hand

and rejects Bond's sexual advances. Finally, as Stephanie Jones notes, it is Bond who is positioned as "the butt of several sight gags in which technologically enhanced objects act as booby-traps and threaten his life."[27] In a reversal of tradition, it is Bond who is taken down a notch by a female agent.

Although Lin is presented as an equitable if not superior agent, she appears onscreen for only (the latter) half of the film. On one hand, Bond's romantic and sexual relationship with Paris Carver is the focus of the first half of *Tomorrow Never Dies*. This frees Lin from the romantic and sexual expectations of the Bond Girl (since the film already has its quota), thus granting her increased heroic agency. On the other hand, Lin's role has to be limited so as not to overshadow Bond, who is the central figure in the film—it is called a Bond film, after all. By limiting her time onscreen and depicting Bond saving her in the end (with his "mouth-to-mouth" doubling as their first kiss), the film strips away some of her agency and reaffirms some of the traditional gender roles in the franchise—albeit somewhat unconvincingly.

What should Bond fans keep in mind as they continue to think about this issue?

Female characterization appears more complex and nuanced when we move away from the colloquial descriptor "Bond Girl" and begin to explore the diversity of women in the franchise.

APPENDIX: QUOTABLE BOND

I was not able to interview every actor who has played James Bond. But their insights are valuable, so I have compiled the following sourced quotes in which some of the notable performers discuss their work and reflect on their contribution to the Bond legacy.

BARRY NELSON—JAMES BOND

Barry Nelson played Jimmy Bond in a live televised production of *Casino Royale* (1954). While Nelson's 007 is often referred to as "Jimmy Bond" throughout the 50-minute production, he is identified as "James Bond" in the closing credits.

Nelson on his approach to the part: At the time, no one had heard of James Bond. . . . I was scratching my head wondering how to play it. I hadn't read the book or anything like that because it wasn't well-known.—*Cinema Retro*, 2004[1]

Nelson assessing the role: I was very dissatisfied with the part. I thought they wrote it poorly. No charm or character or anything.—*Starlog*, 1983[2]

Nelson on being the first to play 007: I always thought Connery was the ideal Bond. What I did was just a curio.—*New York Daily News*, 1995[3]

Nelson on his place in Bond history: It's kind of a novelty for me to be the first one. I've always approached James Bond with humility. Sean Connery was 007. I never pretended to be anything more than 001. No one ever stops me on the street and recognizes me as James Bond.—*Starlog*, 1983[4]

Nelson on *not* being recognized: After a short lift [in an elevator], everything stopped, and we were between floors. Nothing was open and there was nowhere for any air to get in. It got very hot. . . . Everyone started to get a little panicky and someone said, "I wish James Bond were here!" I thought to myself, "If only he knew that he is!"—MI6, October 2004[5]

BOB HOLNESS—JAMES BOND

Bob Holness voiced the character of Bond in a live radio adaption of *Moonraker* (1958) for the South African Broadcast Corporation.

Bob Holness on playing Bond: Well, that just came up through a hole in the floor. I was doing lots of radio plays at the time but I wanted to do something a bit different, so when James Bond came up, I ventured in and said yes. I had never even heard of him at the time, but it became an amazing part to play and the response from listeners was terrific.—BBC, 2008[6]

BOB SIMMONS—JAMES BOND

Stuntman Bob Simmons became the first on-screen 007 when he doubled for Sean Connery in the gun barrel sequence that opens *Dr. No* (1962), *From Russia with Love* (1963), and *Goldfinger* (1964).

Bob Simmons on Bond's approach to fighting: Bond doesn't attack. Ever. He counter-attacks. He waits for the enemy to move first, and then moves in with that license to do whatever ingenuity brings to mind.[7]—*Nobody Does It Better*, 1987

Simmons on dressing like Bond in his personal life: As Sean Connery's double and stunt man I had to be tailored in identical suiting . . . At the end of the picture, I would be given my suits as part of the perks for the job, and as a result I have a wardrobe at my home in Ealing that covers threes walls of my bedroom, the entire space packed with suits. Expensive, hand tailored Savile Row threads. Forty seven of them."[8]—*Nobody Does It Better*, 1987

SEAN CONNERY—JAMES BOND

Sean Connery played James Bond in *Dr. No* (1962), *From Russia with Love* (1963), *Goldfinger* (1964), *Thunderball* (1965), *You Only Live Twice* (1967), *Diamonds Are Forever* (1971), and *Never Say Never Again* (1983). Connery also narrated the *Dr. No* trailer in character and provided the voice of 007 for the video game *From Russia with Love* (2005).

Sean Connery on 007's transition from the page to the screen: I had to start playing Bond from scratch—not even Ian Fleming knew much about Bond at this time. He has no mother. He has no father. He doesn't come from anywhere when he became 007. He was born—kerplump—thirty-three years old. [I play Bond as] a complete sensualist, his senses are highly tuned and awake to everything.—*Cinema Retro*, 2012[9]

Connery on Fleming's books: I had only read two of Ian Fleming's books before filming began, [and] I wasn't all that in sympathy with the character. In fact, I thought to myself that I probably wouldn't even like Bond if I met him on the street. I'm referring to the way he was conceived in the novels of course.—*Cinema Retro*, 2012[10]

Connery on Bond's vices: [If] you take Bond in the situations that he is constantly involved with, you see that it is a very hard, high, unusual league that he plays in. Therefore, he is quite right in having all his senses satisfied—be it sex, wine, food or clothes—because the job, and he with it, may terminate at any minute.—*Playboy*, 1965[11]

Connery on identifying with Bond: Yes, I do identify with him. I too enjoy drinking, women, eating, the physical pleasure—smells and tastes living by my senses, being alive.—*Stuff Nobody Cares About*, 2015[12]

Connery on Bond's stillness: One of the most important things that one learned in the theater particularly is [being] able to stand still.—*Good Company*, 1967[13]

Connery on Bond's physicality: The essence of it for me was to always make everything look easy, simple. So when there was any movement, it was important. It was a message that something was coming.—*The South Bank Show*, 2008[14]

Connery on the tone of the films: I felt that there was a lack of humor [in the Fleming books]. . . . One of the first things one had to do was to imbue [the cinematic Bond with] a humorous aspect. . . . Therefore, one can accept the violence if it had a humorous quality.—*Good Company*, 1967[15]

Connery on typecasting: I would never deny that Bond made me, and I'll be everlastingly grateful to him. But that doesn't make me a Bond slave. I can cut the shackles free any time I want to. And they aren't made of steel chains any longer, either, but smoothest silk.— *Stuff Nobody Cares About*, 2015[16]

Connery on the evolution of the films: As far as gadgets like cars are concerned, fantastic volcanoes and these extraordinary things, [the later films] have developed and developed and gotten away from the personal aspect of the films, which I liked. My favorite one is *From Russia with Love*. Now, he's got to walk on the water or do something which is equivalent.—*Good Company*, 1967[17]

Sean Connery's Bond takes flight in *Thunderball*.

ILLUSTRATION BY PAT CARBAJAL

Connery on the Bond phenomenon: It's a problem because I don't think any other actor has had such . . . exposure in the world. It's like some sort of Frankenstein.—*Good Company*, 1967[18]

DAVID NIVEN—JAMES BOND

David Niven played Sir James Bond in the satire *Casino Royale* (1967).

David Niven describing *Casino Royale*: The picture is a hodgepodge of nonsense, hardly a critic's film. But I bet Charlie Feldman [the film's producer] makes money.—*The Making of Casino Royale (1967)*, 2015[19]

PETER SELLERS—JAMES BOND

Peter Sellers appeared as the expert baccarat player Evelyn Tremble, who is assigned the code name James Bond, in *Casino Royale*.

Sellers on his approach to the role: I wanted to play James Bond the way Tony Hancock would play him. But Ian Fleming's people would never have allowed it. [Hancock was a British comedian known for playing lovable, self-deluding failures in his character-based comedy.]—*Sabotage Times*, 2015[20]

Sellers on Bond's physicality: Sellers said that Bond should have "panther-like" movement.—*The Making of Casino Royale (1967)*, 2015[21]

TERENCE COOPER—JAMES BOND

Terence Cooper played secret agent Cooper, who is also given the code name James Bond in *Casino Royale*.

Terence Cooper on playing Bond: I'm the James Bond that fell into oblivion. I'm not as famous as Sean Connery, George Lazenby, Roger Moore, or Timothy Dalton, but I am proud to be among the men who have portrayed Agent 007 through the years.—James Bond-O-Rama, 2017[22]

GEORGE LAZENBY—JAMES BOND

George Lazenby played Bond in *On Her Majesty's Secret Service* (1969).

George Lazenby on his similarities to Bond: The main similarity I have got with Bond is that I'm a loner. Now, I know a lot of people, but I don't hang around with anybody.—*007 Magazine*, 1981[23]

Lazenby on comparisons to Connery: Sean Connery created James Bond. How could I be better than Sean Connery playing James Bond? . . . He created the character from his [own] character, his personality. I realized very early that people wanted to see Sean Connery's version.—*Becoming Bond*, 2017[24]

Lazenby on the pressures of the role: They wanted me to carry on the James Bond image at all times. . . . It's a tough umbrella to walk under, that James Bond thing.—*Becoming Bond*, 2017[25]

Lazenby on his decision to step away from Bond: I've always done what I thought was the right thing. And it's not always the right thing but I thought it was at the time. When I look back at it, I should have done two [Bond movies] just to prove to people that I wasn't fired. It was a mistake. But in a way, this is who I am. I don't know why. It doesn't make sense to some people [who] say, he's mad, he's crazy. But I lived my life the way I wanted to.—*Becoming Bond*, 2017[26]

Lazenby on whether he has any regrets about being a one-time Bond: No. First of all, I wasn't an actor. I had no desire to be an actor. I just took this on as a challenge and quite liked it. I can take it or leave it. I'm glad I didn't do another Bond, because I would've been totally trapped in the film industry, and I wouldn't have had the life I had. I wouldn't have had the kids I had. I'm quite satisfied with the way my life has turned out so far.—*USA Today*, 2017[27]

ROGER MOORE—JAMES BOND

Roger Moore played Bond in seven movies: *Live and Let Die* (1973), *The Man with the Golden Gun* (1974), *The Spy Who Loved Me* (1977), *Moonraker* (1979), *For Your Eyes Only* (1981), *Octopussy* (1983), and *A View to a Kill* (1985). In the teaser trailer for *The Spy Who Loved Me*, the actor appeared in character to introduce Bond's latest adventure to moviegoers. In 1964, Moore first played 007 in a seven-minute skit on the sketch comedy series *Mainly Millicent* (1964-1966).

Roger Moore on his alleged rivalry with Sean Connery: There was no animosity between Sean and me. We didn't react to the press speculation that we had become competitors in the part. In fact, we often had dinner together and compared notes about how much we'd each shot and how our respective producers were trying to kill us with all the action scenes they expected us to do.—*My Word Is My Bond*, 2008[28]

Moore on violence in the Bond movies: Basically, we have very little brutality in Bond. As Cubby once said, we are sadism for the family. Most of the violence is mechanical, Disney violence.—The 007 Dossier, 2017[29]

Moore on his own similarities to Bond: Well, he looks like the fellow who plays James Bond except he does not wear a dinner jacket to breakfast.—*007 Magazine*, 1985[30]

Moore on what Bond film, other than his own, that he would have liked to make: I thought *Diamonds Are Forever* was a lovely script.—*GQ*, May 2017[31]

Moore on his self-effacing style: It's easier to joke about yourself than to go on about having to work hard as an actor. Bullshit. Get up, say the line, don't bump into the furniture.—Short List, 2017[32]

TIMOTHY DALTON—JAMES BOND

Timothy Dalton played Bond in *The Living Daylights* (1987) and *Licence to Kill* (1989).

Dalton describing what it's like to play Bond: No one, no matter how well someone can communicate, can tell you—and I certainly can't really communicate accurately—what it is like to be the actor playing James Bond. The only actors who can are the other actors who've played the part. It's kind of astonishing, really. You are in kind of a bubble. It's real, it's valuable, it's exciting, and it can give great pleasure. . . . But it's somehow outside the normal course of what we all share in.—AV Club, 2014[33]

Dalton on his approach to Bond: Bond is a flawed hero. How does he deal with himself morally when he's on the side of right and his job is to kill people? He's put in the position where he could call someone a friend one day and be asked to kill him the next. . . . I wanted to capture that spirit of the man—the essence of Fleming's work.—*For Your Eyes Only: Behind the Scenes of the James Bond Films*, 2002[34]

Dalton on deliberately underplaying Bond's famous introduction: You don't suddenly stop acting, turn to face front and go, quotes, "Bond [James Bond]. . . ." If I'd stood outside the movie to do it, we'd have been back in another kind of film."—*Bondage*, 1987[35]

Dalton on whether Bond is a role model: Bond is not a paragon of virtue; he's a man riddled with vices and weaknesses as well as strength. But that is the nature of the man, and the nature of the world he lives in, but I don't think he should be a role model.—*007 Magazine*, 1989[36]

Dalton on the other Bonds: Roger Moore was marvelous at what he did, and his films were successful, so you can't say a word against him. But Connery was shocking. And his movies were shocking. You had never seen women in bikinis in films in those days, and heroes did not shoot unarmed people.—*Entertainment Weekly*, 2010[37]

Dalton on Bond's character: He can be ruthless and determined, yet we're constantly shown what a serious, intelligent, thinking, feeling human being he is. He's a man of principle too, almost an idealist, but one who sees that he's living in a world without principle, in which ideals are cheaply bought and sold. He's a man who wants human contact; the need for love seems to overflow from him. Yet he can't afford emotional involvement, he can't fall in love or marry or have children, because that would prevent him functioning in a world where the possibility of his death is ever-present.—*New York Times*, 1987[38]

Dalton on Bond's sense of duty: Above all, I realized that he hates to kill. He recalls that when he was young, he thought it was all in the cause of righteousness, but now he perceives his assassinations as dirty murders. He kills himself by killing someone who's himself on the other side. Yet he carries on, always regretting it, always trying to shut it out of his mind. Altogether, it seemed to me that Bond was a complex man, with many more facets than I'd realized. Not a shining knight, but someone deeply unhappy with his job, suffering from confusion, ennui, moral revulsion and what Fleming calls accidie.—*New York Times*, 1987[39]

Dalton on leaving the role: When I saw those posters of Pierce standing there, I suddenly thought to myself, "Jesus, I don't have to stand there with a gun to the side of my head anymore!" I suddenly found the most tremendous sense of liberation, and I started feeling more like myself than I'd ever felt in years! I suddenly felt free.—*For Your Eyes Only: Behind the Scenes of the James Bond Films*, 2002[40]

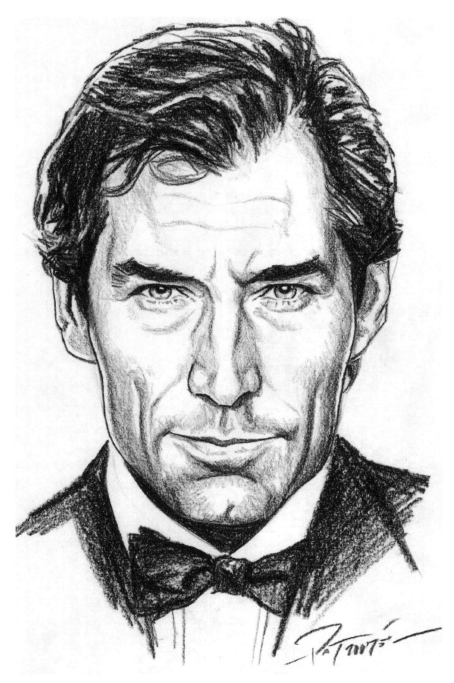

Timothy Dalton as James Bond.
ILLUSTRATION BY PAT CARBAJAL

Dalton on his tenure as Bond: What an experience, indeed. A fantastic experience.—AV Club, 2014[41]

APPENDIX: QUOTABLE BOND

PIERCE BROSNAN—JAMES BOND

Pierce Brosnan played a suave Bond in *GoldenEye* (1995), *Tomorrow Never Dies* (1997), *The World Is Not Enough* (1999), and *Die Another Day* (2002). Brosnan also played 007 in the video game *James Bond 007: Everything or Nothing* (2003) and in a 1997 Visa commercial.

Pierce Brosnan on how Bond fit into his career goals: I grew up with Connery as James Bond, and contrary to what you might have read, I never dreamt of, or wanted to play, this character, until '86 when they offered me the role the first time.—*Huffington Post*, 2015[42]

Brosnan on losing the chance to play Bond in *The Living Daylights* because of his contractual obligations to Remington Steele: "It was a knife in the heart. And not just for me, for my family, because we moved our children back to England and got fucked over by very short people. You get over it. It's just being an actor. Shit happens like that."—*Huffington Post*, 2015[43]

Brosnan on other Bond actors: There's only one man that you want to take the belt from, and that's Connery. So you go into the ring to win. It's a challenge. Connery had a sadistic side to him. . . . I don't know. I live with more heart.—*Huffington Post*, 2015[44]

Brosnan on his characterization: I felt I was caught in a time warp between Roger and Sean. It was a very hard one to grasp the meaning of, for me. The violence was never real, the brute force of the man was never palpable. . . . It was quite tame, and the characterization didn't have a follow-through of reality, it was surface. But then that might have had to do with my own insecurities in playing him as well.—*Telegraph*, 2014[45]

Brosnan on no longer playing Bond: I'll always be known as Bond, but now I don't have the responsibility of being an ambassador for a small country ruled by a character.—*Playboy*, 2005[46]

TOBY STEPHENS—JAMES BOND

Toby Stephens played Bond in a series of radio dramas for the BBC, including *Dr. No* (2008), *Goldfinger* (2010), *From Russia with Love* (2012), *On Her Majesty's Secret Service* (2014), *Diamonds Are Forever* (2015), *Thunderball* (2016), *Moonraker* (2018), and *Live and Let Die* (2019).

Toby Stephens on Bond: As a kid, I used to wish I was 007 because I wanted to be that cool and debonair. And that kind of lone-wolf figure who's completely self-sufficient. That appeals to the male psyche, especially when you're young and reliant on other people's affection.—*Sunday Telegraph*, 2002[47]

DANIEL CRAIG—JAMES BOND

Daniel Craig played 007 in five movies, *Casino Royale* (2006), *Quantum of Solace* (2008), *Skyfall* (2012), *Spectre* (2015), and in the twenty-fifth Eon production (2020). He also provided the voice and likeness for Bond in the video games *007: Quantum of Solace* (2008), *James Bond 007: Blood Stone* (2010), and *GoldenEye 007* (2010). Craig also played 007 in the Heineken commercials "Crack the Case" (2012) and "The Chase" (2015), and in *Happy & Glorious*, the short film that opened the 2012 Olympics and featured Bond and Queen Elizabeth II.

Daniel Craig on preparing for the role: I watched every single Bond movie three or four times, taking in everything I could about how the character had been portrayed in the past—then threw all that away once I started doing the role.—*Entertainment Weekly*, 2006[48]

Craig on Bond: I wanted to play around with the flaws in his character. It was much more interesting than having him be perfect and polished and so suave as to be flawless. I got most of my inspiration from Ian Fleming's books. I reread them. In the books Bond is suave and sophisticated, yes—Sean Connery really nailed it—but there's also a flawed aspect of Bond. In the novels, he is quite a depressive character. When he's not working, he's at his worst.—*Playboy*, 2008[49]

Craig on the importance of Bond to England: There was an identity crisis in England after World War II, with the country figuring itself out, seeing the perceived power we once had dwindling away. And along comes this character who's very British and very charming but at the same time sort of says "F—— you" to the whole world. I think the essence of the character is somewhere in there. I think that's what set this whole thing in motion years ago, and that keeps it going.—*Enter-tainment Weekly*, 2006[50]

Craig on Bond being a perpetual bachelor: In the books, he has relationships and occasionally is nearly getting married when she dumps him because he turns moody and dark. . . . It's that his true personality comes out, and he's impossible to live with. It suits M, his boss, just fine. M is terrified of Bond actually setting down. His inability to have a relation keeps him going.—*Playboy*, 2008[51]

Craig on his advice to the next James Bond: Just make sure you're great. You've got to push yourself as far as you can. But it's worth it. It's James Bond.—*Time Out*, 2015[52]

ACKNOWLEDGMENTS

I want to express my deep gratitude for the many people who helped with this book. I am enormously grateful to Elliot Ravetz, my first reader and biggest advocate. I offer everlasting thanks to my mother Sandra Edlitz, who drove me to see *A View to a Kill* on two consecutive nights, and to my late father Robert Edlitz who is never far from my thoughts and who playfully sang the *Moonraker* theme song while playing charades. I'd like to give thanks to Gail Ravetz, who found the Gilbert action figures at a flea market. I extend love to my sister Tracy who, as she points out, shares the same name as Bond's wife. I am grateful to the support from Joan and Irving Shapiro, who looked after my children while I visited the Bond museum during our trip to London. In addition to enabling my Bond fandom, they have all been consistent sources of joy and love.

Special thanks go to Jerry Kolber and Adam Davis, my dear friends who support me in all my endeavors. Additional thanks go to David Mamet, Charles Salzberg, Mark Viseglia, Renee Jamieson, Ben Ohmart, Paul Talbot, Jim Graham, Vilma Vias, Andrew Read, and Liz Bigger.

I extend my gratitude to the kind people who helped facilitate these interviews, including Gareth Owen, Andrea Stahn, Kyle McGinnis, Marcel Damen, Nikki Weiss, Bruce Kaufman, Adam Sherwin, Ginger Mason, Lauren Macpherson, Chloe Saxby, and Michelle Danso. Additional thanks go to Jim Davis, John Stawarz, and Amber Libke for their assistance with transcriptions.

Bond scholars who have generously supported my efforts and have given me valuable guidance include Raymond Benson of *The James Bond Bedside Companion* and a Bond continuation author, Bruce Scivally of *James Bond: The Legacy*, Brian McKaig of The Bondologist Blog, Peter Lorenz of Illustrated 007, Matt Spaiser of The Suits of James Bond, Mark O'Connell, author of *Catching Bullets*, Clinton Rawls of Comics Royale, and Ajay Chowdhury, coauthor of *Some Kind of Hero*.

I deeply appreciate Lee Pfeiffer, coauthor of *The Incredible World of 007*; Andrew Lane, coauthor of *The Bond Files*; Bruce Scivally, coauthor of *James Bond: The Legacy*; and James Chapman, author of *Licence to Thrill: A Cultural History of the James Bond Films* for their kind words about the book and their support.

Numerous websites exhibit a breathtaking knowledge of 007, including Commander Bond, Artistic Licence Renewed, 007 Magazine, Archivo 007, James Bond 007 Comic Art, Absolutely James Bond, From Sweden with Love, Illustrated 007, MI6, The Bondologist Blog, James Bond Jr. Online, The Spy Command, The Book Bond, Bond Lifestyle, The 007 Dossier, and James Bond Memes. Writers who were instrumental in shaping my interest in Bond include Steven Jay Rubin, Raymond

Benson, John Brosnan, John Cork, John Pearson, Kingsley Amis, Graham Rye, Lee Pfeiffer, Philip Lisa, Philip Gurin, James Chapman, and Richard Schenkman. The passion that the Bondologists of the James Bond Podcast feel for their subject matter is infectious.

I am overjoyed to include Pat Carbajal's stunning illustrations in this book.

I would like to express my deep appreciation to my agents Alyssa Jennette and Ellen Scordato at Stonesong for their support and counsel.

Immeasurable appreciation goes to Rick Rinehart at Rowman & Littlefield, who made working with him a joy and whose instincts and advice were always exceptional. Additional thanks go to Kristen Mellitt, Erin McGarvey, and to the entire team at R&L for their behind-the-scenes efforts and for enhancing this book immeasurably.

I am deeply indebted to all the artists in the book who spoke with me. They were all generous with their time and insights.

Above all, I wanted to express my love and gratitude for Dr. Suzie Shapiro, my wise, supportive, and beautiful wife and for Ben and Sophie, my wonderful, fun, thoughtful, caring, loving, and kooky children.

NOTES

BOND ON FILM

1 *Casino Royale*, directed by Martin Campbell, Eon Productions, 2006.
2 Sarah Marshall, *Daniel Craig: The Biography*, London: John Blake Publishing, 2016.
3 In *GoldenEye*, former MI6 agent Alec Trevelyan states that Brosnan's Bond (like his literary counterpart) is an orphan whose parents were killed in a climbing accident. In *Skyfall*, M tells 007, "Orphans make the best recruits."
4 Christopher Wood, *James Bond, The Spy I Loved*, Great Britain: Twenty First Century Publishers, 2006, 52.
5 Tom Mankiewicz and Robert Crane, *My Life as a Mankiewicz*, Kentucky: University Press of Kentucky, 2012.
6 Albert R. Broccoli with Donald Zec, *When the Snow Melts*, London: Boxtree, 1998, 234.
7 Roger Moore, *The 007 Diaries: Filming Live and Let Die*, Gloucestershire: The History Press, 2018. In 1973, the book was also published under *Roger Moore as James Bond 007* and *Roger Moore's Live and Let Die Diaries*.
8 Leslie Bricusse, LeslieBricusse.com, http://lesliebricusse.com./bio/bio.php.
9 Jon Burlingame, *The Music of James Bond*, New York: Oxford Press, 2012.
10 Paul Simpson, *The Rough Guide to James Bond*, London: Rough Guides, 2003, 228.
11 Playbill.com. http://www.playbill.com/person/don-black-vault-0000005952.
12 The scripted line and lyric "No one ever died from wanting too much" echoes a line from the novel *From Russia, with Love*: "This man died from living too much."
13 Sam Smith's Oscar-winning song "Writings on the Wall" (2016) and a-ha's "The Living Daylights" (1987) are arguably told from Bond's point of view.

BOND IN PRINT

1 Paul Fuhr, "Bad Guys, Bullets & Bookshelves," Buzz Sprout, July 5, 2016, www.buzzsprout.com/56402/397729-ep-019-bad-guys-bullets-bookshelves-raymond-benson.
2 "The Name Is Fleming . . . Ian Fleming," CBS News, November 9, 2008, www.cbsnews.com/news/the-name-is-fleming-ian-fleming.
3 Anthony Horowitz, *Forever and a Day*, New York: HarperCollins, 2018.
4 Anthony Horowitz, *Trigger Mortis*, New York: HarperCollins, 2015.

5 The estate was less strict with William Boyd, who wrote the continuation novel *Solo*, in which Bond sleeps in the nude. In Fleming's *From Russia, with Love*, the agent also appears to sleep naked in the chapter titled "The Soft Life."

6 Tom Sears and Chris Wright, "Raymond Benson Interview—Podcast #11," James Bond Radio, April 18, 2014 and "Raymond Benson Interview," May 11, 2004, MI6, www.mi6-hq.com/sections/articles/interview_raymond_benson _before.php3.

7 "Permission to Die [1989]," October 12, 2016, The Bond Book, www.thebook bond.com/2016/10/permission-to-die-1989.html.

8 John Gardner's *Nobody Lives Forever* was originally published under the title *Nobody Lives for Ever*. "Saab 900 Turbo," Bond Lifestyle, www.jamesbondlifestyle.com/product/saab-900-turbo and John Cox, "Bond's Beast – When 007 Drove A Saab," The Book Bond, https://www.thebookbond.com/p/bonds-beast-when -oo7-drove-saab.html.

9 Mike Grell, *Permission to Die*, California: Eclipse Comics, 1991, 46.

10 "Permission to Die. #3 Review," MI6, September 12, 2004, www.mi6-hq.com/sections/comics/ptd3_review.php3.

BEING BOND

1 Roger Moore, "Bye Bye to Ian Fleming's James Bond?" *London Times*, October 4, 2008.

2 Ian Fleming, *Casino Royale*, Nevada: Thomas & Mercer, 2012.

3 Ian Fleming, *Live and Let Die,* Nevada: Thomas & Mercer, 2012.

4 Ian Fleming, *From Russia, with Love*, Nevada: Thomas & Mercer, 2012.

5 Moore, "Bye Bye to Ian Fleming's James Bond?"

6 Moore, "Bye Bye to Ian Fleming's James Bond?"

7 Ian Fleming, "Octopussy," in *Octopussy* and *The Living Daylights,* Nevada: Thomas & Mercer, 2012. This line became a critical plot point in *Spectre*.

8 Ian Fleming, "From a View to a Kill," in *For Your Eyes Only*, Nevada: Thomas & Mercer, 2012.

9 Fleming, *Live and Let Die*.

10 Fleming, *Casino Royale*.

11 Ian Fleming, *The Man with the Golden Gun*, Nevada: Thomas & Mercer, 2012.

12 Ian Fleming, *On Her Majesty's Secret Service*, Nevada: Thomas & Mercer, 2012.

13 Ian Fleming, *Moonraker*, Nevada: Thomas & Mercer, 2012.

14 Fleming, *Moonraker*.

15 Fleming, *Moonraker*.

16 Fleming, *Moonraker*.

17 Ian Fleming, *Diamonds Are Forever*, Nevada: Thomas & Mercer, 2012.

18 Ian Fleming, *On Her Majesty's Secret Service*, Nevada: Thomas & Mercer, 2012.

19 Fleming, *Diamonds Are Forever*.

20 Raymond Benson's "Blast from the Blast" picks up on this dangling plot point. Raymond Benson, *James Bond: The Union Trilogy; Three 007 Novels*, New York: Pegasus Books, 2008.

21 Fleming, *Moonraker*.

22 Fleming, *Moonraker*.

23 Fleming, *Moonraker*.

24 Fleming, *Moonraker*. Note: Fleming would introduce additional Double-O agents in later books.

25 Ian Fleming, *The Man with the Golden Gun*, Nevada: Thomas & Mercer, 2012.

26 Ian Fleming, *Thunderball*, Nevada: Thomas & Mercer, 2012.

27 Fleming, *Thunderball*.

28 Ian Fleming, *From Russia, with Love*.

29 Ian Fleming, *On Her Majesty's Secret Service*, Nevada: Thomas & Mercer, 2012. As cited by W. Adam Mandelbaum in "Seq Chapter: The Gospel According to Sir James," at Bond Lifestyle, 2008, https://www.jamesbondlifestyle.com/articles/seq-chapter-gospel-according-sir-james.

30 *Goldfinger*. Directed by Guy Hamilton. Eon Productions, 1964.

31 Mark Edlitz, *How to Be a Superhero*, Albany, GA: BearManor Media, 2015.

32 Edlitz, *How to Be a Superhero*.

33 *Playboy*, "Playboy Interview: Sean Connery, November 1965," in *50 Years of the Playboy Interview: James Bond*, Playboy Enterprises, Inc., 2012.

34 Matthew Field and Ajay Chowdhury, *Some Kind of Hero: The Remarkable Story of the James Bond Films*, Stroud, Gloucestershire: History Press, 2015.

35 Mark O'Connell, *Catching Bullets: Memories of a Bond Fan*, Droxford, Hampshire: Splendid Books, 2012.

36 Although the quote, which is attributed to Raymond Chandler, has appeared on the back cover of certain editions of Bond novels, some Bond scholars believe the quote should be credited to Raymond Mortimer, who reviewed the book for *The Sunday Times*. For more on the topic, visit Edward Biddulph's James Bond Memes, http://jamesbondmemes.blogspot.com.

37 *Ian Fleming: The Playboy Interview*, Playboy Enterprises, Inc., 2012.

38 The packaging for the Holly Goodhead action figure eliminated the character's last name and discreetly identified her as "Holly." Dr. Molly Warmflash's name is never spoken but appears in the closing credits of *The World Is Not Enough*.

39 Ian Fleming, *Goldfinger*, Nevada: Thomas & Mercer, 2012.

40 Fleming, *Casino Royale*, 34.

41 Fleming, *Casino Royale*, 49.

42 Fleming, *Moonraker*. I first learned about the reference while reading *The Bond Files* by Andy Lane and Paul Simpson.

43 John Gardner, *Death Is Forever*, New York: Ian Fleming Publications, 1992. I first learned of the reference while reading *The Bond Files* by Andy Lane and Paul Simpson.

44 John Gardner, *Death Is Forever*.

45 Author's correspondence with Brian McKaig in 2018. Also information from the message board user known as "doublenought spy" in the thread "Bob Holness Moonraker adaption," at Commander Bond.net, March 7, 2008," http://debrief .commanderbond.net/topic/45647-bob-holness-moonraker-adaptation.

46 Letter from Bob Holness to Brian McKaig dated February 24, 2003.

47 Letter from Bob Holness.

48 Letter from Bob Holness.

49 Letter from Bob Holness.

50 Letter from Bob Holness.

51 Letter from Bob Holness.

52 Letter from Bob Holness.

53 Letter from Bob Holness.

54 Letter from Bob Holness.

55 Letter from Bob Holness.

56 Letter from Bob Holness.

57 Letter from Bob Holness.

58 Letter from Bob Holness.

59 Letter from Bob Holness.

60 Alan Hayes, "Personnel File: Hugh Rouse," Avengers on the Radio, http://aor .theavengers.tv/bio_hugh_rouse.htm.

61 Robert von Dassanowsky, "Casino Royale at 33: The Postmodern Epic in Spite of Itself," *Bright Lights*, April 1, 2000.

62 Michael Richardson, *The Making of Casino Royale* (1967), Bromley, Kent: Telos Publishing, 2015.

63 Roger Moore with Gareth Owen, *Bond on Bond*, Guilford, CT: Lyons Press, 2013.

64 Ian Fleming, *You Only Live Twice*, Nevada: Thomas & Mercer, 2012, 142.

65 Fleming, *You Only Live Twice*, 144.

66 Fleming, *You Only Live Twice*, 142.

67 Ian Fleming, writer, Fergus Fleming, editor, *The Man with the Golden Typewriter: Ian Fleming's James Bond Letters*, London: Bloomsbury, 2015.

68 Fleming, *The Man with the Golden Typewriter*.

69 Fleming, *The Man with the Golden Typewriter*.

70 Fleming, *The Man with the Golden Typewriter*.

71 Robert Sellers, *The Battle for Bond*, Sheffield: Tomahawk Press, 2008, 53.

72 Sellers, *The Battle for Bond*, 71.

73 Sellers, *The Battle for Bond*, 77.

74 Broccoli, *When the Snow Melts*, 171.

75 Broccoli, *When the Snow Melts*, 227.

76 Broccoli, *When the Snow Melts*, 200.

77 Adrian Lee, "'Diet Coke Is Now My Vice': Sir Roger Moore on Bond, Diabetes and Booze," *Daily Express*, September 1, 2014, www.express.co.uk/entertainment/films/505743/Sir-Roger-Moore-on-Bond-diabetes-and-booze.

78 Hanna Flint, "Hold Old Is 007? Here's the Ages of Each James Bond in Their First and Last Appearances," *Metro UK*, September 27, 2015, https://metro.co.uk/2015/09/27/how-old-is-007-heres-the-ages-of-each-james-bond-in-their-first-and-last-appearances-5409515.

79 Fleming, *The Man with the Golden Typewriter*.

80 Raymond Benson wrote three film novelizations, six original novels, and three short stories.

81 Benson was comparing Lazenby to Connery and Moore. Benson's book was published in 1984, before Timothy Dalton, Pierce Brosnan, and Daniel Craig assumed the role of Bond. Raymond Benson, *The James Bond Bedside Companion*, New York: Dodd, Mead and Company, 1984, 198.

82 Steven Soderbergh, "A Rambling Discourse," Extension 765, November 1, 2013, http://extension765.com/soderblogh/2-most-irrelevant-no-1.

83 Sinclair McKay, *The Man with the Golden Touch*, New York: Overlook Press, 2008, 123.

84 McKay, *The Man with the Golden Touch*, 127.

85 Broccoli, *When the Snow Melts*, 212.

86 *You Only Live Twice*, Directed by Michael Bakewell, BBC-Radio 4, 1990.

87 *You Only Live Twice*, 1990.

88 *You Only Live Twice*, 1990.

89 *You Only Live Twice*, 1990.

90 Jon Burlingame, *The Music of James Bond*, New York: Oxford Press, 2012.

91 Unidentified writer using penname "M," James Bond Dossier, originally posted November 15, 2013, www.the007dossier.com/007dossier/post/2013/11/15/James-Bond-007-at-the-1982-Academy-Awards.

92 R. D. Mascott is a pseudonym that many Bondologists believe to be Arthur Calder-Marshall, an English author. Andy Lane and Paul Simpson, *The Bond Files*, London: Virgin Publishing, 2002, 63.

93 Lane and Simpson, *The Bond Files*, 103.

94 Simon Vance, SimonVance.com.

95 Tim Bentinck Interview, MI6, November 3, 2004, www.mi6-hq.com/sections/articles/interview_tom_bentinck2.php3.

96   In *Rogue Agent*, Scaramanga is revealed to be working for SPECTRE and not, as depicted in *The Man with the Golden Gun*, an independent assassin.

97   The Casting Directors' Guild, www.thecdg.co.uk/members/debbie.

98   Erik Olsen, "No Country for Subtitles (Just Voices)," *New York Times*, August 27, 2014, www.nytimes.com/2014/08/28/movies/dietmar-wunder-the-german -speaking-voice-of-james-bond.html?_r=0.

99   In the witty audio documentary "Tape Secret! The Audiobooks of James Bond," Dan Gale points out that Christopher Cazenove, who played 007 in the 1973 documentary *Omnibus: The British Hero*, recorded the audiobook version of John Gardner's Bond book *SeaFire* (1994). Cazenove also recorded Gardner's final Bond book *Cold* (1996), under its US title *Cold Fall*. Dan Gale, "Tape Secret! The Audiobooks of James Bond," *James Bond Radio*. 2016, http://jamesbond radio.com/tape-secret-audiobooks-james-bond-documentary.

100 The producers of the video game *007 Legends* intentionally played with that enjoyable but uncanny sensation when they inserted Daniel Craig into missions from each previous Bond movie era. The result of the continuity-blurring premise is that Craig's Bond supplants all prior cinematic Bond actors by appearing in *Goldfinger*, *On Her Majesty's Secret Service*, *Moonraker*, *Die Another Day*, and *Licence to Kill*. Toby Stephens is another example of an established Bond actor portraying different versions of the character. He's an eight-time Bond in BBC Radio 4's dramatizations of Ian Fleming's books and he has also narrated Deaver's *Carte Blanche* and Fleming's *From Russia, with Love*.

101 Chris Hewett, "Sam Mendes Talks Gun Barrel Sequence," *Empire Online*, November 6, 2012, www.empireonline.com/movies/news/sam-mendes-talks -gun-barrel-sequence.

102 Unidentified author, "Who Played James Bond: A Complete History," 007 James, www.007james.com/articles/who_played_james_bond.php.

103 Over the years, many brave stuntmen have left their mark on the franchise. That group, as reported by Jon Auty and Anders Frejdh, includes Bob Simmons (who doubled for Connery and Moore, Alf Joint (Connery), George Leech (Connery, Lazenby, and Moore), Vic Armstrong (Connery, Lazenby, and Moore), Martin Grace (Moore), B. J. Worth (Dalton and Brosnan), Simon Crane (Dalton and Brosnan), Wayne Michaels (Brosnan) and Ben Cooke (Craig). Jon Auty, "Stuntmen Who Have Played Ian Fleming's James Bond on Film," From Sweden with Love, https://jamesbond007.se/eng/artiklar/stuntman-som-james-bond.

104 "James Bond: 50 Years of the Best 007-Related Records to Mark 50 Years on the Big Screen," Guinness World Records, October 5, 2017, www.guinness worldrecords.com/news/2012/10/james-bond-50-of-the-best-007-related- records-to-mark-50-years-on-the-big-screen-45200.

DESIGNING 007

1 The nature of the McGinnis/McCarthy collaboration is complicated and varies with the different posters on which they both worked. However, they worked separately and contributed different elements to the poster. To see a treasure trove of their Bond art, read *James Bond: 50 Years of Movie Posters* by DK Publishing, visit Peter Lorenz's website, the Illustrated 007, and seek out the Nixdorf collection.

2 Edward Biddulph, "The James Bond art of Robert McGinnis: The *Sunday Times* magazine 007 collectors' issue," James Bond Memes, May 10, 2015, http://jamesbondmemes.blogspot.com/2015/05/robert-mcginnis-james-bond -artwork-for.html.

3 Peter Lorenz, Illustrated 007. http://illustrated007.blogspot.com/search/ label/Artist%3A%20Robert%20McGinnis.

4 In addition to the classic stance, McGinnis has also illustrated Bond in different positions. For a variety of reasons, several images, not just one, are used for marketing.

5 Robert E. McGinnis: The Official Website, www.mcginnispaintings.com/ about-robert-mcginnis.

6 Bob Simmons with Kenneth Passingham, *Nobody Does It Better*, New York: Sterling Publishing, 1987, 31.

7 Peter Lorenz, Illustrated 007, http://illustrated007.blogspot.com.

8 The international poster by Italian artist Renato Casaro is closer to the look of a traditional Bond poster.

9 RudyObrero.com.

10 MI6, "Designing 'Never Say Never Again' – Rudy Obrero Interview, August 7, 2010 www.mi6-hq.com/sections/articles/interview_rudy_obrero.php3.

11 Emovieposter.com.

12 The unused images can be found on the Bond fan website, Illustrated 007, and in the Nixdorf collection.

13 A teaser poster presents a strong graphic image that is intended to whet the audience's appetite while being slightly enigmatic about the forthcoming movie. The teaser poster is usually meant to raise questions about the movie. The final poster provides the answers. The final poster is usually more descriptive and less mysterious than the teaser.

14 Marcel Damen, "Dan Goozee Galactica.TV Interview," Galactica.TV, www .galactica.tv/battlestar-galactica-1978-interviews/dan-goozee-galactica.tv -interview.html.

15 Peter Lorenz, "Moonraker Artwork," Illustrated 007, and the Thomas Nixdorf collection, http://illustrated007.blogspot.com/2015/01/moonraker-artwork .html.

16 Although it's not his normal practice, Bond briefly carried two guns during the finale of *Tomorrow Never Dies*. As in the video game, the second gun belonged to a fallen adversary.

BOND WOMEN

1 [*Note:* Dr. Lisa Funnell provided notes for her detailed answers.] For a detailed discussion of the lover literary tradition, see Harriet Hawkins, *Classics and Trash: Traditions and Taboos in High Literature and Popular Modern Genres* (Toronto: University of Toronto Press, 1990).

2 For a detailed discussion of sex and (hetero)sexuality in James Bond, see Jeremy Black, *The Politics of James Bond: From Fleming's Novels to the Big Screen* (London: Praeger, 2001).

3 Lisa Funnell, "From English Partner to American Action Hero: The Heroic Identity and Transnational Appeal of the Bond Girl," *Heroes and Heroines: Embodiment, Symbolism, Narratives and Identity,* edited by Christopher Hart (Kingswinford, UK: Midrash, 2008), 63.

4 For example, Catherine Haworth examines the influence of music on the depiction of Pussy Galore in *Goldfinger* ("Pussy Galore: Women and Music in *Goldfinger*," in *For His Eyes Only: The Women of James Bond*, edited by Lisa Funnell [London: Wallflower, 2015], 157–66). Andrea Severson uses costume theory to explore the depiction of femininity and power of the Bond Girls featured in *Dr. No* and *Casino Royale* ("Designing Character: Costume, Bond Girls, and Negotiating Representation," in *For His Eyes Only*, 176–84). Thomas Barrett explores how the depiction of Tatiana Romanova in *From Russia with Love* reflects the changing geopolitics of the time as the Soviet Union was opening up to the West ("Desiring the Soviet Woman: Tatiana Romanova and *From Russia with Love*," in *For His Eyes Only*, 41–50). Marlisa Santos examines how *On Her Majesty's Secret Service* fits the formula of the "woman's film" by centralizing women in the narrative, especially Bond Girl Tracy di Vicenzo ("'This Never Happened to the Other Fellow': *On Her Majesty's Secret Service* As a Bond Woman's Film," in *For His Eyes Only*, 101–9). Robert von Dassanowsky examines the depiction of Ursula Andress as Vesper Lynd in the spoof *Casino Royale* (1967) and the ways in which her character intertexts with her previous role as Honey Ryder in *Dr. No* ("'Never Trust a Rich Spy:' Ursula Andress, Vesper Lynd, and Mythic Power in *Casino Royale* 1967," in *For His Eyes Only*, 91–100). Finally, Jeffrey A. Brown discusses Angelina Jolie's rejection of an offer to play a Bond Girl and how the action film *Salt* (2010) attempts to create a female Bond franchise ("'Who Is Salt?' The Difficulty of Constructing a Female James Bond and Reconstructing Gender Expectations," in *For His Eyes Only*, 224–33).

5 For instance, Alexander Sergeant explores the representation of Electra King in *The World Is Not Enough* and how the depiction of female desire in the film challenges Bond's phallic authority ("Bond Is Not Enough: Elektra King and the Desiring Bond Girl," in *For His Eyes Only*, 128–36).

6 For example, Charles Burnetts explores the different narrative treatments of three categories of Bond women: Bond Girls, Bad Girls, and secondary female characters who he likens to "fluffers" in the porn industry ("Bond's Bit on the Side: Race, Exoticism and the Bond 'Fluffer' Character," in *For His Eyes Only*, 60–69). Travis Wagner discusses how race and colonialism influence Bond's treatment of black women across the film series ("'The Old Ways Are Best': The Colonization of Women of Color in Bond Films," in *For His Eyes Only*, 51–59). Dan Mills examines the differences between Bond Girls, Bad Girls, and Secondary Women to discuss the issue of female empowerment ("'What Really Went on up There James?' Bond's Wife, Blofeld's Patients, and Empowered Bond Women," in *For His Eyes Only*, 110–18). Finally, Eileen Rositzka describes supportive female characters as "Secondary Girls" (a wordplay on the term "Bond Girls") and explains their form and function in the narrative ("Random Access Mysteries: James Bond and the Matter of the Unknown Woman," in *For His Eyes Only*, 148–56).

7 For instance, Klaus Dodds discusses the various ways in which Eve Moneypenny in *Skyfall* is depicted differently from her predecessors and other figures who make up Bond's (institutional) support system ("'It's Not for Everyone': James Bond and Miss Moneypenny in *Skyfall*," *For His Eyes Only*, 214–23).

8 For example, Brian Patton explores the casting of Judi Dench as M and the depiction of female authority across the Brosnan and Craig eras ("M, 007, and the Challenge of Female Authority in the Bond Franchise," in *For His Eyes Only*, 246–54).

9 For a discussion of gender and communication, see Julia T. Wood, *Gendered Lives: Communication, Gender, and Culture*, 9th ed (Boston: Wadsworth, 2011).

10 Andrew Roberts, "Nikki van der Zyl: The Bond girl you've never seen who voiced some of the films' best known heroines," *Independent*, October 11 2015, https://www.independent.co.uk/arts-entertainment/music/features/nikki -van-der-zyl-the-bond-girl-youve-never-seen-who-voiced-some-of-the-films -best-known-heroines-a6689701.html.

11 Lisa Funnell, "From English Partner to American Action Hero," 63–64.

12 Funnell, "From English Partner to American Action Hero," 69.

13 Funnell, "From English Partner to American Action Hero," 77–78.

14 Christopher Holliday, "Mothering the Bond-M Relation in *Skyfall* and the Bond Girl Intervention," in *For His Eyes Only*, 267–69.

15 Lisa Funnell, "Objects of White Male Desire: (D)Evolving Representations of Asian Women in Bond Films," in *For His Eyes Only: The Women of James Bond*, 86.

16 Peter C. Kunze, "From Masculine Mastermind to Maternal Martyr: Judi Dench's M, *Skyfall*, and the Patriarchal Logic of James Bond Films," in *For His Eyes Only*, 242.

17 Lori L. Parks, "'M'(O)thering: Female Representation of Age and Power in James Bond," in *For His Eyes Only*, 262.

18 Michael W. Boyce, "Property of a Lady: (S)Mothering Judi Dench's M," in *For His Eyes Only*, 281.

19 For example, in *GoldenEye* M dismisses criticism by stating, "If I want sarcasm, Mr. Tanner, I'll talk to my children, thank you very much."

20 Lisa Funnell, "'I Know Where You Keep Your Gun': Daniel Craig As the Bond–Bond Girl Hybrid in *Casino Royale*," *Journal of Popular Culture* (2011): 443.

21 Funnell, "'I Know Where You Keep Your Gun,'" 462.

22 Funnell, "'I Know Where You Keep Your Gun,'" 466–68.

23 Funnell, "'I Know Where You Keep Your Gun,'" 467.

24 Ian Fleming, *Diamonds Are Forever*, Nevada: Thomas and Mercer, 2012, 200.

25 Fleming, *Diamonds Are Forever*, 201.

26 Stephen Nepa, "Secret Agent Nuptials: Marriage, Gender Roles, and the 'Different Bond Woman' in *On Her Majesty's Secret Service*," in *For His Eyes Only*, 195.

27 Stephanie Jones, "'Women Drivers': The Changing Role of the Bond Girl in Vehicle Chases," in *For His Eyes Only*, 212.

APPENDIX: QUOTABLE BOND

1 *Cinema Retro*, 2004, quoted in MI6, www.mi6-hq.com/sections/articles/obituary_nelson.php3.

2 Lee Goldberg, "Barry Nelson: The First James Bond," *Starlog* 75, 1983.

3 *New York Daily News*, 1995, quoted by Dennis McLellan for the *Los Angeles Times*, April 14, 2007.

4 Goldberg, "Barry Nelson: The First James Bond."

5 Lee Pfeiffer, "The Curious Legacy of *Casino Royale*," MI6, October 22, 2004. www.mi6-hq.com/sections/articles/history_casino_royale.php3?id=0593.

6 Robert Dex, "Quiz Host Bob Holness Dies," *Independent*, January 6, 2012, www.independent.co.uk/news/people/news/quiz-host-bob-holness-dies-6286014.html.

7 Simmons and Passingham, *Nobody Does It Better*, 6.

8 Simmons and Passingham, *Nobody Does It Better*, 62.

9 Matthew Field, "Connery in His Own Words," quoted in *Cinema Retro*'s "Celebrating 50 Years of James Bond in the Cinema," 2012: 1323, which found it in the *Observer*, March 1, 1998.

10 Matthew Field, "Connery in His Own Words," which found it in Peter Haining's *James Bond: A Celebration* (London: Planet 1987); the original source is unknown.

11 *Playboy*, "Sean Connery, November 1965."

12 *Newsday*, 1963, quoted in Stuff Nobody Cares About, http://stuffnobodycares about.com/2015/11/12/sean-connery-on-james-bond.

13 F. Lee Bailey, *Good Company*, 1967, www.youtube.com/watch?v=VZzbIIQ2OH4.

14 Melvyn Bragg, *The South Bank Show*, October 2008.

15 Bailey, *Good Company*.

16 *New York Times*, 1964, quoted in Stuff Nobody Cares About, http://stuffnobody caresabout.com/2015/11/12/sean-connery-on-james-bond.

17 Bailey, *Good Company*.

18 Bailey, *Good Company*.

19 Richardson, *The Making of Casino Royale* (1967), quoting from *The Blade*, April 30, 1967.

20 Richard Luck, "A Cocktail Recipe for Disaster: Peter Sellers and Orson Welles on the Making of Casino," *Sabotage Times*, November 2, 2015; original source unknown.

21 Michael Richardson, quoting from BBC's *Film Night*, November 8, 1970; original source unknown.

22 Karen Glahn, "Terence Cooper—The Forgotten Agent 007," *Morgenavisen Jyllands-Postens*, May 21, 1996, quoted in "Casino Royale (1967): Terence Cooper—the Forgotten Agent 007 (1996)," Bond-O-Rama, February 15, 2017, www.bond -o-rama.dk/en/cr67-terence-cooper-1996-eng. Bragg, *The South Bank Show*.

23 Paul Riddell, "The George Lazenby Interview," *007 Magazine* (9–10): 1981. www.007magazine.co.uk/archive/archive_01.htm.

24 *Becoming Bond*, documentary, directed by Josh Greenbaum, 2017.

25 *Becoming Bond*.

26 *Becoming Bond*.

27 Patrick Ryan, "'Forgotten' James Bond Actor Says He Had a Fan in Roger Moore," *USA Today*, June 2, 2017, 2017, www.usatoday.com/story/life/ movies/2017/06/02/becoming-bond-george-lazenby-hulu/102313230.

28 Roger Moore, *My Word Is My Bond*, Sydney: HarperCollins, 2008, 248.

29 The 007 Dossier quoting Lee Goldberg, "Roger Moore: His Name Is Bond," *Starlog*, July 1985, www.the007dossier.com/post/2017/03/27/1985-Starlog -Interview-with-Roger-Moore.

30 David Giammarco, "Roger—Over and Out!" originally published in *007 Magazine* 16 (1985), www.007magazine.co.uk/archive/archive_05.htm.

31 David Walliams, "Sir Roger Moore: 'I'm a Lover, Sean Connery's a Killer,'" *GQ*, May 2017, www.gq-magazine.co.uk/article/roger-moore-dies-89.

32 Kevin Perry, "Roger Moore on Bond, Brexit and Gin," Short List, 2017, www.short list.com/entertainment/roger-moore-interview-james-bond-brexit-gin/104477.

33 Will Harris, "Timothy Dalton on *Penny Dreadful*, Serenading Mae West, and Being James Bond," AV Club, May 9, 2014, www.avclub.com/article/timothy-dalton-penny-dreadful-serenading-mae-west--204395.

34 David Giammarco, *For Your Eyes Only: Behind the Scenes of the James Bond Films*, Toronto: ECW Press, 2002, 199.

35 Richard Schenkman, "A Conversation with Timothy Dalton," *Bondage* 15 (1987): 22.

36 Raymond Benson, "Poetic Licence,"originally published *007 Magazine* 21 (1989); www.007magazine.co.uk/archive/archive_06-1.htm.

37 Christian Blauvelt, "Timothy Dalton Talks 'Chuck,' 'The Tourist,' and, of course, 'Bond,' *Entertainment Weekly*, November 1, 2010, http://ew.com/article/2010/11/01/timothy-dalton-chuck-the-tourist-bond.

38 Benedict Nightingale, "007: A New Bond Meets the New Woman; Timothy Dalton Finds a Hero in the Hero," *New York Times*, July 26, 1987, www.nytimes.com/1987/07/26/movies/007-a-new-bond-meets-the-new-woman-timothy-dalton-finds-a-hamlet-in-the-hero.html.

39 Nightingale, "007."

40 Giammarco, "For Your Eyes Only," 207.

41 Harris, "Timothy Dalton on *Penny Dreadful*, Serenading Mae West, and Being James Bond."

42 Alex Simon, "Great Conversations: Pierce Brosnan," *Huffington Post*, June 24, 2015, www.huffingtonpost.com/alex-simon/great-conversations-pierc_b_7656846.html.

43 Simon, "Great Conversations: Pierce Brosnan."

44 Simon, "Great Conversations: Pierce Brosnan."

45 Horatia Harrod, "Pierce Brosnan: I Was Never Good Enough As Bond," *Telegraph*, April 12, 2014, www.telegraph.co.uk/culture/film/10755167/Pierce-Brosnan-I-was-never-good-enough-as-Bond.html.

46 Stephen Rebello, "Playboy Interview: Pierce Brosnan, December 2005," in *50 Years of the Playboy Interview: James Bond*, Playboy Enterprises, Inc., 2012.

47 James Inverne, "Villain with a Past," *Sunday Telegraph*, December 2002.

48 Benjamin Svetkey, "The Man Who Would Be Bond," *Entertainment Weekly*, August 18, 2006, 46.

49 David Sheff, "Playboy Interview: Daniel Craig, November 2008," in *The Playboy Interviews: James Bond*, Playboy Enterprises, Inc., 2012.

50 Svetkey, "The Man Who Would Be Bond," 49.

51 Sheff, "Playboy Interview: Daniel Craig, November 2008."

52 Dave Calhoun, "Daniel Craig Interview: 'My Advice to the Next James Bond? Don't Be Shit!'" Time Out New York, October 7, 2015, www.timeout.com/london/film/daniel-craig-interview-my-advice-to-the-next-james-bond-dont-be-shit.

INDEX

INDEX

misogyny/attitude toward women, Bond and, 4, 8, 10, 38, 175, 182, 252
Mission: Impossible (movie franchise), 15
Moneypenny (aka Miss Moneypenny), 45, 94, 226, 248–49, 252, 279n7
  relationship with Bond, 254–55
Monro, Matt, 86
Monro, Caroline, 244
Moonraker
  1955 book, 96
  Bond-girls, 273n18
  illustrations and posters, XI, 208, 211, 215–18, 222
  Moore as Bond, 262
  radio dramatization, 144–49, 162, 165, 267
  video game, 276n100
  writing the screenplay, 44, 55, 73
Moore, Deborah, 154
Moore, Mary Tyler, 20–21
Moore, Roger
  as heir to the Bond throne, IX, 40
  as the character, Bond, 61, 134
  cast in the Bond role, 152
  comparison to other Bonds, 4, 42, 58, 73–74, 98, 140–41, 153, 174
  contributions to the Bond legacy, IX, 40–42, 262–63
  death of, VIII, 127
  on following Connery as Bond, 127–28, 140
  reflections on being Bond, 127–41
  relationship with David Niven, 153, 154
  work for UN ICEF, 127, 138–39
Moriarty (Horowitz, 2014), 94
Morrison, Lee, 199, 201
Mower, Patrick, 166
"Mr. Kiss Kiss, Bang Bang" (song, 1965), 77–79, 82, 88
MTM Enterprises, 20–21
"Murder on Wheels" (Fleming, unpublished), 95
music and lyrics
  Don Black interview, 86–92
  Leslie Bricusse interview, 77–85

The Mystery of Natalie Wood (TV film, 2004), 245
My Word Is My Bond (Moore, 2008), 156

N
Nelson, Barry, 144, 149, 257
Nepa, Stephen, 255
Never Say Never Again
  Connery as Bond, 64–72, 153, 231, 258
  illustrations and posters, 211–14
  making the movie, 30, 63
  tango dance scene, 168
  writing the screenplay, 57, 63
Never Send Flowers (Gardner, 1993), 114
Newley, Anthony, 77, 79
Newman, Paul, 11
New York Times, 156
Niven, David, 75, 150–54, 191, 261
Niven, David, Jr., 150–54
Niven, Fiona, 154
Nobody Lives Forever (Gardner, 1986), 114
Nolte, Nick, 12
Noreiga: God's Favorite (movie, 2000), 12
North, Harry, 106
novels. *See* Bond continuation novels
nudity, 272n5
Nuns on the Run (movie, 1990), 53–54

O
Obrero, Rudy, 211–14
O'Connell, Mark, 133
OCTOPUS, 231
Octopussy
  allusions to other Bond films, 132–33
  Bond in a monkey suit, 24
  Glen role as director, 20
  illustrations and posters, 211, 215–18, 221
  making the movie, 30, 65
  Moore as Bond, 134, 262
  music and lyrics, 86
  writing the screenplay, 29, 44
"Octopussy" (Fleming, short story), 130
O'Donnell, Peter, 106
Olympic Games (London, 2012), 267

S

Sakata, Harold, 168

Saltzman, Harry, 32, 55, 88, 127, 152, 178, 210

The Scent of Danger (comic strip, 1983), 106

Schofield, Glen A., 231–39

Schwartzman, Jack, 66, 72

Schwarzenegger, Arnold, 12

Scorupco, Izabella (actor), 53

Scott, A. O., 156

Scrooge (theatrical musical, 1992), 77

SCUM (Saboteurs and Criminals United in Mayhem), 172

Seafire (Gardner, 1994), 114, 276n99

Sellers, Peter, 150, 152, 261

Sellers, Robert, 152

Semi-Tough (illustrations/posters), 208

Semple, Lorenzo, Jr., 64

Separate Tables (movie, 1958), 151, 152

sexuality, James Bond
   acknowledging AIDS, 38
   affair with Paris Carver, 39, 256
   Bond-girls challenge to, 39, 250, 279n5
   Bond-girls rejection of, 254
   disarmed by Miranda Frost, 248
   Lazenby on, 160
   Moore on, 129, 134, 137, 139
   natural magnetism of Connery, 68
   passing the screen test, 2
   relationship with Moneypenny, 254–55
   relationship with Wai Lin, 255–56
   showering with Tanya Roberts, 134
   sleeping naked, 102
   virginity, Bond losing his, 130
   women as distraction, 255

Seydoux, Léa, 1

Seymour, Jane, 57

Sherlock Holmes: The Musical (theatrical musical), 77

Shoot to Kill (movie, 1988), 12

Shout at the Devil (movie, 1976), 21

Simmons, Bob, 198, 258, 276n103

Simpson, Paul, 274n43

To Sir, with Love (movie, 1967), 86

Skyfall
   Bond-girls, 250–52
   Craig as Bond, 267
   dressing for the part, 224, 226–28
   insights into Bond, the man, 8, 224–25, 271n3
   making the movie, 5–6, 133
   M depiction as Bond-girl, 250–52
   Moneypenny, Bond relationship with, 254–55, 279n7
   stunts/stunt doubles, 198, 202
   ticket sales/income, 8

Snake Goddess (comic strip, 1983–84), 106

Soderbergh, Steven, 155

Solo (Boyd, 2013), 193, 272n5

Some Kind of Hero (Field, 2015), 133

Somewhere in Time (movie, 1980), 57

Sondheim, Stephen, 80, 83

South African Broadcasting Corporation, 144–48

Spectre
   author's note on, XI
   Bond-girls, 63, 247, 251
   Craig as Bond, 267
   dressing for the part, 75, 224, 226–28
   insights into Bond, the man, 8, 133
   linkage to earlier movies, 6–8
   making the movie, 5–8
   photos/illustrations, 229
   stunts/stunt doubles, 198, 203
   ticket sales/income, 8, 100

Spottiswoode, Roger, 12–19

Star Wars Holiday Special (TV program, 1978), 178

Stephens, Toby, 165, 267, 276n100

Stop the World - I Want to Get Off (theatrical musical, 1961), 77

Straw Dogs (movie, 1971), 12

Streisand, Barbra, 66

stunts/stunt doubles, 26, 29, 59, 140, 192, 198–206, 258

The Suits of James Bond (website), 230

Sunday Times Magazine (England), 208

Sunset Boulevard (Broadway production, 1994), 86

Superman (movie franchise), 55, 57, 156

ABOUT THE AUTHOR

Mark Edlitz has worked as a writer and producer for ABC News, NBC-Uni, CNBC, Discovery ID, and for National Geographic Channel's *Brain Games*.

Edlitz's writings about pop culture have appeared in *The Huffington Post*, *Los Angeles Times Hero Complex*, *Moviefone*, and *Empire* magazine online.

He wrote and directed the award-winning independent film *The Eden Myth* and directed *Jedi Junkies*, a documentary about extreme Star Wars fans.

His book *How to Be a Superhero* includes interviews with actors who have played superheroes over the past seven decades.

Edlitz lives in New York with his wife and two children.